WANDERING WOMEN

NEW DIRECTIONS IN NATIONAL CINEMAS
Robert Rushing, editor

WANDERING WOMEN

Urban Ecologies of Italian Feminist Filmmaking

LAURA DI BIANCO

INDIANA UNIVERSITY PRESS

This book is a publication of

Indiana University Press
Office of Scholarly Publishing
Herman B Wells Library 350
1320 East 10th Street
Bloomington, Indiana 47405 USA

iupress.org

© 2023 by Laura Di Bianco

All rights reserved
No part of this book may be reproduced or utilized in any form or by any means, electronic or mechanical, including photocopying and recording, or by any information storage and retrieval system, without permission in writing from the publisher. The paper used in this publication meets the minimum requirements of the American National Standard for Information Sciences—Permanence of Paper for Printed Library Materials, ANSI Z39.48-1992.

Manufactured in the United States of America

First printing 2023

Cataloging information is available from the Library of Congress.

ISBN 978-0-253-06464-6 (hardback)
ISBN 978-0-253-06465-3 (paperback)
ISBN 978-0-253-06466-0 (ebook)

*To all the women of my family: a lemon picker,
a trader, workers in a toy factory, all of them mothers,
housewives, caretakers, and fast-paced walkers.*

CONTENTS

Preface: Women Make Movies in Italy   ix

Acknowledgments   xvii

Note on Translation   xxi

Introduction: Mapping Italian Women's Filmmaking   1

1. Walking in Resilient Cities: *Traveling with Cecilia*   16

   Fegatello: *The Nightless City*   43

2. Urban Wandering, Scrapbooking, and Filmmaking: *As the Shadow, My Tomorrow, Poetry You See Me*   45

   Fegatello: *Ophelia Does Not Drown*   83

3. Mothers and Daughters—Stories of Survival and Care: *The White Space, I Like to Work*   85

   Fegatello: *All About You*   111

4. Coming of Age in the City—Garbage, Corpses, and Miracles: *Corpo Celeste, Domenica, Lost Kisses*   113

   Fegatello: *The Macaluso Sisters*   149

5. A Psychogeology of the City: *N-Able*   151

   Fegatello: *In This World*   179

   Epilogue: The Cities of Women   182

Filmography   189

Bibliography   193

Index   207

PREFACE

Women Make Movies in Italy

IN 2019, LINA WERTMULLER RECEIVED an honorary Oscar at the Governors Awards. As the first woman to be nominated for an Academy Award for Best Director for *Pasqualino settebellezze* (*Seven Beauties*) in 1976, for decades Wertmuller—along with Liliana Cavani—was the only Italian woman director to have captured the attention of international film critics and audiences. Returning to the Academy forty-three years later at the age of ninety-one, she playfully proposed giving the little golden statue a female name. She picked "Anna."

The occasion honoring Wertmuller's distinguished career was certainly one that celebrated cinema made by women. At the ceremony, director Greta Gerwig affectionately categorized Wertmuller's feminism as "naughty and playful." And yet, the significance of Wertmuller's award as a form of redress for the Academy's decades-long disregard for women's cinema was questioned by Jane Campion, who in 1993 became only the second woman ever to be nominated for Best Director. From the stage, Campion bluntly declared, "I have been asked to speak about women in the directing category at the Academy. It's a very short history. It's more of a haiku.

> First it was Lina,
> four more were nominated,
> —then Catherine won.

So, the number of nominations for women is five. For men, it's a different story . . . 350 nominations and seventy Oscars. Staggeringly unequal. . . . How do you correct centuries of patriarchal domination?"[1]

Nevertheless, Wertmuller's "Anna" may serve as a portent of coming change. While it was only at the end of the past decade that Wertmuller received international recognition for her life's work, in Italy, growing numbers of women have conquered spaces in a male-dominated film industry during the first twenty years of the twenty-first century, many of them making female-centered films. What is driving this change?

Social and cultural factors on both a national and global scale have alternately compelled and enabled women to make movies. The advent and evolution of digital technology profoundly transformed the cinematic language and the economics of the film industry. The size of crews needed to make a film has shrunk, and rigid hierarchies have been loosened somewhat, empowering greater numbers of independent filmmakers.[2] There has been, too, an urgent need to tell female-centered stories as a response to the sexism, sexual harassment, and alarming violence faced by women. These two elements have combined to produce a proliferation of women filmmakers in Italy and beyond.

The rising profile of women directors seems more significant during the cultural climate of the #MeToo movement, despite the common opinion that it never happened in Italy.[3] This assumption has been questioned by several feminist journalists and activists, such as Carla Cossutta, a member of the transfeminist grassroots collective Non una di meno (Not a Single One Less), who rightly points out that the lack of judicial or social consequences for producers or directors accused of sexual harassment or abuse and the lack of media attention to the phenomenon is not proof that the movement was nonexistent. As a corrective, feminist journalist Ida Dominijanni asserts, "We did not miss the MeToo movement; we anticipated it, and that has been held against us." She reminds us that in Italy "the denunciation of the exchange of sex and power and money that underlies the political, ethical, and aesthetic system of [Silvio] Berlusconi started in 2009 thanks to women's accusations."[4]

Right before the beginning of the #MeToo movement in the United States, writer Giulia Blasi launched, in 2017, the narrative project #quellavoltache (that time when), inspiring women to share their stories of abuse on social media. In February 2018, a group of 124 female representatives of the media industry, among whom was actor Asia Argento, one of the first to break the silence (and one shamefully discredited by Italian newspapers), along with several women's organizations, signed a letter addressed to the president of the Italian Republic, Sergio Mattarella. The letter was later published by the prominent left-wing newspaper *Il Manifesto*; it expressed solidarity with those actors who raised the alarm around sexual harassment and called for sisterhood and support for all women abused in the workplace: "Gender inequality in workplaces makes women—all women—vulnerable to sexual harassment, always subjects to implicit blackmail. It happens to secretaries, factory workers, migrants, students, interns, housekeepers.... The time has come when we are no longer scared."[5]

This breaking of the silence, the need to assert one's own autonomy, integrity, and worth, whatever one's vocation or social position, is very much part of a trajectory that started well before but was amplified by the #MeToo movement. It has driven the discourse toward women's stories and the rising profile of women directors.

Against the historical scarcity of female role models, the increased visibility of women directors around the world and in the Italian national context, even if not yet a significant presence in mainstream cinema, empowers other women to enter the field. For instance, Alina Marazzi's stunning documentary films have forged a path for other women filmmakers in Italy and revived the use of found footage and mixed media, tools that are rich in content and possibility and not too costly. Her documentary film *Vogliamo anche le rose* (*We Want Roses Too*, 2007) revisited the women's liberation movement of the 1960s and 1970s by masterfully suturing various types of archival material: films directed by other feminist filmmakers from previous generations, commercials, educational films from the period, and photo magazines, all accompanied by the personal journals of three women. The title of Marazzi's film references the political slogan "Bread for all, and roses too" that women workers chanted during the 1912 textile strike in Lawrence, Massachusetts.

In addition to reviving historical moments in her own films, Marazzi gives an afterlife to hard-core feminist documentary films from the mid-1970s that had very limited circulation, if any, beyond the small circles that might have viewed them. Moreover, she encourages archivists and historians to search for lost women's cinema. Anna Bella Miscuglio and Roni Daopuolo's *L'aggettivo donna* (The Adjective Woman, 1971), long since given up for lost, was recovered from a moldy basement of the National Film Archive in Rome when Marazzi insisted it be searched for.[6] Significantly, one of the most recent publications on the work of women directors published in Italy is called, paraphrasing the title of Marazzi's film, *We Want Cinema*. Women have thus claimed the right to the camera.[7]

Literature may also be empowering women to undertake film projects. In a 2019 *New York Times* article, "The Ferrante Effect," journalist Anna Momigliano argues that the global success of Elena Ferrante's Neapolitan Quartet, which has sold over fifteen million copies worldwide and was adapted into an HBO-RAI TV series, has been "inspiring female novelists and shaking up the country's male-dominated literary establishment." The international critical acclaim and the popular consensus for what is mostly a woman's bildungsroman as a writer and academic is inspirational not only for women authors but also for women artists at large. In other words, the "Ferrante effect" might well reverberate into cinema, and while no Italian film made by a woman has yet had the global resonance of Ferrante's books, it seems that in Italy, women directors, like women writers, "are ascendant."[8]

International film festivals are essential to the circulation of films directed by women. In Italy, Cinema e Donne di Firenze is on its forty-third edition in Florence; Sguardi Altrove has been held in Milan since 1993; Immaginaria, International Film Festival of Lesbian and Rebellious Women, also founded in 1993, takes place in Bologna and Rome; and many other women's film festivals and retrospectives are starting in all regions of Italy. Despite the struggle to obtain funds, they continue to promote the work of early-career directors and play a significant role in retrieving neglected women's work from the archives.

Still, while ever more women manage to secure funds to produce their *opera prima*, they still represent less than 10 percent of Italian filmmakers, a significantly lower percentage than many other European countries. A 2015 report by the European Women's Audiovisual Network indicates that in Austria, Croatia, France, Germany, Sweden, and United Kingdom, between 2006 and 2013, 21 percent of films were directed by women. In Italy, a recent study, DEA (Donne e audiovisivo; Women in Audiovisual Industry, 2018), conducted by the Consiglio Nazionale di Ricerca (National Research Council) documents "gender discriminations in hiring and unequal pay, precarious conditions of work, and difficulties in gaining access to decision-making and prestigious positions." "A woman-led project," writes Ilaria De Pascalis, "requires a greater effort in finding multiple funding partners, and it inevitably has a smaller budget."[9] The same was confirmed by all the directors I interviewed while writing this book.

In 2016, Italy adopted a law that reformed the allocation of public funds for use in the film industry. Known as the Franceschini law, the statutes included for the first time a gender quota, which, through a gendered point system, has encouraged film companies to propose films directed by women. While this ranking system might not ensure diversity within predominantly male juries, this new legislative framework may contribute, in time, to correcting the gender gap. After all, if the gender gap remains wide and female directors continue to work predominantly from the industry's margins, they are most likely to remain invisible.

In her remarkable 2015 book *Women's Cinema, World Cinema*, Patricia White raises a question that many female film scholars are addressing: "Where in the world are women making movies, and for whom, and who is seeing and writing about them?"[10] White's book includes an impressive number of films from twenty-two countries, yet no Italian woman director is represented.[11] Marc Cousins's thirteen-hour documentary film *Women Make Film: A New Road Movie* (2018), encompassing over one hundred films worldwide from the silent era to the present, includes only the work of Liliana Cavani, Lina Wertmuller, and, from the new generation, Alice Rohrwacher.

These omissions and limited recognition are the by-product of the invisibility of Italian women's cinema in the international film industry and in scholarly discourse outside the field of Italian screen studies. A few isolated cases aside, this is a cinema rarely distributed beyond the borders of Italy, often not even in Italy, and despite the proliferation of streaming platforms, it is essentially unavailable. All of which is to say, the work of Italian women film directors is still largely absent from the map of global cinema.

Investigating women's cinema from a feminist perspective has always been a matter of making the invisible visible, of rewriting film history in ways that reposition women filmmakers within it. Such an endeavor, in the Italian context, has been initiated by Giuliana Bruno, who sheds light on the work of Elvira Notari, Italy's "first and most prolific woman filmmaker," and demonstrates how her independent, street filmmaking practice constituted a countercinema to the mainstream national cinematic production of the time, characterized as it was by the "super spectacle."[12] Between 1906 and 1930, Notari wrote, directed, and produced nearly "sixty feature films and over a hundred documentaries and short films" while running her own film production company, Dora Film, in Naples.[13] Concerned with the hardships of the lower classes, especially women, and shooting on location with nonprofessional actors and inserting intertitles in Neapolitan dialect, Notari appears, Bruno argues, as a precursor of the celebrated Italian neorealist cinema. However, Notari's remarkable work was suppressed, first by fascist censorship and later by critical neglect. It is largely lost, except for three films.

Streetwalking on a Ruined Map showed me how the figure of Elvira Notari and her pioneering work are relevant to my study, which concerns a much more recent cinematic production. Not only does Notari's story exemplify the exclusion from the canon that many women artists suffered over the centuries, but her city films also foreshadow the female and place-centered urban narratives that I identify as a recurrent trope in the work of contemporary Italian women filmmakers. Bruno's spatial approach to cinema and the "reappropriation of geography in history" that her book develops have been a major source of inspiration, as has been her "reclaiming of marginality and difference," a guiding principle of my own scholarly endeavor.[14]

Many other scholars give Italian cinema "a second take on gender" as advocated by Danielle Hipkins, either by studying the work of single directors, as Gaetana Marrone did in her 2000 monograph on Liliana Cavani, *The Gaze and the Labyrinth*, or by offering comprehensive studies such as Bernadette Luciano and Susanna Scarparo's *Reframing Italy*, which explores how the Italian cinematic tradition has been embraced and transformed in Italian women's films.[15] Maristella Cantini's collection of essays entitled *Italian Women Filmmakers and the Gendered Screen* assembles the work of artists from the past and the present who, in addition to being directors, are also writers, painters, and scrapbookers.

In Italy, Lucia Cardone founded FAScinA (Forum annuale delle studiose di cinema e audiovisivi/Annual Forum of Women Scholars of Film and Audiovisual), based in Sassari, Sardinia. Now in its tenth edition, this forum endeavors to brings together female international scholars to promote their scholarship on women's work in film and media. It has built an online video gallery of contributions on a vast array of topics from cinema's representations of feminism and women's liberation movements, actors' engagement in writing, and women's experimental cinema.[16] Similarly, Stefania Benini and Barbara Zecchi are building an online archive of oral history, The Gynocine Project, collecting the increasingly numerous voices of women directors.[17]

Finally, in Rome, Veronica Pravadelli had a leading role in the creation of the international network Global Women's Cinema, "whose role is to investigate women's agency in film production, distribution and reception in contemporary global and transnational contexts," and she has also made important contributions to scholarship on the subject, such as the volume *Contemporary Women's Cinema* (2017), which explores how "women's cinema now tends to merge women's personal and private trajectories with historical, social, political, and religious dynamics."[18]

Wandering Women participates in all these scholarly efforts in the field of Italian and cinema studies to inscribe contemporary Italian women's filmmaking in a global film scenario.[19] Furthermore, as a book that takes a specific theoretical approach to Italian women's filmmaking—a feminist ecocritical one—it also builds on the significant body of works that in the last decade has been placing Italian studies in dialogue with the environmental humanities.

Pathbreaking books such as Marco Armerio and Marcus Hall's *Nature and History in Modern Italy* (2010), Monica Seger's *Landscapes in Between* (2015), Serenella Iovino's *Italy and Ecocriticism* (2016), and Enrico Cesaretti's remarkable *Elemental Narratives* (2020), along with rich edited volumes like Pasquale Verdicchio's *Ecocritical Approaches to Italian Culture and Literature* (2016), Iovino, Elena Past, and Enrico Cesaretti's *Italy and the Environmental Humanities*

(2018), and, most recently, *Posthumanism in Italian Literature and Film* (2020), edited by Enrica Maria Ferrara, have delineated a new, ethically engaged scholarly landscape in Italian studies.

Finally, *Wandering Women*, as a book that engages with the field of ecomedia, is intellectually indebted to Past's *Italian Ecocinema: Beyond the Human* (2018), which inaugurates a new approach to Italian cinema studies, reading cinematic texts "in terms of pressing environmental questions" and interrogating the nonhuman actors (hydrocarbons, dirt, nonhuman sounds, animals, especially goats, and volcanoes) involved in the process of filmmaking, as well as in the narratives. I was particularly inspired by Past's awareness that "to understand the complexity of film's engagement with the world, we should examine what happens before the film makes it to the screen" and her invitation to explore "the ways a film shapes the world, while also seeing the reciprocal ways the world writes itself on film."[20] All these environmentally conscious works paved my way and contributed to what Rosi Braidotti calls "the decentering of Man" in the humanities. They convinced me of the urgency to continue writing about women's cinema in Italy.[21]

NOTES

1. Greta Gerwig and Jane Campion, "Greta Gerwig and Jane Campion Honor Lina Wertmuller at the 2019 Governors Awards," Oscars, October 27, 2019, YouTube video, https://www.youtube.com/watch?v=AcaTL9oGahU&ab_channel=Oscars.

2. During the silent era, when the roles of writer, director (at the time, artistic director), producer, and even distributor converged, women found spaces they would progressively lose later when motion pictures acquired a more regimented structure. The digital era, to a certain extent, has re-created that freedom.

3. See Horowitz, "In Italy, #MeToo Is More Like 'Meh'"; and Siviero, "È vero che in Italia il #MeToo non c'è mai stato?"

4. Siviero, "È vero che in Italia il #MeToo non c'è mai stato?" (my translation).

5. "Dissenso Comune" (my translation).

6. I acquired this information from Alina Marazzi during her visit to Johns Hopkins University in 2017.

7. Buffoni, *We Want Cinema*.

8. Momigliano, "'The Ferrante Effect': In Italy Women Writers Are Ascendant."

9. See De Pascalis, "La ricerca DEA-Donne e Audiovisivo," 262.

10. White, *Women's Cinema*, 7.

11. The October 2015 issue of *Sight & Sound*, "The Female Gaze," lists one hundred overlooked films directed by women from all over the world and from different decades. Italy is represented only by Liliana Cavani's 1981 *La pelle*.

A more recent list compiled by the BBC includes Alice Rohrwacher's *Lazzaro felice* (*Happy as Lazzaro*, 2018).

12. Bruno, *Streetwalking on a Ruined Map*, 18.

13. Bruno, 3.

14. Bruno, 4. Bruno employs an "archeological intertextual approach." She uses film journals and advertising material to investigate the reception of Notari's films and draws connections between her films and nineteenth-century and regional women's popular literature. She masterfully reconstructs the cultural context in which Notari's work was produced and received in order to inscribe her work into a genealogy of women's cultural production.

15. Hipkins, "Why Italian Film Studies Needs a Second Take on Gender."

16. Lucia Cardone, Elena Marcheschi, and Giulia Simi, eds. "FAScinA 2020_Sperimentali: i contributi video," *Forum Annuale delle Studiose di Cinema e Audiovisivi*, accessed October 18, 2021, https://fascinaforum.org/fascina-2020-home/galleria-video-fascina-2020/.

17. The Gynocine Project, accessed October 18, 2021, https://www.gynocine.com/.

18. Pravadelli, *Contemporary Women's Cinema, Global Scenarios and Transnational Contexts*, 1.

19. I would like to acknowledge that Dalila Missero's book *Women, Feminism and Italian Cinema: Archives from a Film Culture* was published in 2022, while my book was already in the late stage of production. Missero's book adds to the literature on Italian cinema a much-needed study of feminist filmmaking practice in the period between 1960s and 1970s. Although its subject is relevant to the treatment of contemporary expressions of feminist cinema, I was not able to incorporate its findings in my treatment of contemporary women's cinema.

20. Past, *Italian Ecocinema beyond the Human*, 12, 2.

21. Braidotti, *The Posthuman*, 2. See also, Braidotti, "Afterword: The Proper Study of the Humanities Is No Longer 'Man.'"

ACKNOWLEDGMENTS

THIS BOOK IS DEDICATED TO all the women of my family: my grandmothers, aunts, and my mother—a lemon picker, a trader, workers in a toy factory, all of them mothers, housewives, caretakers, and fast-paced walkers. They are my models of courage, resilience, and resourcefulness. I am grateful to all of them for their hard, often unrecognized, work of care that contributed to my chance for an education. My gratitude goes, above all, to my mother, Margherita, for imagining a different path for me, along with my father, Luigi, who never left me while I was writing this book.

Academic family members offered fundamental support. I am exceptionally grateful to Aine O'Healy, whose work as a feminist film scholar set a paradigm for my research project on Italian women filmmakers. I thank her for providing attentive and rigorous feedback on early drafts of the manuscript and for her guidance and continuous encouragement. I also offer deep, special thanks to Giancarlo Lombardi, a dedicated mentor, who also became a personal advocate during challenging times, always inspiring me to move forward with excellence. I am indebted to David Forgacs for his pathbreaking scholarship on Italian culture and for his guidance and support over the years.

Infinite thanks to my colleague and mentor at Johns Hopkins University, Bernadette Wegenstein, for inspiring me with her documentary filmmaking and dedication to women's world cinema, for bringing brilliant scholars and filmmakers to the Center for Advanced Media Studies, and for building a community of cinephiles. I am also grateful to Sharon Achinstein for her dear advice and guidance and to my colleagues Sam Spinner and Marina Bedran for their solidarity and friendship.

I wish to thank, too, the department of Modern Languages and Literature and the Krieger School of Arts and Sciences at Johns Hopkins University for the vibrant intellectual environment that nourished my work. I am especially grateful to have been able to participate in a research boot camp, the Faculty Success Program with the National Center for Faculty Diversity and Development (FDD), in the summer of 2018. Thanks to the FDD for granting me a scholarship that allowed me to repeat the program in 2019. Both programs were deeply transformative experiences that equipped me with academic survival skills and guided me to forge a daily writing practice that was instrumental to the completion of this book.

Through FDD, I met an extraordinary developmental editor and writing coach, Rose Ernst. While traveling around the world, she accompanied this project from the crafting of the book proposal to the final manuscript. Rose, thank you for getting me unstuck, helping me to recognize my strengths as a researcher and writer, and, when it was necessary, urging me to stop researching and start writing.

Many people eased the incessant research process that preceded and unfolded in parallel with writing. First, the librarian Mackenzie Zalin, from the Sheridan Library at Johns Hopkins University. Mack, your help was essential during the lockdown of the COVID-19 pandemic, when we all lost access to libraries and archives. Natalia Rolla, Viridiana Rotondi, and Lisa Sacchi, my former colleagues at the Centro Sperimentale di Cinematografia, and Luca Ricciardi and Claudio Olivieri from the AAMOD, Audiovisual Archive of the Democratic Labor Movement in Rome, provided me with invaluable noncommercial copies of films and images that enriched my book and connected me with directors whose works compose my map of women's filmmaking.

I am most grateful to directors Cecilia Mangini, Mariangela Barbanente and their producer Gioia Avvantaggiato from GA&A Productions, Marina Spada, Francesca Comencini, Alina Marazzi, Wilma Labate, Alice Rohrwacher, Eleonora Danco, Anna Kauber, and Paola Randi for the interviews they granted, some of which turned into conversations in their homes, museums, gardens, cafés, and hotels, in Rome, New York, Baltimore, or on computer screens and phones. I deeply appreciate the experiences you shared, the doubts you raised, and the time you took to engage in long, insightful discussions about your filmmaking practice. My double gratitude goes especially to Marina Spada for generously sharing her beautiful scrapbooks and allowing me to share them with my readers.

ACKNOWLEDGMENTS   xix

I am indebted to Robert Rushing, editor of the book series New Directions in National Cinemas at Indiana University Press, and to Allison Blair Chaplin, acquisitions editor, for choosing and caring for this book. And I cannot thank enough the three anonymous readers engaged to review the manuscript. You all provided the most generous, thoughtful feedback and illuminating suggestions that enabled me to sharpen the feminist ecological framework of my book. I shaped and reshaped this book in an inner dialogue with you. And thank you for loving my *fegatelli* and for wanting more of them!

I wish to acknowledge the ISSNAF (Italian Scientists and Scholars in North America Foundation) for selecting me as a finalist for the RnB4Culture Award for Innovation in the Study of Italian Culture. I thank them for their consideration and for the joy of first presenting the completed version of *Wandering Women* at the 2021 symposium.

I wrote most of this book at my desk, in my apartment in New York. On the wall, there is a map of New York City called "The City of Women," but it has nothing to do with Federico Fellini's film. It is a map of the New York City subway, designed by Rebecca Solnit and Joshua Jelly-Schapiro, with each station renamed after a woman who lived in NYC and shaped its history. The epigraph says, "What kind of silence arises in places that so seldom speak of and to women? This map was made to sing the praises of the extraordinary women who have, since the beginning, been shapers and heroes of this city that has been always, secretly, a City of Women." This map marked my writing space, and the words written underneath were my abracadabra at the beginning of long, often frustrating days of work. More meaningful was the fact that this framed female cartograph was a gift from my friend and colleague, the historian Martha Jones. Martha, thank you for your friendship, mentorship, and for celebrating every step forward.

And thanks to my brilliant friend Victor Zarour Zarzar for his meticulous copyediting, his phenomenal attention to detail, and his imperturbable positive attitude. To Hopkins graduate student Marta Cerreti, thank you for your infectious intellectual enthusiasm.

I also wish to thank friends who provided spaces with nonhuman writing companions, like Annie Paulson and Jeff Brown (and their cats Tequila and Black Velvet), and a room with a view on the water, like Abigail Carrol. Childhood friends back in Italy, Roberta Rustichelli and Arianna Azzolina, took care of me when I most needed it and cheered for me from the other side of the ocean. And finally, one special friend, who over the years became more like a sister, has my infinite gratitude: Valeria Castelli. She was my accountability buddy, silenced my inner critic, read rough drafts, and gave me unlimited affection.

Finally, every atom of me is grateful to my loving husband, Jamal Rayyis, for his unwavering support, for his unlimited patience, for listening to every evolving idea, for reading every word, for pushing me to strive for clarity, for feeding me and providing exquisite wines, and for encouraging me to work with joy. I could not have done this without you. *Grazie, amore mio.*

NOTE ON TRANSLATION

ALL ENGLISH TRANSLATIONS OF THE interviews, originally conducted in Italian, are mine. When the original language is salient for poetic reasons, I maintain the Italian and offer the English translation in parentheses.

WANDERING WOMEN

INTRODUCTION

Mapping Italian Women's Filmmaking

IN HER ENCHANTING BOOK *On Looking: A Walker's Guide to the Art of Observation*, Alexandra Horowitz writes about the effects of selective attention and mobility. What we see while walking is determined by our "internal monologue on what we are doing." "Attention," she says, is "an intentional, unapologetic, discriminator [that] asks what is relevant right now, and gears up to notice only that."[1]

As a film student in Rome and later in New York, I was spellbound by Federico Fellini, Pier Paolo Pasolini, Michelangelo Antonioni, the lesser-known Antonio Pietrangeli, and other Italian auteur directors, and I focused my attention on the wandering women populating their films. Iconic films such as *Le notti di Cabiria* (*The Nights of Cabiria*, 1957), *La notte* (1961), *Mamma Roma* (1962), *Il deserto rosso* (*Red Desert*, 1964), and *Io la conoscevo bene* (*I Knew Her Well*, 1965) show women searching for a place within the shifting landscapes of an Italy transitioning from an agricultural to an industrial society, rushing toward modernity. Embodying the multiple, cultural gendered meanings of walking—they streetwalk, embark on pilgrimages, sleepwalk, march, wander, migrate, saunter, or strut the catwalk—their perambulations are infused with melancholy, mental illness, fear, desperation, desire, joy, pride, and hope.

Feminist film studies urged me to investigate if and how women in Italy, a country whose cinematic tradition continues to have a global impact, could infiltrate a male-dominated industry and artistic scene. When I turned my attention toward women's cinema, a cinema made by, representing, and addressing women, as advocated by Teresa De Lauretis, I discovered a vibrant new generation of women directors whose work, like that of women directors of previous generations, had been completely neglected or confined to the footnotes.[2]

While researching and charting a map of this cinematic production, my understanding of women's cinema has been informed by Alison Butler's notion of "minor cinema."[3] As she elaborates on women's marginality in the image-making industry, "The distinctiveness of women's filmmaking is not based on an essentialist understanding of gendered subjectivity, but on the position—or positions—of women in contemporary culture ... neither included within nor excluded from cultural tradition, lacking a cohesive collective identity, but not absolutely differentiated from each other."[4]

Concerned with the marginal positions women occupy in the Italian cultural scene, as recognized by Butler, and with "the imprint that exclusion of women's perspectives has made on films, audiences, and the cultural imaginary," I assembled a body of nomadic narratives, stories shaped by roaming characters.[5] I use *nomadic* as Rosi Braidotti intends it in *Nomadic Subjects*, as "the entire process of becoming-subject" shaped by "the will to know, the desire to say, the desire to speak," and, as in the case of the women represented in films discussed in this book, the desire to be the subject of the gaze, to take up the camera, thereby shaping a way of seeing.[6]

Wandering Women traces an urban geography of contemporary women's cinema in Italy from feminist and ecocritical perspectives by investigating the work of eight remarkable women film directors spanning three generations: Cecilia Mangini, Mariangela Barbanente, Marina Spada, Francesca Comencini, Alice Rohrwacher, Wilma Labate, Roberta Torre, and Eleonora Danco. Their films, released in the first two decades of the twenty-first century, tell stories of displacement and liminality that unfold through the act of walking in the city.

In the process of mapping this cinema, the tendency to situate and investigate women's subjectivity in urban contexts and configure female characters as city walkers raised several questions: How do women assert their authorship? How and where do they position themselves in the cinematic worlds they create? And if the spatial practice of walking in the city can be considered a "pedestrian speech act" (indicating that walks are not only mute ambulatory acts but also forms of discourse), what statements do these filmmakers convey through their female city dwellers? Thus, a critical starting point for this book has been the conceptualization of the spatial practice of flânerie in literary criticism and the feminist debate around it.

In the context of mid-nineteenth-century Paris, flânerie was a spatial practice involving a shift from the private sphere to the public, two realms undergoing increasing separation due to industrial development since the beginning of the eighteenth century.[7] The flaneur is the male hero of modernity, as introduced by Charles Baudelaire inspired by Edgar Allan Poe. He leaves the intimacy of home to escape loneliness while simultaneously sustaining his isolation among the multitudes of the metropolis, which he infiltrates to find nourishment for his art. As inconceivable as it seems in today's pandemic-afflicted world, the flaneur found it "an immense joy to set up house in the heart of the multitude, amid the ebb and the flow of movement, in the midst of the fugitive and the infinite." Flânerie concerns being "away from home and yet to feel oneself everywhere at home, to see the world, to be at the center of the world, and yet to remain hidden from the world."[8]

Walking and looking, and seeing without being seen, are essential elements of this urban experience. "A passionate spectator," like the (future) filmgoer, the flaneur absorbs images in movement while being incognito. He sits at the window of a café, again rejoicing while gazing at the crowd. Both present but absent, involved but removed, engaged but detached, *he* is "an artist who is always, spiritually, in the condition of that convalescent."[9] For the flaneur, the modern city is a phantasmagoria: lights, carriages, women, and prostitutes are the objects of his gaze. Flânerie was a distinctly male activity.

The increasing rationalization of time and space and the opening of wide boulevards for traffic and public conveyance transformed the urban landscape and challenged a pedestrian experience that had been "more or less independent of the clock."[10] In *The Arcades Project*, Walter Benjamin, for whom "the great cities of modern European culture were both beautiful and bestial," isolated new incarnations of the flaneur, nomadic figures produced by the industrial economy and the logics of consumption: the sandwich man, the rag-picker, and the prostitute—"seller and sold in one."[11] None of these marginal figures "meet the poet as his equal."[12]

If the male flaneur's idleness and vagabondage lead to a creative end, female vagabondage is equated to prostitution and needs to be tamed, regulated, or prohibited. Susan Buck-Morss reiterates the idea of prostitution as the female version of flânerie: "The *flâneur* was simply the name of a man who loitered; but all women who loitered risked being seen as whores, as the term 'street-walker' or tramp, applied to women makes clear."[13] The Italian language confirms such a sexist distinction. The terms *peripatetica* or *passeggiatrice* (feminine) mean street prostitute, while the former's masculine *peripatetico* (from the Greek verb *peripateo*, to walk around) means follower of the philosophical school of the Peripatetics, founded by Aristotle.[14] Elizabeth Wilson reiterates this point: "Certainly, prostitutes, 'women of the streets,' never inhabited the streets on the same terms as men."[15]

However, common social practices like dining, shopping, and cinemagoing have permitted women to occupy public spaces for leisure without the presumption of streetwalking. Appropriate for the emergent age of consumer-driven modernity, the arcade, a predecessor of the contemporary shopping mall, functioned as a hybrid between private and public urban space that created a legitimate space for women to wander.[16] As Giuliana Bruno observes about the Galleria Umberto I, in late nineteenth-century Naples, such convenient spatial organization enabled women a double form of flânerie: that of shoppers and also that of cinemagoers and city viewers. In Bruno's words, cinema and flânerie share "the montage of images, the spatio-temporal juxtaposition";[17] therefore, cinema elicits a virtual form of flânerie (i.e., a spatiotemporal mobility) and an activation of the female gaze as a female spectator. But then again, the flaneuse spectator receives a preordained view of reality mediated through a representation in which women can be caught again in being the object of the gaze.[18] Moreover, it is doubtful that, at that time, women could be undisturbed film viewers if unaccompanied.

Thus, the figure of the flaneuse, which carries deeply embedded assumptions about the masculine nature of public urban space, is the result of a long process of ongoing female struggle to gain the freedom to safely occupy public spaces while being the subject rather than the object of the gaze. Again, Bruno reminds us, "It is not by chance that one of the first acts of Italian feminism was for women to 'streetwalk' together through the city at night, a gesture that aligns female emancipation with spatial appropriation of the city."[19]

From every era of world cinema, women filmmakers—essentially flaneuses equipped with cameras—have revisited the trope of flânerie and often restored the agency of the female city walker. At the beginning of the twentieth century, pathbreaking filmmaker Alice Guy Blaché produced and directed dozens of short films for the film production company Gaumont, many of them informed by a playful feminism. *Une dame vraiment bien* (*A Very Fine Lady*, 1908) charmingly represents a woman in the street as a disruptive presence. An elegantly dressed woman carrying a parasol leaves her house for a walk. Drawing the attention of male passersby as she innocently trots along the street, comic catastrophes unfold: a man walks into a lamppost, a distracted bicyclist crashes into the table of other male admirers, and marching soldiers with rifles trip as they fall out of formation. Finally, two policemen grab her by the arms, conceal her with a black cloth, and deliver her home.

Agnès Varda's *Cléo de 5 à 7* (*Cléo from 5 to 7*, 1962) is a classic of cinematic flânerie, a film I kept close to my heart and mind while writing about women strolling through Italian cities. Cléo, a comely singer anxiously awaiting the results of a cancer test, is preoccupied with the fear that the illness will take away her beauty. During a walk to distract herself from the wait, she is suddenly struck by the fact that it is life itself, not her beauty, that is threatened. Her senses awakened, she notices the world around her and starts engaging with others in the city—not as the object of admiration she had been previously but as an active participant. In short, she assumes agency. Having experienced a similar anxious wait over an illness, I reacted viscerally to the film. Affirming Horowitz's idea of selective attention described at the opening of this chapter, it is not coincidental that the theme of waiting is present in nearly all the films discussed in this book.

Women's urban filmmaking in Italy represents a claim for belonging. *Wandering Women* explores how women directors place themselves and their female characters both literally and figuratively as flaneuses in the landscape, and it analyzes their methods of cinematic self-reference. By roving through urban space and contemplating their surroundings, women question the gaze as an inherently male privilege and challenge the notion of urban space as a masculine domain. This wandering exemplifies an ongoing process whereby female subjectivity is constructed while also symbolizing a woman's search for a place within the confines of a largely patriarchal society. The errant female protagonists replicate the gaze of the directors and function as authorial self-inscriptions in the cinematic text.

In *Women's Cinema*, Butler refers to the experimental cinema of artists like Maya Deren and Chantal Akerman, writing, "Within alternative cinema, women filmmakers have addressed 'the difficulty of saying I' by appearing in their own films, performing as themselves and others, using their voices on the soundtrack and working with autobiographical content."[20] While most Italian filmmakers considered in *Wandering Women* generally adhere to conventional narrative cinema and, with the exception of Mangini, Barbanente, and Danco, do not physically appear in their own films, I observe similar degrees of self-reflexivity in their works. Italian women filmmakers express "the difficulty of saying I" (their anxiety of authorship) by formulating explicit statements of concern with the female gaze over the city, therefore affirming their appropriation of the cinematic medium through place-centered narratives.

But the female director's gaze does not only look inward in a postmodern, self-reflexive fashion. My aim is not only to acknowledge that women filmmakers appropriated the trope of female urban wandering in the transition from modernity to postmodernity to continue dismantling the persistent male-gendered nature of urban spaces; I must also emphasize that, in doing so, their films articulate an ecological discourse. While walking, looking, and actively engaging with their surroundings, they reimagine the places that shape their stories and bring into view landscapes that we, the viewers, ought to see. These films' nomadic characters wander along the margins of Italian cities, often represented as nonplaces, places of abandonment, and the ruins of postindustrial societies. By conveying ecological concerns about the fate of the human and nonhuman world, the films offer a broad exposé of the alienation and social invisibility endured by marginal subjects, especially by women.

I argue that while articulating a claim for belonging and asserting cinematic and social agency, women's urban filmmaking brings into view landscapes of the ecological crises in which urban decay and the erasure of nature intersects with human alienation. The emptied cities they traverse show the inability of contemporary cities to sustain communities and encapsulate humans' fear of extinction, but they also represent the possibility—the space—for a life-sustaining community to form.

To attain this positive outlook, however, it is essential to understand the state we are in. The characters' walks allow us to observe the effects of Italy's untrammeled industrialization, pollution of the sea and other bodies of water, the cementification of land, the abandonment of mountains, and the erasure of nature in the city. These are landscapes of the Anthropocene: "the new geological epoch defined by overwhelming human activity."[21]

Anthropocene is an unwieldy and powerful word that has generated intense debates in the field of environmental humanities and inspired new artistic practices. Considering human-induced massive environmental crises, not only have the debates proposed the renaming of the current geological era, the Holocene, but they have inspired an intellectual and imaginative shift. As Serenella Iovino writes, "The Anthropocene is both a landscape and a discourse, a dynamic composition of corporeal elements and sociopolitical narratives. . . . Its landscape is made of continuous cities swallowed by their own metabolism; it is a land swathed by an asphalt-and-concrete crust, a territory covered in rubble or knitted by wires."[22] This sort of landscape, mostly produced during the period of the economic boom, is recurrent in *Wandering Women*.

How does a solitary walker observe Anthropocene landscapes? One recurrent strategy adopted by filmmakers is to film from above. All the films discussed in this book contain these "views from above," often in the opening sequences. Views from above serve multiple functions: they signal the beginning of a journey, they showcase the landscapes of place-centered narratives, and they position women as storytellers. They are not views from nowhere; they are women's landscapes, with female protagonists almost always included in the view as observers. In *Italian Ecocinema*, Elena Past (in dialogue with Stacy Alaimo and Jussi Parikka) observes that "the view from 'above' and 'nowhere' comes frequently into play in the Anthropocene." As a view that replicates the camera's reference, removing the human eye from the field of vision, a bird's-eye view is a view from nowhere: an "abstract and potentially alienating" one that replicates a mechanism of control over and exploitation of the environment.[23]

However, a framing strategy including an observer, and particularly a female observer, works against that kind of control and opposes what Alaimo critiques as an "invisible, unmarked, ostensibly perspectiveless perspective."[24] A view from above that includes its observer works as a "recognition of our material interconnection with the wider environment that impels ethical and political responses."[25] Therefore, each of the five chapters of *Wandering Women* opens with a view from above, followed by street views retracing the nomadic spatial trajectories of the films analyzed, working against a sense of alienation from the surrounding world.

My approach to film analysis is informed by feminist ecocriticism, "a vitally important branch of ecocriticism" that asserts, as the compound term suggests, the inseparability of feminist and environmental issues.[26] As Serpil Oppermann, Simon C. Estok, and Greta Gaard explain, feminist ecocriticism embraces the critical premise of ecofeminism: the interconnection of gender, racial, and species oppression combined with environmental deterioration. Such a convergence is based on the "premise that how we treat nature and how we treat each other are inseparably linked."[27] Iovino, in dialogue with leading ecofeminist thinkers such as Karen Warren and Val Plumwood, emphasizes that at the core of ecofeminist thought is the dismantling of dichotomies such as human/nature, nature/culture, and mind/matter, as well as the undoing of the master narrative "in which the master subject (whether humankind, man, or colonizer) tends to 'devour' every form of otherness (respectively, non-human, women, or the colonized)."[28]

While I do not claim the films in *Wandering Women* address all the concerns of feminist ecocriticism (just as women's experiences in the films are not representative of all women), the book's theoretical perspective and activist approach can provide tools to recognize women's contributions to environmental struggles, bring awareness of women's marginal social positions and invisibility in deteriorating urban environments, and potentially transform the narratives about the world we inhabit. Ultimately, this framework illuminates new expressions of feminist filmmaking in contemporary Italy.

Reflecting on the trajectories of women's transnational cinema, Ann E. Kaplan observes that "if in the past, feminist issues (domestic violence, sexuality, motherhood, and the politics of discrimination and exclusion in the public sphere) preoccupied directors, as humans enter the Anthropocene, so female filmmakers explore dangerous environmental practices that foreshadow future [and present] disasters."[29] While it is true that issues of ecological crises might be more central in the films of a new generation of directors, the filmmaking practices (at the level of both representation and film production) of the films discussed in this book demonstrate a continuity and entanglement of those themes. Thus, I argue that feminist cinema or women's "countercinema," as Claire Johnston famously defined it in 1973, is ecocinema.

Wandering Women provides various examples of such ecocinema. As I write elsewhere, "Ecocinema studies emerge from an all-embracing method of critical inquiry at the intersection of film theory and criticism, material ecocriticism, bioregionalism, ecofeminism, environmental history, philosophy, and animal studies."[30] The interdisciplinary nature of this interpretative approach expands the realm of film criticism and theory and offers the tools, as advocated by Past, to "ask new questions about how and what films signify."[31] Most relevantly to the films treated in this book, ecocinema is a strategy of reading films and the landscapes they frame from women's perspectives, as well as in the context of film history, "in light of a changed perception of the world, with the knowledge of the devastation and social inequalities wrought by unrestrained industrialization, reckless over-construction, and abusive environmental practices."[32]

My critical approach also draws on Scott MacDonald's theorization of ecocinema, identifying it as composed of films that provide a slow, contemplative visual immersion into the natural world, counteracting the consumption of images to which mainstream cinema inures viewers. As he puts it, "The fundamental job of an ecocinema is to provide *new kinds of film experience* that demonstrate an alternative to conventional media-spectatorship and help to nurture a more environmentally progressive mindset."[33] Such cinematic experience, he argues, engages viewers in "a retraining of perception."[34]

While nearly all the films I discuss have a slow pace, they offer an immersion into peripheral urban lives, with rare moments of respite in nonbuilt environments (often solitary moments on beaches). However, in the vein of MacDonald's idea of "retraining of perception," I probe the cinematic framings, making visible what remains off-screen and bringing the cinematic text into dialogue with the world. While retracing the trajectories of peripatetic characters, I often engage in cine-geographical investigations about the places represented and that the films capture in their process of becoming. Integrating film analysis with urban cultural insights, I foreground the ecological discourse these films reveal. By doing so, I aim to widen the view to perceive the significance of environmental problems and how they relate to women's conditions in contemporary Italy, even when the films do not explicitly convey environmental concerns.

My dialogue with the filmmakers featured in the chapters infuses this book. In these conversations, the directors discuss their approach to filmmaking and their idea of a female gaze, while the filmmakers of earlier generations also describe the challenges of daring to undertake a profession still perceived as the exclusive province of men, as well as their struggle to finance their films, especially early in their careers. Financial obstacles present themselves to artists of all generations, but they are aggravated for women due to a deeply rooted reluctance on the part of producers, even when female, to entrust them with projects involving conspicuously large budgets.

Through my own experience on the set, I learned that what ends up on the screen, especially for low-budget film productions like the ones discussed in this book, often moves beyond the intention of the director and her crew; it is often influenced, if not determined, by the constraints of budgets or fortuitous circumstances. Nevertheless, the stories these directors told me enriched my appreciation of their process.

I chose the directors as interlocutors while being aware that cinematic work is a collaborative effort. That said, it seems fair to talk about single authorship for each film. With the exception of Barbanente and Mangini's *In viaggio con Cecilia* (Traveling with Cecilia, 2013), these films are written and directed (and even sometimes performed) by a solo filmmaker, an artist who leaves a distinctive signature on each film she produces by deploying specific stylistic strategies and themes. Most importantly, she is an artist whose gender affects the vision of the world presented in the film and the way she situates herself within it.

Each chapter of *Wandering Women* presents the work of one or a group of filmmakers. The opening chapter, "Walking in Resilient Cities," acknowledges the prominent role of a "minor" filmmaker—Cecilia Mangini—in the genealogy of women's filmmaking, and more specifically, of a filmmaking animated by a commitment to environmental and social justice.

The case study is Mangini and Mariangela Barbanente's *Traveling with Cecilia*, a documentary film set in the postindustrial cities of Taranto and Brindisi. The film features the two directors traveling to places where a younger Mangini, during the period of the so-called economic miracle (1958–1965), shot films that investigated the traumatic transition from agrarian to industrial society and uncovered the entanglement of social inequalities and environmental decline.[35] Four decades later, Mangini's films appear prophetic, as industry collapsed and left those cities both impoverished and heavily polluted. Incorporating extracts from Mangini's films such as *Essere donne* (Being Women, 1965), *Brindisi 65* (1966), *Tommaso* (1965), and *Stendalì, suonano ancora* (Stendalì, Playing On, 1960), and engaging in dialogue between the directors and the inhabitants of these agonized Apulian cities, *Traveling with Cecilia* gives Mangini's original work a new audience while also giving voice to a resilient and mourning population.

Taking us from the south to the north of Italy, chapter 2 examines three films set in Milan directed by Marina Spada: *Come l'ombra* (As the Shadow, 2006), *Il mio domani* (My Tomorrow, 2011), and *Poesia che mi guardi* (Poetry You See Me, 2009). This chapter is enriched by extracts from the director's film diaries containing captivating collages of paintings, photos, maps, and frames from films that inspired her, mixed with her own directorial notes in preparation for shooting.

By engaging with film texts and pages of diaries, I show how Spada constructs her authorship by inscribing herself into a place-centered artistic production rooted in Milan that includes film, poetry, photography, and painting, while also contributing to the recovery of other women artists' work, such as poet Antonia Pozzi. Utilizing the narrative strategy of an errant character in a deserted city, these films convey a critique of women's invisibility while exposing landscapes of the Anthropocene: neglected working-class neighborhoods, postindustrial areas, construction sites of soon-to-be-gentrified districts, peripheries where naturally flowing water has been covered by concrete. By eschewing the absolutism of the patriarchal gaze, Spada's transient Milanese narratives weave a fabric of the city that allows for gaps, temporal and spatial continuities and discontinuities, urban and rural voids, and uncertainties about the past and future.

Building on the discussion of Spada's films in which women's lives are transformed by gestures of hospitality, friendship, compassion, and love, chapter 3 explores the different dimensions of care, intended both as predisposition (caring for) and the practice of care (taking care of someone or something). I provide a feminist ecocritical analysis of two films by Francesca Comencini: *Lo spazio bianco* (The White Space, 2009) and *Mi piace lavorare—Mobbing* (I Like to Work—Harassment, 2003).

In a compelling and innovative way, Comencini tackles the experience of single motherhood in contemporary society: the emotional conflict of maternal ambivalence, the social isolation in which motherhood is often experienced, and the struggle to reconcile motherhood and paid work. These stories of survival and care unfold in the urban environments of Naples and Rome, cities that are surviving and transforming, much as the subjects who inhabit them. Drawing from Adriana Cavarero's concept of maternal inclination and feminist ecological conceptions of care, I argue that by showing how women take up the burden of care and condemning the violence of a neoliberal economy on women's bodies, these films contribute to an understanding of how care is vital to the survival of humans, nonhumans, and places.

Expanding on the theme of female childhood raised in the discussion of Comencini's *I Like to Work*, chapter 4, "Coming of Age in the City: Garbage, Corpses, and Miracles," presents three stories of girls surviving in the impoverished southern cities of Reggio Calabria, Naples, and Librino: Alice Rohrwacher's *Corpo Celeste* (2011), Wilma Labate's *Domenica* (2001), and Roberta Torre's *I baci mai dati* (Lost Kisses, 2010). Reconfiguring a strong motif from neorealist cinema that recurrently presented male children as witnesses of a wounded postwar society and as hope for the future of the nation, these films show a contemporary society that has lost control of its present and risks losing control of its future, all from the perspective of female adolescents.

While transitioning from girlhood to womanhood and undertaking journeys of self-discovery, Marta (*Corpo Celeste*), Mimì (*Domenica*), and Manuela (*Lost Kisses*) direct their gazes toward deteriorating urban environments. Simultaneously, they expose the collapsing structures that family, state, and church supposedly provide for building life-sustaining communities. Though different in genre and aesthetic approaches (the first two are dramas, the third a comedy), they all, in line with feminist ecocritical thought, critique the city as a toxic environment and a place of patriarchal violence while also endeavoring to create a *naturecultural* continuity in their narratives. The protagonists' walks through cities, though seemingly detached from nature, all end at the sea. Yet, this end is not an end at all; rather, it signals possibilities for the future, maybe chthonic, possibly elysian, unsettled, or even just happy.

The concluding chapter, "A Psychogeology of the City," is devoted to *N-Capace* (N-Able, 2015), a mesmerizing, visionary, and sophisticated film by performer, playwright, and filmmaker Eleonora Danco. The theme of liminality returns once again: liminality of genre, times, spaces, and emotions. Blurring the boundaries of fiction, documentary, and art performance, *N-Able* explores the emotional struggle of an artist haunted by her childhood memories. She is fraught with doubts and questions her ability to function in society as an adult woman, as well as her creative ability to make a film. It is another coming of age that unfolds through a journey on foot, this time between Rome and the director's coastal hometown of Terracina, with an errant protagonist who loiters, runs, throws herself on the floor, rolls around while probing, scrutinizing her surroundings. She bears a name appropriate for all the female characters portrayed in *Wandering Women*: Anima in Pena (Lost Soul).

I interpret Danco's nomadic narrative through the concept of psychogeography, "the art of moving through space according to feelings and effects rather than ordinary purposes," and its related term *dérive* (drifting), introduced by the Parisian Situationists in the late 1950s.[36] Danco's urban performances are acts of appropriation and a reimagining of public space; they protest urban deterioration through a call to protect ancient beauties and act as symbolic gestures to stop the transformation of the Eternal City. Danco builds what I call a *psychogeology* of the city: she digs in both the earth and in her soul to comprehend "the undecipherability of life." Similarly, I bore into the affective landscapes in which the protagonist places herself, unearthing both their symbolic and material significances to foreground on- and off-screen urban ecologies.

In intellectually engaging and playful ways, *N-Able* weaves together many themes explored in *Wandering Women*: walking as a form of introspection and self-discovery, the mother-daughter relationship, film as a form of mourning, the critique of relentless construction upon and extraction of resources from the earth, and women's claim for social and artistic agency. It seems to be an appropriate concluding walk.

I provide additional case studies through brief treatments in the liminal spaces of the book (in-between chapters). I call these snapshots *fegatelli*. In Italian film jargon, a *fegatello* (literally, a small liver) is a simple connecting scene or a detail that might be shot during the crew's spare time, or perhaps when the shooting schedule is disrupted by a rainy day.[37] These scraps of analysis suggest future trajectories for this book and offer possibilities to expand the map of Italian women's filmmaking and give voices to more women. Further highlighting the dialogue among the films presented in *Wandering Women*, each chapter is followed by a page or two on a film that speaks to the film or group of films discussed in the preceding chapter. These might give readers the impression of wandering off the path, but I ask them to welcome the *spaesamento* (disorientation) that might come from the brief digression.

Films such as Alessandra Pescetta's *La città senza notte* (The Nightless City, 2015), Francesca Fini's *Ofelia non annega* (Ophelia Does Not Drown, 2016), Alina Marazzi's *Tutto parla di te* (All About You, 2012), Emma Dante's *Le sorelle Macaluso* (The Macaluso Sisters, 2020), and Anna Kauber's *In questo mondo* (In This World, 2018) address local and global ecological catastrophes, rewrite histories, recover memories, commemorate losses, and show *modi vivendi* outside the logic of profit and consumption in rural environments. Some of these recent films gesture toward a posthuman cinema and an environmentally aware cinematic practice. With the final *fegatello*, dedicated to Kauber's *In This World*, we leave the city for the Alps and Apennines's high pastures and encounter shepherds from all regions of Italy, women of different ages, social backgrounds, and education who truly embrace a nomadic life in the care of nonhuman animals.

This is a cinema that embodies a feminist ecocritical ethos in *ars et praxis*. Kauber, in fact, is a one-woman crew, who despite the budget constraints of self-production, travels in a yellow Fiat Panda running on methane and films at a slow pace, always aware of cinema's ecological footprint.

Embracing the feminist ecocritical practice of situated knowledge that recognizes the importance of the author's position, both social and geographical, I take a personal and narrative approach to film criticism. I often introduce the analysis with my encounters with the filmmakers, imbued with reflections on how these films resonate with me: the first woman in my family with a university education; a breast cancer survivor; a white, privileged, yet "nomadic subject" myself, thinking between two languages, Italian and English, feeling at home in two countries, Italy and the United States, living between two cities, New York and Baltimore, and producing scholarship from the vibrant, multidisciplinary crossroads of Italian studies and environmental humanities.

I grew up in the coastal town of Fiumicino, about twenty miles from Rome. There, my father, a shipwright from the Amalfi coast, built his own shipyard on the banks of the Tiber. A fishermen's town with a marina for sailboats, bisected by a river flowing into the warm waters of the Tyrrhenian Sea, and now home to Rome's international airport Leonardo Da Vinci, Fiumicino is a transitional place, defined by mobility. Yet, while geographically close to the city of Rome, it is quite far away from that reality. With no movie theater, no bookstore, and no efficient public transportation that would easily connect me to the city, I experienced as a child and teenager the profound sense of immobility and social and cultural exclusion that every desolate periphery can transmit. There, I engaged in my anxious adolescent wandering, there is rooted my sense of nonbelonging, and from there originates my critical obsession with mobility and liminal spaces.

In *Happy Objects*, Sara Ahmed writes that "to be affected by something is to evaluate that thing. Evaluations are expressed in how bodies turn towards things. To give value to things is to shape what is near us."[38] Along the same lines, anthropologist Anand Pandian writes that "cinema draws its vitality from affective encounters with many kinds of worlds: those of the characters and the landscapes within which they engage one another, those of filmmakers seeking and remaking resonant environments for cinematic elaboration, and those of audiences who may or may not be moved by the horizons of these works."[39] As I contemplated how each of the landscapes of *Wandering Women* has affected me, I realized how the trope of wandering between the city and the sea is indeed my own. That is the horizon that moves me, and this is my homecoming journey.

NOTES

1. Horowitz, *On Looking*, 12, 13.
2. See De Lauretis, *Technologies of Gender*.
3. Butler borrows the concept of "minor cinema" from Gilles Deleuze and Felix Guattari's notion of "minor literature," which is produced by a minority in a dominant language. Butler, *Women's Cinema*, 19.
4. Butler, 22.
5. White, *Women's Cinema, World Cinema*, 2.
6. Braidotti, *Nomadic Subjects*, 5.
7. See Wilson, "The Invisible *Flâneur*."
8. Baudelaire, "The Painter of Modern Life," 9.
9. Baudelaire, 7.
10. Tester, *The Flâneur*, 15.
11. Gilloch, *Myth and Metropolis*, 1. Benjamin, "Paris, The Capital of the Nineteenth Century," 40.
12. Wolff, "The Invisible *Flâneuse*," 42.
13. Buck-Morss, "The *Flâneur*, the Sandwichman and the Whore," 119.
14. See "The Peripatetic School," *The Oxford Classical Dictionary*, 4th ed., Oxford University Press, https://www.oxfordreference.com.proxy1.library.jhu.edu/view/10.1093/acref/9780199545568.001.0001/acref-9780199545568-e-4870.
15. Wilson, "The Invisible Flaneur," 105.
16. The edited volume *The Invisible Flâneuse?* (2010) explores women's spatial practices in nineteenth-century Paris. Most relevant to this discussion is Greg Thomas's account of Parisian parks as urban spaces where women could exercise the freedom of strolling and looking. D'Souza and McDonogh, *The Invisible Flâneuse?*, 13.
17. Bruno, *Streetwalking on a Ruined Map*, 48.
18. See Friedberg, *Window Shopping*, 2.
19. Bruno, *Streetwalking on a Ruined Map*, 50.
20. Butler, *Women's Cinema*, 61.
21. Grusin, *Anthropocene Feminism*, vii.
22. Iovino, *Italy and the Environmental Humanities*, 68, 69.
23. Past, *Italian Ecocinema Beyond the Human*, 191.
24. Alaimo, "Insurgent Vulnerability and the Carbon Footprint of Gender," 28.
25. Alaimo, 26.
26. Gaard et al., *International Perspectives on Feminist Ecocriticism*, 30.
27. Gaard et al., 158.
28. Iovino, "Ecocriticism and a Non-Anthropocentric Humanism," 36.
29. Kaplan, "Traumatic Dystopian Futurist Scenarios," 15.
30. Di Bianco, "Ecocinema *Ars et Praxis*," 152–53.

31. Past, 3.
32. Di Bianco, "Ecocinema *Ars et Praxis*," 153.
33. MacDonald, "The Ecocinema Experience," 20.
34. MacDonald, "Toward an Eco-Cinema," 109.
35. See Crainz, *Storia del miracolo italiano*.
36. "Psychogeographic Destination Kit," *Bureau of Unknown Destinations*, accessed September 10, 2020, http://unknowndestinations.org/files/destination_kit_1_0.pdf. This is an art project by Brooklyn-based artist Sal Randolph developed at the interdisciplinary gallery Proteus Gowanus in 2012.
37. Apart from cinematic jargon, a *fegatello*, or small liver, is generally understood as a *panino* made from skewered liver cooked on a grill; in other words, a liver kebab sandwich.
38. Ahmed, "Happy Objects," 31.
39. Pandian, "Landscapes of Expression," 53.

ONE

WALKING IN RESILIENT CITIES
Traveling with Cecilia

THE FIRST CHAPTER[1]

In December 2018, in a bookstore café near Ponte Milvio in Rome, I met director Cecilia Mangini. She walked in and immediately asked the server in a gracious but peremptory tone to turn off the music so that we could have a quiet environment for our interview. "A book about Italian women filmmakers?" she asked abruptly, opening the conversation. She rolled her eyes. Thankfully, knowing the common yet puzzling-to-me refusal among Italian female directors to be identified as "a woman filmmaker," I prepared myself for her skepticism. "I know about your statement 'Cinema is not male nor female, it is cinema. And that's it!'," I said. "Can you deny that being a woman had any influence on your path as a filmmaker?" I asked.[2]

She did not answer my question directly but told me her origin story: "In the midforties I took a train to Rome, and I went to the Centro Sperimentale di Cinematografia.[3] I wanted to apply to study film directing. They told me: '*Signorina, lei è pazza!*' (Young lady, you're crazy!) They encouraged me to try editing or production, more suitable areas of study for a woman. I walked away. I bought myself a photo camera and went out into the street . . . respectable women in those years would not be out in the street. I became a photographer"[4] (see figs. 1.1, 1.2, and 1.3).

Street photography led to documentary filmmaking and film criticism. An encounter with poet Pier Paolo Pasolini was instrumental to the realization of her stunning first short films, *Ignoti alla città* (Unknown in the City, 1958) and *La canta delle marane* (The Chant of Ditches, 1961), which were inspired by Pasolini's early novels on the life of children on the outskirts of Rome. In

Figure 1.1. Lipari Islands, 1952. Pumice pickers. Photo by Cecilia Mangini. Fondo Fotografico Cecilia Mangini, Roma (Photo Archive Cecilia Mangini, Rome, Italy).

the same year, continuing her collaboration with Pasolini, she directed the critically acclaimed *Stendalì, Suonano ancora* (Stendalì, Playing On, 1960), which presents the mourning ritual of a group of peasant women in Salento, Apulia.

She was a forerunner of the contemporary trend of using found footage, which she employed masterfully in *All'armi siam fascisti* (To Arms! We Are Fascists, 1962), codirected with her husband, Lino Del Fra, and the film historian Lino Miccichè. The latter is an antifascist reconstruction of the rise and fall of the fascist regime made entirely from archival material. Then came *Essere donne* (Being Women, 1965), a documentary film commissioned by the Communist Party on the conditions endured by women workers in Italy. Tired of the struggle to secure funds to produce her films, by the mid-1970s she devoted herself only to scriptwriting.

In 2010, journalist and documentarian Mariangela Barbanente challenged Mangini to codirect a film, *In viaggio con Cecilia* (Traveling with Cecilia, 2013),

Figure 1.2. Sesto San Giovanni, 1957. Witnesses of the economic miracle. Photo by Cecilia Mangini. Fondo Fotografico Cecilia Mangini, Roma. (Photo Archive Cecilia Mangini, Rome, Italy.)

which would bring her back to her native Apulia and, for the first time, place her both behind and in front of a digital camera.[5]

In the 2013 film, the two directors travel to Apulia to revisit the places where, in the late 1950s and mid-1960s, a younger Mangini shot many of her documentary films, projects that focused on poverty and social marginality in both urban and rural environments. During the so-called economic miracle (1958–1965), the process of industrialization had just begun in the agrarian south. Today, decades of untrammeled industrialization have made the region's cities among Italy's most polluted, and the social inequalities Mangini uncovered in her early films have been exacerbated. Mangini's documentary films foresaw the ecological disaster happening today.

Figure 1.3. Milan, 1955. Preindustrial laundry. Photo by Cecilia Mangini. Fondo Fotografico Cecilia Mangini, Roma. (Photo Archive Cecilia Mangini, Rome, Italy.)

When I came across *Traveling with Cecilia*, I felt that it encapsulated the meaning and the trajectory of this book project. The film emerges from a feminist gesture: one woman director paying homage to another. Barbanente, a native of Apulia like Mangini, grew up worshipping her. One of the few women who succeeded in entering what in the late 1950s was almost exclusively a male profession, Mangini represented the female model of the militant, independent documentary filmmaker who nevertheless occupied a marginal position in the Italian film industry and history. Her ten-minute documentary films, per custom in Italy in the 1960s and 1970s, were projected in theaters before feature films, most likely to impatient viewers who wanted to be entertained rather than educated. Having died in January 2021, Mangini is currently regarded as a *grande maestra* by independent filmmakers and scholars, although her films are inaccessible outside the festival circuit and retrospectives and are thus not widely known.[6]

By incorporating extracts from Mangini's previous films and featuring the dialogue between the directors and the inhabitants of the blighted Apulian cities of Brindisi and Taranto, *Traveling with Cecilia* retrieves Mangini's work from the archive to give it visibility and to make it signify again, while tackling Italy's present ecological crises. It is an archive of Mangini's work but also an ecofilm in and of itself.

The term *ecocinema*, as Paula Willoquet-Maricondi and David Ingram agree, encompasses a great variety of films that, through different aesthetic approaches and modalities of storytelling, "engage with environmental concerns either by exploring specific environmental justice issues or, more broadly, by making 'nature,' from landscape to wildlife, a primary focus."[7] While *Traveling with Cecilia* is mostly concerned with the effect of environmental ruin on the human urban communities of Taranto and Brindisi, it falls into the broad definition of the ecofilm, or environmental justice documentary.

In addition to showing women as agents of change, this film acknowledges Mangini's prominent, one might say prophetic, role in the genealogy of women's filmmaking and highlights how her earlier opera, informed by a feminist ecocritical vision, revealed the connections among the oppression of women and marginal subjects, abusive environmental practices, poverty, and social injustice.

The dialogue between the two directors takes place largely as they walk, wandering through places each has visited before in different contexts, listening, taking in, and commenting on what they now find together. This chapter follows the spatial trajectories of the journey that unfolds in the film. Beginning with a view from above that frames the two directors on a stone bridge marking the entrance to the region (thereby announcing a place-centered story) and asserting the authorship of both women, the film heads toward Taranto and Brindisi. Highlighting the multiple temporalities of the film, and retracing the research path that *Traveling with Cecilia* propelled me down, I pause to reflect on Mangini's documentary films *Being Women, Brindisi 65* (1966), *Tommaso* (1965), and *Stendalì, suonano ancora* (Stendalì, Playing On, 1960), fragments of which are incorporated in *Traveling with Cecilia*, suturing, via editing, past and present. As the journey unfolds, I focus my attention on the symbolic meanings that emerge from the multiple walks that Mangini takes with Barbanente and with the people of Taranto and Brindisi in the environments in which they are immersed as they give voice to their protests and grievances.

I also highlight the film's narrative elisions, notably on issues around racial diversity and, strikingly, women's bodily experiences of environmental degradation. Finally, in a coda, I briefly discuss Mangini's last film projects, both codirected with Paolo Pisanelli, *Due scatole dimenticate* (Two Forgotten Boxes, 2020) and *Grazia Deledda, la rivoluzionaria* (Grazia Deledda, the Revolutionary, 2021), and her contributions to the construction of a female genealogy of women's art.

My encounter with Mangini infused the writing of this book with her passion and courage. As the dialogue that Barbanente undertakes with Mangini mirrors the dialogue I undertook with all the filmmakers of *Wandering Women, Traveling with Cecilia* feels like an appropriate starting point.

A VIEW FROM THE BRIDGE: WOMEN, THE LANDSCAPE, AND THE ARCHIVE

A car drives through a wind farm, and two women, Mariangela and Cecilia, their backs to the camera, converse along the way. Cecilia, the older of the two, finds the windmills scenic as they make the landscape more dynamic, "not frozen." "My body changed so much, why shouldn't the world around me change?" she comments.

"When was the last time you were behind the camera, 1974?" asks Mariangela.

Cecelia replies, "1974 or 1975, I am not sure. *La briglia sul collo* (The Bridle on the Neck), a documentary film I am very fond of. My husband, Lino, did the interviews. Every time it is shown I hear his voice."

We understand that this is a journey back home. When the car stops before crossing a stone bridge, Cecilia recounts a childhood memory, when she used to travel with her father to his homeland, Apulia. The women get out of the car and walk over the bridge (see fig. 1.4). "Why do you want to start the film from here?" asks Mariangela.

"This bridge over the Ofanto River represents the entrance into the Apulia of my childhood, the Apulia I then explored in my documentary films years later. Apulia reminds me of my father," Cecilia answers.

The view from the bridge urges us to reflect on the idea of landscape and also the question of who is looking at it. Feminist geographer Gillian Rose argues that a landscape is not merely that which falls into the visual field of the observer; it is a partial worldview (like that of the filmmaker), a form of

Figure 1.4. Cecilia and Mariangela on the bridge over the Ofanto River. Screen capture, *Traveling with Cecilia* (2013), directed by Mariangela Barbanente and Cecilia Mangini. © GA&A Productions.

representation. At play is a "visual ideology," a way of looking that implicates issues of gender.[8] The view from the bridge presents women as "bearer[s] of the look," in Laura Mulvey's terms.[9] As we shall see repeatedly in *Wandering Women*, through views from above and street views, this modality of framing the landscape, one that includes its observers, suggests an assertion of female authorship. As in Danco's *N-Able* (chap. 5), in *Traveling with Cecilia* these features shape the narrative itself insofar as the directors are also "actors" who stage the making of the film.

The scene on the bridge addresses the film's self-reflexivity and tells us what we are about to participate in: the journey of two women directors from different generations who are making a film together. The younger woman revisits the work of her older colleague, and together they take a stance on the present. Adopting a participatory modality of documentary filmmaking, the directors of *Traveling with Cecilia*, as Valeria G. Castelli writes, "purposely fashion their persona on screen in order to enhance the trustworthiness of their narration and advance their political agenda.... Their performances attest to their ethical care for collective problems as well as their role as active political agents."[10]

The camera frames the two women in an extremely long take while they are standing on the bridge and looking at the murky water of the river (fig. 1.4).

Figure 1.5. Olive pickers in Apulia. Screen capture, *Being Women* (1965), directed by Cecilia Mangini, © Fondazione AAMOD.

The music marks this as a solemn moment. Cut. Black-and-white footage shows women picking olives in a field in the proximity of a factory (fig. 1.5). This is an extract from Mangini's 1965 *Being Women*, as mentioned, a film about the conditions of women workers in Italy during the economic miracle. "Today industry peered out among the olive groves of the south—those that have not [yet] been uprooted to make space for factories," says the voice-over. Almost fifty years later, Mangini returns to the places where she shot that film.

Traveling from north to south, visiting factories, farms, and houses, *Being Women* reveals how, in Mangini's own words, "Italy was taking off thanks to women's hidden work, thanks to the housewives who were taking care of the houses and the children. Italy was becoming a modern nation thanks to women, who were only starting to understand their importance."[11]

In this film, Mangini merges the idea of planetary destruction with an awareness of the debasement of women, an association that will become a foundational concept of ecofeminism in its early stages in the mid-1970s. As widely acknowledged, the term *écoféminisme* was coined by Françoise d'Eubonne in *Le féminisme ou la mort* (*Feminism or Death*, 1974), in which she identified "patriarchal man" as a toxic and destructive force, called for an urgent shift of power, and incited women to environmental activism.[12] While today the term *ecofeminism* is "irretrievably tainted," in Catriona Mortimer-Sandiland's words, for its essentialism, insofar as it implies that women are inherently close to nature and therefore perpetuates the nature/culture dichotomy whose dismantlement is central to feminist ecocriticism in all its current manifestations, its core idea still offers an understanding of the logic of anthropocentrism and its consequences. The oppression of women and the destruction of the environment are tightly interconnected, and a feminist ecocritical ideology and practice must expose those connections.[13]

Footage of atomic mushroom clouds opens and closes *Being Women* and is repeatedly intercut with scenes of exploited young girls in factories and women working in insalubrious environments, living in extreme conditions of poverty, and confessing to illegal abortions. Notably, Mangini mixes interviews of "real" women with images from the media showing glamorous, happy housewives. As the voice-over comments, "Those are the images of the myth of wealth, behind which our society hides contradictions and violence." In other words, by denouncing women's poverty, exploitation, illiteracy, and lack of agency, Mangini provides a counternarrative to the triumphalist rhetoric of the economic miracle.[14] In the finale, showing women peasants silently marching for peace, Mangini anticipates women's commitment to the feminist peace movement of the mid-1980s.

The transition from color to black and white, from present to past, and the alignment of gazes created in the process (Mangini and Barbanente's with those of the olive pickers) suggests that the olive pickers from Mangini's *Being Women*, as well as others who will be shown throughout *Traveling with Cecilia*, are inscribed in that landscape, part of the story of the place. Remembering these women—their labor and their relationship to the land—is crucial to understanding the present crisis.

TARANTO: THE CITY OF STEEL

From the bridge that opens the film, we head to the city of Taranto, the city of steel. Another view from above provides viewers with a map of the city. This time Mangini is off-screen, and Barbanente meets with a local citizen. Piles of dark raw material as vast as sand dunes in the desert appear in various shades of black, gray, and yellow. In the background, tangles of pipes, conduits, and conveyors. Cut. Barbanente and a young woman, their backs to the camera, stand on a terrace overlooking the industrial landscape (see fig. 1.6). While the

Figure 1.6. Mapping Taranto. Screen capture, *Traveling with Cecilia* (2013), directed by Mariangela Barbanente and Cecilia Mangini. © GA&A Productions.

camera slowly pans, the woman comments on the view and tells her story. She is a young doctor who migrated to the United States and has returned to her hometown of Taranto to "face the problem," as she puts it.

She oversees the city's cancer registry, which, it turns out, indicates neoplasm rates that are significantly higher than the national average. As she tells Barbanente, studies since the 1990s attest to excess cancer mortality in Taranto, but they have been ignored. The industrial landscape now extends beyond the piles of iron and charcoal to steam columns and smokestacks, with the sea, barely visible, on the horizon. What we see are the Ilva steel plant's mineral parks—the tracts of land where the raw materials required for the plant's production are amassed. As the camera continues to pan, it shows, in disquieting proximity to the steel plant, houses, a bell tower, a cemetery, and typical Italian cypress trees—features of the neighborhood of Tamburi.

Throughout the film, sequences of mapping and landscape views provide a sense of place. In the scene described above, we are offered a closer look at the city's source of pollution (the plant is inaccessible to cameras, which contributes to its demonization or nonrepresentability) as well as a glimpse into Taranto's everyday poisoning: "On windy days like this, the dust rises. So, they try to avoid the dust spreading by soaking it with water sprinklers. The parks and the piles are so huge that it is almost ridiculous to see puffs of water trying to dampen the dust," explains the doctor. As in Calvino's visionary 1958 *La nuvola di smog* (Smog), tons of dust covered the city of Taranto for over fifty years before the plant's management started implementing a plan to partially cover the mineral parks.[15]

Taranto's steel plant began operations in 1965, when, as Guido Crainz writes in his history of the economic miracle, the country experienced great economic growth, and new industrial geographies rapidly took shape in the underdeveloped south.[16] The plant was welcomed as a promise of modernization. Soon, it radically changed the topography and the social fabric as well as the identity of the city. Ironically, before the construction of the steel mill, the streets of the district of Tamburi used to be named after plants and trees. Their renaming speaks to the erasure of nature in the city.[17] Indeed, the construction of the steel plant (and the process of industrialization in general) entailed from the very beginning vast environmental damages that included the uprooting of centuries-old olive trees and the shredding of the landscape.

Today, Monica Seger writes, "despite rich histories of agricultural production, maritime trade, and artistic expression, Taranto is largely in a state of despair, struggling to survive amid deadly, decades-long industrial pollution."[18] Indeed, suffocated by heavy emissions of dioxin, accounting for 90 percent of national dioxin emissions, and afflicted by frightening cancer rates, especially among infants, Apulia has been dubbed in an investigative report in the Italian news weekly *L'Espresso* "la Puglia dei veleni" (Poisoned Apulia) and the steel plant Ilva a "source of national contamination."[19]

While the steel industry has undoubtedly been one of the main sources of pollution since the mid-1960s, it is not the only one. In addition to ENI, the major Italian oil and gas company, Taranto, given its strategic position on the Mediterranean, has been home to the maritime military arsenal since 1889. A fisherman Cecilia interviews laments, "The government knows how much stuff, all kinds of carcinogenic chemicals, is dumped in the sea, every day. They took our jobs, our future." The scene, which poignantly takes place right in the Mar Piccolo (the Small Sea), the lagoon around which the old city developed, shows how an entire harvest of mussels, cultivated over a year and a half, is lost to pollution with no compensation for the fishermen (see fig. 1.7).

As the granddaughter of a fisherman and the daughter of a *maestro d'ascia* (shipwright), I felt a great sense of loss and profound sadness over this scene. Food, the fruit of his labors, has turned to waste. The fisherman standing on his boat amid piles of corroded mussels appears as a contemporary and even more tragic version, if that's possible, of the impoverished fishermen from Giovanni Verga's 1881 *I malavoglia* (*The House by the Medlar Tree*), whose *mare amaro* (bitter sea) has turned into *mare tossico* (toxic sea). "We are dead, we're sinking," he

Figure 1.7. Cecilia and the Fisherman. Screen capture, *Traveling with Cecilia* (2013), directed by Mariangela Barbanente and Cecilia Mangini. © GA&A Productions.

says while he bails water out of his boat and catches his breath. His questions remain unanswered: Who polluted this sea? Will the citizens ever be compensated for their loss? How long will the process of decontamination take? Our position, as spectators, aligns with Cecilia's, who, seated on another small boat, leans toward the fisherman, showing great compassion.

Parts of Taranto we glimpsed in the view over the mineral parks and from the sea are shown later from a streetview perspective. Moving inland, the obituaries of former Ilva workers placed on the walls of Taranto signal that Ilva has brought illness and death. To press the point, a long camera car takes us through a dilapidated part of Taranto (fig. 1.8). The facades of the crumbling buildings are black, as though charred by a fire or a bomb, and the windows are bricked up. A western-sounding tune by Egisto Macchi, Mangini's longtime collaborator, connotes the *città vecchia* (the old town) as a ghost town.

As we shall see in the following chapters, the deserted city is a haunting visual trope in the films selected in this study. It conveys a sense of anxiety, alienation, loneliness, and immobility. In all of Marina Spada's films, *Come l'ombra* (As the Shadow, 2006), *Poesia che mi guardi* (Poetry You See Me, 2009), and *Il mio domani* (*My Tomorrow*, 2011), characters continuously roam the deserted streets of Milan.[20] In Comencini's *Lo spazio bianco* (*The White Space*, 2009), a quiet and uneventful Naples serves to underscore the existential immobility of the main character and the social isolation mothers often experience

Figure 1.8. Evacuated city. Screen capture, *Traveling with Cecilia* (2013), directed by Mariangela Barbanente and Cecilia Mangini. © GA&A Productions.

in a still largely patriarchal society. In Wilma Labate's *Domenica* (2001; see chap. 4), a deserted Naples (again) symbolizes the loneliness the protagonist experiences as an orphan and a raped child. All of the abovementioned films are very much defined by their place, and yet they simultaneously explore the feelings of rootlessness and unbelonging.

Unlike the previously noted films, though, *Traveling with Cecilia* does not place women's individual identities at the center of an isolating urban narrative. Rather, the city is portrayed as the place where a community lives; the deserted city does not signify individual alienation but rather the rupture of community. Its crumbling buildings reveal the impoverishment of the city, the unfulfilled promises of modernization and wealth; they speak of illness and death caused by pollution. In a film that deals with toxicity, a deserted city represents an evacuated city—a city too perilous to maintain the community that built it.

MOURNING WALKS

Taranto is a resilient city, and *Traveling with Cecilia* captures the ways the environmental crises dramatically impact its life. When Barbanente and Mangini traveled to Apulia for the shooting in the summer of 2012, a historical change was taking place. After decades of the state's inaction and corruption, a judge,

Patrizia Todisco, ordered the requisition of part of the Ilva plant and the arrest of its owner, Emilio Riva, for violation of EU environmental regulations and other crimes.[21] This event created much agitation in the city. It fired up local environmental activists and brought citizens into the street to demonstrate their rage and grief.

Mariangela and Cecilia, two adult women from different generations, camera in hand, walk, listen, and talk, interacting with others as they go, engaging their surroundings in a concrete, conscious manner. Narrating while walking is a strategy often adopted in documentary films to avoid the tedious repetition of static talking heads. In *Traveling with Cecilia*, a film that heavily relies on interviews, it represents much more.

The walking interview with the filmmakers (showing, alternatively, Mangini or Barbanente or both together) allows the "characters" to be immersed in their environment while reinforcing the self-reflexivity of the film. Most importantly, the process of walking reveals the two filmmakers' quest to understand the status quo. Listening becomes, as Deborah Bird Rose suggests, "an active verb," a way of paying attention.[22] Elaborating on Rose's feminist approach to communication, Greta Gaard reminds us that communication has been long conceived in terms of power hierarchies: "Speaking is associated with power, knowledge, and dominance, while listening is associated with subordination."[23] Debunking such dualism, a feminist documentary filmmaking practice is based on listening as a form of understanding, expressing solidarity, and giving voice to the oppressed as well as participating in their protests and grievance. Many of the walks Cecilia and Mariangela take, in fact, address people's need to mourn their losses.

In one of the most touching scenes in the film, Cecilia takes a walk inside Taranto's cemetery. (This is also a segment of the film that adeptly illustrates the continuity between past and present by incorporating extracts from Mangini's early films.) There, she engages in conversation with Cosimo, a retired worker afflicted by asbestosis, who started an inventory of Taranto's "victims of work," people who supposedly died from illnesses caused by toxic work conditions.

Taking one uncertain step after another and struggling to catch his breath, Cosimo says, "I am one of thousands of people afflicted with asbestosis. It's all the state's fault. A lot of my colleagues, unfortunately, are not here to tell their story. Many workers would have been saved if the state had protected our health and safety." He shows Cecilia a modest memorial stone along the alley in the cemetery: "Honor to those who lost their lives working."

The memorial stone acknowledges the absence of members of a community while helping the survivors cope with grief. Furthermore, it stands as a j'accuse

Figure 1.9. The mourners of Martano. Screen capture, *Stendalì, Playing On* (1960), directed by Cecilia Mangini.

for the impossible choice citizens of Taranto and Apulia had to face: work or health. Ultimately, as Cosimo's statement makes more explicit, it represents a collective demand for the responsible party's contrition.

Suturing past and present, the memorial stone in today's Taranto's cemetery is juxtaposed with images from Mangini's 1960 short *Stendalì, Playing On*. Inspired by the groundbreaking work of the anthropologist Ernesto De Martino, *Morte e pianto rituale* (*Death and Ritual Crying*, 1958), and most likely by Carlo Levi's novel *Cristo si è fermato a Eboli* (*Christ Stopped at Eboli*, 1945), it reenacts the ancient ritual lamentation of a group of women from the peasant village of Martano in the Griko-Salentino area (see fig. 1.9).

As described by historian James Amelang, drawing from De Martino, the practice of lamentation consists of "a dramatic mixture of words, gesture and music that moderated by ritual means the 'crisis of presence' or tendency to disintegration that threatened persons in moments of extreme mental danger, such as the aftermath of the death of a close relation."[24] Mangini's short film masterfully captures the repetitive gestures of the women swinging their

Figure 1.10. A mourning community. Screen capture, *Traveling with Cecilia* (2013), directed by Mariangela Barbanente and Cecilia Mangini. © GA&A Productions.

handkerchiefs and tearing at their hair while surrounding the body of the dead youth in a dramatic crescendo enhanced by the overlapping of voices: those of the women lamenting in the Griko language and that of the voice-over in standard Italian. The text, written by Pasolini, articulates the cry of a mother who has lost her child: "Piangete, madri che avete figli, piangete con tutto il vostro dolore, che vi venga dalle foglie dell'anima che vi abbandonano prima del tempo. Viene la morte che non ci rispetta, che ci ha tutti quanti segnati." (Cry, mothers that have children, cry with all your sorrow, that comes to you from the leaves of the soul that abandons you before time. Crude death arrives, which has for us all these marks.)

Returning once more to Taranto, viewers witness a contemporary form of ritual mourning: people gathered on the pier hang paper silhouettes of Taranto's dead while reciting their names (fig. 1.10). These are not anonymous bodies like those evoked on the memorial stone. They were women, men, and children whose lives, as the fluttering simulacra suggest, were fragile. It is a seemingly endless list; less haunting, perhaps, than the Griko lamentations from Martano, but it nonetheless provides an echo of ancient, solemn rites of grief, acknowledging both individual losses and the collective loss of community and environment.[25]

THE CITY OF OIL AND PLASTICS

Mariangela and Cecilia's journey through Apulia eventually takes them to Brindisi. As we discussed in the section devoted to Taranto, Mangini's archive offers viewers insights into the modern history of that place. Brindisi is an ancient coastal town located on the east coast of the beautiful Salento peninsula, the heel of the Italian boot. With its natural harbor, the city had been for centuries a crossroads for trade with Greece and the Middle East. In the late 1950s, it became the site of the country's greatest petrochemical complex, along with Porto Marghera, near Venice. Rapidly built from 1959 to 1962 and dubbed simply "Il Petrolchimico," it produced polyvinyl chloride and oil.

The city of oil and plastics, with its own internal road system, railroad, and buildings for workers and managers that covered an area of more than seven hundred hectares, devoured both countryside and beaches.[26] Like the steel plant in Taranto constructed later, Brindisi's petrochemical complex was presented by the national press as an almost supernatural event. A 1963 newspaper heralds, "The petrochemicals arrive in the quagmires of the old farms. The splendid adventure of the petrochemical pioneers; the city of oil is four times bigger than the town for the people. An immense city, a wonderful creation, a marvelous new page in the book of the history of the South."[27]

In 1965, just a few years after the plant started operations, Mangini made two documentary films, *Brindisi 65* and *Tommaso*, that counter that celebratory narrative by uncovering the worsening social inequalities and the already apparent environmental deterioration of the place. As Mariangela and Cecilia travel to a postindustrial Brindisi, extracts from Mangini's short films show, once again, that the current crises are the result of decades of what Rob Nixon defined as "slow violence," which "occurs gradually and out of sight; a delayed destruction often dispersed across time and space."[28]

Taranto, at least in the past decade, has been recurrently in the national news and has proved the source of inspiration for several documentary films and novels.[29] Brindisi, conversely, is almost forgotten.[30] Mangini's old films, in this sense, are rare historical documents, and *Traveling with Cecilia*, to my knowledge, is the only contemporary film that shows the social and environmental effects of the collapse of the petrochemical industry. *Brindisi 65*, a ten-minute reportage with some fictional twists, investigates the factory from both inside and outside. A rudimentary map of the south of Italy is followed by a rapid series of gigantic and alienating views of the chemical complex with its burning smokestacks juxtaposed against desolate streets of impoverished urban areas populated by malnourished, barefoot children. The voices of people too scared to be filmed bear witness to the aggravated poverty among farmers and day laborers, the exploitation of workers, the lack of safety measures, and the harassment of the workers who would rebel against such conditions. A pedantic male voice-over (alas, recurrent in all Mangini's films and in documentary films from the same period more generally) alludes to the lack of class consciousness among the workers and highlights how the social change and supposed modernization did not bring a change to the subordinate position of women.[31]

Tommaso, presumably shot at the same time and in the same locations, focuses on the life of a young man who aspires to work at Il Petrolchimico so he can make enough money to buy a motorcycle. It is a literal and metaphorical dream of social mobility. "The other Italians," the protagonist says, alluding to the urban middle-class people who arrived with the industry, "they buy everything." Establishing a conceptual association between consumerism and the production of waste, a man is seen on the banks of the river, rummaging through the garbage: "I'm looking for bottles to sell. They pay five lire each. It's bad. I'm forced to do that so that I don't have to steal. Four years ago, when they built the factory, I was a manual laborer, and I hoped to get a job in the factory, but to get in you needed a leg-up." As he speaks, the camera pans over the body of water that is colored an almost fluorescent white, most likely polluted by the factory's waste.

Finally, Mangini records the heartbreaking lament of a peasant who lost her son. He had left the countryside to work in the Brindisi complex, where he fell to his death in a storage tank. Reminiscent of Taranto's memorial stone and *Stendalì*'s ritual crying, Mangini juxtaposes the obituary with images of this mother crying while watering her vegetable garden. The scene alludes to the collapse of rural culture, a process accelerated by reckless industrialization.

Brindisi's chemical industry, Tatiana Schirinzi explains in one of the few studies on the subject, started declining in the mid-1970s with the energy crisis and rising oil prices following the 1973 Arab-Israeli war. Aggravating the crisis, a 1977 explosion in a section of a plant killed three workers and injured seventy. The plant, one of the most important of the complex, was never rebuilt but was instead progressively abandoned. The industrial area, with the exception of a few factories, was closed in 2000, leaving a legacy of environmental disaster: "What the petrochemical plant has left behind is a very large area to reclaim, filled with non-identified harmful substances, polluted aquifers, an interrupted food chain, a blackened (polluted) harbor, destroyed beaches—they were precious gems, part of the city's collective patrimony, some destinations of the working class, others of the bourgeoisie since the days of the belle époque."[32]

On one of those ruined beaches of Brindisi, Mariangela and Cecilia take a walk with a local resident, Silvio. As in Taranto, they collect stories along the way, allowing viewers to learn about the life of an individual while perceiving, through the observation of the landscape, the entanglement of humans and their environment. On a deserted beach scattered with refuse, Silvio shares his vision of the global economic dynamics that affect a "dying" postindustrial city like his hometown Brindisi, and his own personal story: "Today, the state no longer gets involved in giant industries, and at some point, it became obvious that it was more convenient to produce in Bhopal . . . here decontamination of the territory never took place. I am happy to see those smokestacks muted. Those smokestacks kill. They killed my father." As Silvio recounts with contained rage, his father, a former worker of the Petrolchimico, was diagnosed with cancer soon after retirement. Aware that his illness had been caused by exposure to polyvinyl chloride, he attempted to start a legal battle involving the judge Felice Casson. The latter had started an investigation on the Marghera Petrochemical complex in the Veneto region.[33] Unlike the investigation in Marghera, which ended in 2006 with the conviction of the management of the companies Enichem and Montedison, Brindisi's was inconclusive. "There are no culprits for those deaths. They died for nothing," concludes Silvio.

An epidemiological study published in 2013 (the same year *Traveling with Cecilia* came out) by Emilio Antonio Luca Gianicolo and colleagues documents that in addition to the devastation brought by the petrochemical complex, the city is exposed to toxic emissions from pharmaceutical, metallurgical, manufacturing, and cement industries; two power plants; and, finally, from illegal waste dumping. Shockingly, these massive pollution emissions "associated with increased mortality and hospital admissions due to respiratory and cardiovascular diseases" are below the legal limit, which makes Brindisi "a government-designed environmental risk area."[34]

Nevertheless, as *Traveling with Cecilia* shows, the majority of people are still scared and reluctant to speak the truth in Brindisi, like the doctor featured in the film, who observes an abnormal number of infant cardiac malformations yet refuses to state that they might be induced by pollution. Lowering his voice, he warns Cecilia to refrain from incautious accusations: "Stai attenta" (Be careful). Outraged by such intimidation, she keeps it in the final cut of the film to highlight that a code of silence prevents people from expressing their dissent—but she is not bound by such a code.

NARRATIVE OMISSIONS

As the opening view from the bridge announces, *Traveling with Cecilia* brings the perspective of women to the environmental crises in Taranto and Brindisi.

The filmmakers, who chose a participatory modality of documentary filmmaking, are "present" in the scene, asserting their position, not only as "bearers of the look" but also as speakers and listeners.[35]

Traveling with Cecilia builds a choral tale of shared vulnerability and collective grieving. However, some narrative omissions diminish its feminist political power and raise questions about the ethics of documentary filmmaking, and, more specifically, environmentally concerned filmmaking. For instance, at the end of the film, a young black man casually appears in the shot, sitting on a bench and holding a laptop. We are therefore casually informed that a nonwhite population lives in the city, although this is not given voice in the film. Such a problematic ending reminds us how overwhelmingly white Italian cinema is.

More relevant to the topic of this chapter, it is striking that the film devotes little space to women and the ways that poverty and a toxic environment might affect their lives. This omission becomes apparent when we reconsider the film's opening with footage from Mangini's *Being Women* that features female olive pickers by the edge of a factory. Awareness of the dire effects toxic exposure could have on women first came to light in 1976, through the story of Italy's first modern, industrial accident that took place in the small town of Seveso, near Milan. That catastrophe showed that exposure to dioxin in pregnant women causes miscarriages and fetal deformities.[36] And how do women experience toxicity in their bodies in today's Taranto and Brindisi?

In their independent documentary film *Non perdono* (*I Do Not Forgive*, 2016), Grace Zanotto and Roberto Marsella include an interview with activist and writer Daniela Spera.[37] Based on data from the 2015 epidemiological study "Sentieri" (Paths), Spera affirms that "approximately one out of two women in Taranto will see her child born ill or about to become ill." Although *Traveling with Cecilia* addresses in part the issue of infant illnesses, we are left wondering: Why aren't mothers given a voice? The reluctance to speak in front of the camera encountered by Mangini and Barbanente might explain, at least partially, these narrative elisions.

It is important to realize that all films elide and omit and that many activist voices are not explicitly political. Indeed, some of the most impactful scenes in *Traveling with Cecilia* are those that bear witness to and document contemporary forms of mourning gleaned through conversation. Mariangela and Cecilia walk and listen to the young female doctor in charge of the cancer registry, to an environmental activist, to another doctor reluctant to speak the truth, to a son who lost his father, and to a fisherman who lost his sea, all of whom suffer the loss of cities that sustained life for millennia. By breaking silence and bringing mourning to the public space of the screen, *Traveling with Cecilia* turns their private grief into a shared one, an act of contrition that is necessary to the survival of endangered communities and to raise collective environmental consciousness.

The silence around the toxic effects of polyvinyl chloride and the massive emission of dioxins by major chemical and steel industries, as well as the silence of disempowered communities like Brindisi's and to a different degree Taranto's, somehow reflect the destiny of Mangini's neglected films. In this regard, the story of *Brindisi 65* is particularly significant. A film shot in a couple of days, with a single reel of film, that admittedly tried to cover too much material, was censored. Mangini and her husband, Del Fra, risked the accusation of industrial espionage by the management of the Petrolchimico, and, over the decades, the film had very limited circulation. *Traveling with Cecilia* offers *Brindisi 65*, as well as other Mangini films, the opportunity of a new life with new audiences.[38]

Filmmaking, like scholarship, has the capacity to make the invisible visible and "to do justice to peripheral narratives," tasks that Serenella Iovino identifies as essential to the fostering of "an inclusive environmental culture."[39] *Traveling with Cecilia* gives visibility to the work of Mangini, a woman director who, from the margins of the film industry, committed herself to a form of political filmmaking that confronts a question that, as Willoquet-Maricondi writes, is "central to environmental justice struggles: How do injured bodies come to matter within the larger sociopolitical community?"[40] Despite narrative omissions, films like *Traveling with Cecilia* give voice to disempowered communities while turning us into "activist viewers," and they impel other directors to engage in filmmaking as a form of environmental activism and to be agents of change.[41]

CODA

During our interview, Mangini was reluctant to talk about *Traveling with Cecilia* and in general about the past. But she was eager to tell me about her most recent film in collaboration with Paolo Pisanelli: *Two Forgotten Boxes*, 2020. Almost entirely made of black-and-white photos accompanied by a voice-over and combined with footage of Mangini in her home in Rome, the film is about an unfinished project, *Le Vietnam sera libre* (Vietnam Will Be Free), one of the many saved in Mangini's archive at the Cineteca di Bologna.

In 1964, Mangini and her husband, Lino Del Fra, embarked on a documentary project on the war in Vietnam (see fig. 1.11). After months of preparation and field research, during which Mangini had undertaken a photo reportage documenting the Vietnamese resistance to the United States, they were forced to leave the country when the conflict intensified. A selection of the photos

Figure 1.11. Cecilia Mangini in Vietnam. Screen capture, *Two Forgotten Boxes* (2020), directed by Cecilia Mangini and Paolo Pisanelli.

featuring women warriors was published in the magazine *Noi Donne*, along with Mangini's article "Le caste guerriere del Vietnam" (The Chaste Women Warriors of Vietnam). The rest was forgotten.

Decades later, she discovered two boxes in her basement containing her entire Vietnam reportage and decided to close "an open wound." Working together with Paolo Pisanelli, she created a montage of the recovered photos and made a poetic documentary film, a meditation on photography, memory, and resistance.[42]

In January 2020, *Two Forgotten Boxes* was presented at the International Film Festival in Rotterdam. On that occasion, the *New York Times* published an article by Elisabetta Povoledo entitled "A Legendary Documentary Maker Closes 'an Open Wound,'" which told the compelling story of this film and retraced Mangini's career from the mid-1950s, exploring her collaboration with Pier Paolo Pasolini and her lifelong artistic and personal partnership with Lino Del Fra.[43] I rejoiced in seeing such acknowledgment of Mangini's work, who while popular among film critics and documentary filmmakers in Italy is almost unknown in the United States. Interestingly, the article headline was reedited the following day, deleting the word *legendary*. I suppose the *New York Times* editor thought defining Mangini as "a legendary filmmaker" was a bit of an overstatement since she was unknown in the United States. Though the incident might seem but a minor detail, it speaks, once again, to the ongoing marginality of contemporary Italian women directors on the global film scene, a marginality that *Wandering Women* seeks to address.

In January 2021, Mangini passed away, leaving another "open wound," a documentary film on prominent Italian writer Grazia Deledda. In the film that Mangini's longtime collaborator Paolo Pisanelli completed, *Grazia Deledda, the Revolutionary*, Mangini "is present" in front of the camera, as she is in *Traveling with Cecilia*.[44] Leafing through handwritten manuscripts in Deledda's archives or contemplating the Sardinian landscapes dominant in Deledda's stories, she presents the film project as an expression of gratitude to the woman writer "whose courage guided her to become who she became." She recounts how Deledda's novels, "informed by a sense of justice, a desire for peace on earth, and compassion for the excluded," strongly influenced her documentary filmmaking, and, in dialogue with Pisanelli, she speaks of the contemporary relevance of Deledda's attention to nature and all forms of life.[45]

When Deledda won the Nobel Prize for Literature in 1926, the greatest achievement a writer can obtain, she was still on the margins of the Italian literary canon; today, she is largely forgotten.[46] Mangini's last cinematic effort bears testimony to the work that feminist directors, writers, poets, artists, and scholars have been doing in the twentieth century to "uncover zones of repressions of knowledge," to use the words of Giuliana Bruno, expanding cultural boundaries and continuing to build a genealogy of women's art.[47]

NOTES

1. I debated if this chapter would be the first or the last because the other films examined in this book do not have such explicit environmental intent, whereas the films discussed here fall under the category of environmental documentary. I was inspired by the first part of Laura Mulvey's *Afterimages: On*

Cinema, Women and Changing Times, which was titled "A Last Chapter," perhaps because Mulvey is returning for the last time to the subject of her famous essay on feminist film studies, "Visual Pleasure and Narrative Cinema."

2. Cecilia Mangini, interview by author, Rome, December 22, 2018 (my translation).

3. The Centro Sperimentale di Cinematografia (Experimental Center for Cinema) is the leading film institution in Italy. Founded by the Italian government, it was established in 1935 during the fascist era to promote film culture and train film professionals. Directors Michelangelo Antonioni and Liliana Cavani and cinematographers such as Vittorio Storaro graduated from the Centro Sperimentale, which is considered one of the major film schools in Europe.

4. Cecilia Mangini, interview by author, Rome, December 22, 2018 (my translation). Figures 1.1, 1.2, and 1.3 represent some of the concerns that early-career Mangini had as a photographer of industrialization and its social impacts.

5. For Mangini's complete filmography, see Sciamanneo, *Con ostinata passione*.

6. I obtained an English subtitled version of *Traveling with Cecilia* from producer Gioia Avvantaggiato at GA&A Productions, and all Mangini's documentary films I discuss in this chapter came from AAMOD (Fondazione Archivio Audiovisivo del movimento operaio e democratico) and Cineteca di Bologna. Paolo Pisanelli provided with me with a private screener of *Two Forgotten Boxes*.

7. Willoquet-Maricondi, ed., *Framing the World*, 9.

8. Rose, *Feminism and Geography*, 189.

9. I'm referencing the third section of Laura Mulvey's seminal article "Visual Pleasure and Narrative Cinema," entitled "Woman as Image, Man as Bearer of the Look." As Mulvey famously argued, "In a world ordered by sexual imbalance, pleasure in looking has been split between active/male and passive/female." Women are not bearers of the look, nor the makers of meaning, but the passive recipients of the look, objects of voyeuristic pleasure. "Visual Pleasure and Narrative Cinema," 11.

10. Castelli, "The Filmmaker Is Present," 235.

11. Mangini, "I corti di Cecilia Mangini," *Cortoreale: Gli autori del documentario italiano*, YouTube video, 36:01, posted by "Kathryn Morris," January 18, 2018 (my translation), https://www.youtube.com/watch?v=4hPrUYST6KE.

12. D'Eaubonne, *Le féminisme ou la mort*, 213. Demonstrating the relevance of Françoise d'Eaubonne's ideas today, an English translation of her book has been published recently, half a century after the original publication in French. See d'Eubonne, *Feminism or Death: How the Women's Movement Can Save the Planet*.

13. Mortimer-Sandilands, "An Ecofeminist Perspective in the Urban Environment," 192.

14. See Missero, "Cecilia Mangini."

15. For an ecocritical analysis of Calvino's novella *Smog*, see Seger, *Landscapes in Between*. The covering of the mineral parks was expected to be completed in 2020, but the work is still ongoing and the parks remain only partially covered. See Casula, "Ex Ilva, ecco la copertura dei parchi minerali."

16. Crainz, *Storia del miracolo italiano*, 128.

17. I found a reference to the naming of streets after plants and trees in the neighborhood of Tamburi in the opening titles of Maria Tilli's *La gente resta* (*People Stay*, 2015), an observational documentary film about a family of fishermen in Taranto.

18. Seger, "Thinking through Taranto," 184.

19. Riva, "La puglia dei veleni."

20. As in the films directed by Spada and Comencini, in Elisa Fuksas's debut film, *Nina* (2012), the young female protagonist rambles through deserted city streets, here, in Rome's EUR. The latter film explicitly references Michelangelo Antonioni's *L'eclisse* (*The Eclipse*, 1962).

21. See Seger, "Thinking through Taranto," 191. Riva would be a fugitive for two years before his arrest in 2015. As Barbanente recounted, this event radically changed the nature of the film project, which was initially intended to be a portrait of Mangini and to revisit the places where she shot her early documentary films. "It became imperative to talk about the present," she said. Mariangela Barbanente, interview by author, Skype, October 22, 2018 (my translation).

22. Rose, "Val Plumwood's Philosophical Animism," 102, quoted in Gaard, *Critical Ecofeminism*, XVIII.

23. Gaard, XVII.

24. Amelang, "Mourning Becomes Eclectic," 9.

25. For further analysis of naming those who have died in the Mediterranean as a form of recognition, see Verdicchio, "This Nostrum that Is Neither Sea nor Remedy."

26. Schirinzi, *Il Petrolchimico a Brindisi (1969–1972)*, 26.

27. "Il Petrolchimico all'avanguardia dei più moderni servizi sociali," *La Gazzetta del Mezzogiorno*, April 25, 1963, quoted in Crainz, *Storia del miracolo italiano*, 128.

28. Nixon, *Slow Violence and the Environmentalism of the Poor*, 2.

29. For an in-depth analysis of Taranto-based narratives with an environmental focus, see Seger, *Toxic Matters*.

30. One of the rare films to address Brindisi's social and environmental deterioration is Valentina Pedicini's *My Marlboro City* (2010). The DVD was

released with Barbara Garlaschelli and Valentina Pedicini's *Nostalgie urbane* (Florence: Ed.it, 2021).

31. *Traveling with Cecilia*, and the subsequent documentary films *Two Forgotten Boxes* and *Grazia Deledda, the Revolutionary*, the latter two codirected with Paolo Pisanelli, are the only films in which Mangini speaks in voice-over and appears in front of the camera. In almost all previous films, including *Being Women*, the voice-over, in line with the fashion at the time but in contradiction to the female authorship that Mangini's films assert, is male. In our interview, Mangini lamented this, considering the current trends in documentary filmmaking, and she perceived it as a limit of her work.

32. Schirinzi, *Il Petrolchimico a Brindisi (1969–1972)*, 26.

33. The investigation of Marghera's petrochemical industry was reconstructed in Felice Casson's memoir *La fabbrica dei veleni* (The Factory of Poisons), published in 2007 and reissued in an expanded version in 2015.

34. Gianicolo, "Acute Effects of Urban and Industrial Pollution in a Government-Designated 'Environmental Risk Area.'"

35. Mulvey, "Visual Pleasure and Narrative Cinema," 11.

36. Feminist struggles to legalize abortion in Italy were catalyzed by this event. The story of this industrial accident is dramatized in Laura Conti's novel *Una lepre con la faccia di bambina* (*A Hare with the Face of a Child*, 1978). For an analysis of this work, see Iovino, "Toxic Epiphanies." See also Seger, "Narrating Dioxin."

37. *I Do Not Forgive* is an independent film with significantly more modest production resources than Barbanente and Mangini's film (which was granted state funds and benefitted from the Apulia Film Commission). It delves into local initiatives to resuscitate the economy, like the farmer who, after living through the forced slaughter of his dioxin-contaminated livestock, started cultivating hemp because of its supposed detoxing properties; it also explores efforts to reconfigure postindustrial spaces into spaces of social aggregation and infuse in young people a sense of belonging to their hometown.

38. The Cineteca di Bologna intends to produce a DVD collecting all of Mangini's short films and *Traveling with Cecilia* with English subtitles. Currently, the films I analyzed are available for consultation at the Cineteca di Bologna. I received a copy of *Traveling with Cecilia* from the producer at GA&A Productions and all the short films from the Cineteca and the AAMOD (Archivio del movimento operaio).

39. Iovino, "Ecocriticism and a Non-Anthropocentric Humanism," 38.

40. Willoquet-Maricondi, *Framing the World*, 15.

41. Mayers, *Political Animals*, 37.

42. Povoledo, "A Legendary Documentary Maker Closes 'an Open Wound.'"

43. Povoledo.
44. I am referencing the title of Castelli's article, "The Filmmaker Is Present."
45. Cecilia Mangini in *Grazia Deledda, the Revolutionary*.
46. For an in-depth analysis of Grazia Deledda's literature, see Heyer-Cáput, *Grazia Deledda's Dance of Modernity*. See also Lucamente, "A Quiet Revolution."
47. Bruno and Nadotti, eds., *Off Screen*, 152.

Fegatello: *The Nightless City*

LA CITTÀ SENZA NOTTE (The Nightless City, 2015) is an independent film directed and produced by multidisciplinary artist Alessandra Pescetta. It is a work that, for its hallucinatory tone, visionary aesthetics, and hybridity of language, resists the classification of narrative film and gears toward video art.

It tells a strange but compelling story: a woman relocates to Palermo, Italy, after surviving the 2011 Fukushima earthquake, tsunami, and subsequent nuclear incident. Tormented by insomnia and obsessed by the fear of contamination through food, Mariko, the protagonist, finds ways to come to terms with her traumatic experience through art.

Unlike in Alain Resnais's *Hiroshima Mon Amour* (1959), explicitly referenced in the opening sequence, the destruction and horror brought by radiation remain off-screen. And despite the fact that a sense of death informs the entire film, a glossy, beautifying gaze permeates its aesthetics. The female protagonist, always impeccably dressed, is very often fetishized on the screen and deprived of agency, and the reconstruction of the events in Fukushima that followed the tsunami is entrusted to the male protagonist, Salvatore.

The most fascinating parts of the film are those in which the protagonist's hallucinations are staged. In a sequence that represents the emotional climax of the film, Mariko, who has been accumulating food waste, creates with it a sculpture that resembles a weapon. Embracing this weapon, she places herself in the frame and takes a self-portrait (see fig. 1.12). It is a visually powerful authorial self-inscription that comments on the healing force of art.

Figure 1.12. Mariko transforms food waste into art. Screen capture, *The Nightless City* (2015), directed by Alessandra Pescetta. Director's personal archive.

This film, while problematically revealing a fetishizing gaze on the female body and perpetuating urban/rural and nature/culture binaries, engages in a compelling self-reflective discourse on cinema as a means of raising environmental consciousness while mirroring the audience's cognitive and emotional responses to global environmental catastrophes.

TWO

URBAN WANDERING, SCRAPBOOKING, AND FILMMAKING

As the Shadow, My Tomorrow, Poetry You See Me

WHEN I REACHED OUT TO director Marina Spada to arrange my first interview with her, she invited me to her house in Milan, where "her cinema happens." As I walked in, I recognized a strangely familiar space: it was one of her film locations, Claudia's apartment from *Come l'ombra* (As the Shadow, 2006)—an overlapping of art and life independent filmmakers so often embrace.[1]

She laid a pile of bulky notebooks on the kitchen table: "I collect flyers, images of all sorts.... These are images that I find, and pictures I take. I pick up a lot of paper out and about, I take everything home, then I process it.... I write down where it comes from, and then I put it in a box. I have been doing this for years," she said, leafing through one of them with pride. "Then I glue them in notebooks. I search for meaningful links."[2]

Part of a process somewhere between scrapbooking and storyboarding, those notebooks documented the preparation of her films (see figs. 2.1, 2.2, 2.4, 2.7, and 2.9). Every page, charmingly messy and colorful, had its own chromatic tone and mood. They compiled reproductions of paintings, old photos, maps, and even pictures of the television screen. These were mixed with shot sketches and handwritten notes (often whited out) describing camera angles and movements, light and sound directions, images and words that would find their way into the fabric of the story through props, characters, and landscapes. The journals contained the emotional maps of the films and a visual atlas of her filmmaking practice: urban wandering, gleaning of images, visual tapestry, and production of new images. She shared the notebooks with her recurrent collaborators, then with me, inviting me to engage in an archaeology of images. Here I share them with my readers.

Figure 2.1. Claudia looks at Milan from Branca Tower. Screen capture, *As the Shadow* (2006), directed by Marina Spada.

In this chapter, examining extracts from the director's fascinating film diaries and engaging in textual film analysis supported by urban history, I discuss three of Spada's films set in the city of Milan: *Come l'ombra* (As the Shadow, 2006), *Il mio domani* (My Tomorrow, 2011), and *Poesia che mi guardi* (Poetry You See Me, 2009). The first film I analyze, *As the Shadow*, is a story of an alienated middle-class woman who, while searching for a friend who met an untimely end, reconnects with the world; the second, *My Tomorrow*, is about a woman who, following her father's death, finds a way to reconcile herself with her long-deceased mother and start anew. *Poetry You See Me* is the story of a filmmaker who investigates the life and work of the neglected poet Antonia Pozzi, who died by suicide in 1938. In all these films, female characters—caught in similar situations: immobility, crisis, searching, and questioning—are shown perpetually crossing and observing the city, either from above or from street level.

Integrating film analysis with urban cultural insights and using Spada's diaries to reveal the genesis of these works, I foreground their feminist ecologies. I focus on three recurrent aspects of these films: women's position in the landscape, the representation of an urban void, and the construction of authorship. As in my previous chapter, I follow the films' spatial organization, which often opens with a view from above and proceeds with a journey on foot, from the center to the peripheries (*As the Shadow* and *Poetry*) and between city and countryside (*My Tomorrow*). I investigate the places the female protagonists traverse during their soul searching: neglected working-class neighborhoods, postindustrial areas, construction sites of soon-to-be-gentrified districts, peripheries where water has been covered by concrete, and areas where the city's homeless have been ghettoized.

Spada's films, while conveying a critique of women's invisibility and marginality and reclaiming women's place in the city, engage in a self-reflective discourse on cinema as mapping, montage, and suture. An education of the gaze and self-fashioning as a director is at play in the fabrication of the notebooks as well as in the films. Eschewing the absolutism of the patriarchal gaze, Spada's transient Milanese narratives weave a fabric of the city that allows for gaps, temporal and spatial continuities and discontinuities, urban and rural voids, and uncertainties about the past and future.

WOMEN IN THE DESERTED CITY

A beep and the sound of an engine over a black screen suggest the confines and the movement of an elevator; a cityscape fades in. In the foreground, a few trees and red-roofed buildings. More buildings almost fill the entire frame, stretching to the horizon. A woman enters the scene and stands at the right edge of it, looking at the view, her back to the camera (see fig. 2.1). As she momentarily exits the scene, the camera pans slowly in a semicircle, following the woman as she walks and looks pensively at the view, now double framed both by the camera and by large windows. Cut. The woman descends in a glass-paneled elevator through which trees can be seen. This is the opening of Spada's *As the Shadow*, and it presents the female protagonist, Claudia, in front of a panoramic view of Milan from the Branca Tower, located in the central district of Porta Sempione.[3]

As discussed in the introduction and in the analysis of *Traveling with Cecilia* in chapter 1, the view from above, a recurrent visual trope in the body of films presented in this book, conveys multiple meanings and plays a key narrative function: it heralds a place-centered story, it signals the beginning of a journey, and, most importantly, it positions a woman as an observer, a witness, and a storyteller.

Spada's shooting journals contain multiple aerial views of Milan, or reproductions of paintings or photos taken from high angles, images she collected that informed her own image of the city (see fig. 2.2). The above-described sequence, as well as similarly constructed sequences I discuss later in this chapter, show how a strategic, feminist reconfiguration of those views from above is at play in this film. The framing strategy makes it clear that we are not presented with a totalizing view from nowhere. The latter, to recall Stacy Alaimo's words, is an "invisible, unmarked, ostensibly 'perspectiveless perspective,'" which replicates a mechanism of control over the environment.[4] Instead, by incorporating the female observer into the landscape, this strategy recognizes the interconnectedness between human and nonhuman.[5]

This scene is a quotation of the opening sequence of *La Notte* (1961), directed by Michelangelo Antonioni, an auteur Spada references explicitly throughout her films. In *La Notte*, shot in the midst of the so-called economic miracle, the camera accompanies an external elevator's downward movement while showing the urban landscape reflected in the glass walls of Gio Ponti's Pirelli skyscraper ("Pirellone"). Both Spada's and Antonioni's views of Milan are, in different ways, landscapes of the (Italian) Anthropocene. In this perspective, the overconstructed cityscape brought into view bears witness to the cementification of the Italian landscape while linking these new spaces to urban speculation and alienation.

By changing the point of view and placing the camera inside the tower and including a female observer, however, Spada subtly "reframes" Antonioni's scene, foregrounding women's perspective.[6] Furthermore, this scene functions as a *mise-en-abîme* of the film itself, featuring the auteur making a film. Spada, perhaps more than other directors discussed in this book, manifests an anxiety of authorship in her films, a condition that she seems to legitimize by repeatedly inscribing herself, and her female characters, both in the text and in the landscape. That is, they became part of a visual culture rooted in *her* city, Milan.

Set in a desert-like summer in Milan, *As the Shadow* narrates an encounter between a native Milanese, Claudia, and Olga, a young Ukrainian woman who has recently arrived in Italy. Claudia is a single, independent, but socially awkward woman who maintains routines she rarely strays from, alienating herself from much of the city. She works in a travel agency and studies at a Russian language school, where she becomes attracted to her teacher, Boris. On the verge of starting a relationship, Boris asks her to host his "cousin" from Ukraine while he is on a business trip. Reluctantly, Claudia accepts on the condition that it will be for just one week.

Olga, a curious newcomer eager to explore Milan as fully as possible, inevitably disrupts Claudia's semicloistered existence. However, despite Claudia's initial diffidence, the two women become friends. One night, after they start developing a warmer relationship, Olga fails to return home. Panicked, Claudia journeys through unfamiliar parts of Milan, only to be interrupted by a call from the police announcing Olga's death.

The film tells the story of two women walking separately in the same city. Their paths cross briefly. Claudia, a white-collar worker who presumably grew up in Milan, is estranged from her hometown. The idea of separation and immobility is reiterated through a framing strategy that reverses the opening sequence where the character is looking at the city. In the first part of the film, she is shown repeatedly within indoor spaces, alone in her apartment, standing by the window, or behind a streetcar or café window—"under glass," as Spada put it. To the same effect, the camera is often kept at a distance and frames the subject through glass, suggesting a sense of entrapment while impeding full identification with the protagonist.

Olga, by contrast, is a stranger (though not estranged) eager to embrace the city and is mostly shown outdoors, in the street. Again, Spada revisits and reinvents the cinema of a master of self-reflexivity, Jean-Luc Godard. In fact, as the shooting diaries reveal (see fig. 2.2), Olga's character is modeled after Nana, the Parisian prostitute of *Vivre sa vie* (*My Life to Live*, 1962), and like the latter, she will be murdered in the street. Dismantling the masculine association of female walking with streetwalking, as well as pervasive, stereotypical representations in Italian cinema of Eastern European immigrants as prostitutes, Olga is configured as a flaneuse, "a modern legitimized 'streetwalker,'" who, as Scarparo and Luciano observe, "wanders through the city window-shopping, purchasing cheap imitation commodities, thus buying rather than selling pleasure."[7]

Flânerie, as conceived by Charles Baudelaire in mid-nineteenth-century Paris and later elaborated on by Walter Benjamin, is a spatial practice involving a shift from the private sphere to the public one (two spheres that were undergoing increased separation due to industrial development) and an immersion in the anonymity of the crowds. In the postindustrial city of the twenty-first century, as represented in many of the films examined in this book, the (male) crowds have disappeared—that is, the public sphere is no longer masculine (or gendered at all) if it is empty. This allows us to go beyond the critique of the gendered nature of urban space and see the female city walker as a vehicle for a feminist critique of the postmodern city. The deserted city underscores individuals' isolation, but it also represents the possibility—the space—for a life-sustaining community to form.

Only twenty minutes from the beginning of the film, like Anna from Antonioni's *L'Avventura* (1960), Olga disappears from the landscape. As the film diaries show, she enters "un campo vuoto" (an empty frame), looks around, and addresses the camera by gazing directly into it (see figs. 2.3 and 2.4). The narration is suspended, and the absence of sound creates a disquieting atmosphere. Louis Althusser would describe this moment as the interpellation, the moment in which the film's ideological message is conveyed to the audience as its subject. Olga's gaze is finally active and directed toward the viewers to whom she

Figure 2.2. Film diary of *As the Shadow* (2006), directed by Marina Spada. Director's personal archive.

Hopper - The city 1927

VISTE DALL'ALTO

Sironi 1922

Il tram e la gru

Figure 2.3. Olga disappears. Screen capture, *As the Shadow* (2006), directed by Marina Spada.

exposes her vulnerability. In Spada's words, she is addressing them by saying, "And now you must look at me."[8] Olga's gaze into the camera is followed by the recurrent empty landscape, which thus foreshadows her death.

When I asked Spada about her choice to represent Milan, one of the most populous European cities, as deserted, she answered, "I like the empty city because it allows me to highlight the lines and shapes of architecture... the empty city stands as a metaphor for the character's loneliness. Where did the people end up? Did they run away from the plague? Or perhaps they are all beyond the windows, they don't want to have contact with the rest of the world."[9] But the deserted city is not only a metaphor or an effect obtained by shooting in August (as Spada recounts). Some of the neighborhoods featured in the film, in fact, were empty at the time of shooting because the buildings were under construction and therefore not yet inhabited. "The area where Claudia drives around looking for Olga is the Leoni district," Spada recounts. "It was built where there once was an enormous metalwork factory (the OM). After it was decommissioned, the factory remained abandoned for years until the land was sold, and they built beautiful apartments, they created a park." In this sense, void represents an absence, yes, but also a space for the possibility of new life in the city. This idea also informs the treatment of emptiness in *My Tomorrow*, a film I will discuss later in this chapter.[10]

By depriving the city of human presence, Spada is revisiting the visual tradition of "beautiful voids."[11] As the journals again reveal, the work of contemporary Italian photographer Gabriele Basilico, known for his portraits of global cities, is an important source of inspiration. In one of Basilico's first and better-known works, *Milano, ritratti di fabbriche* (Milan, Factory Portraits), between 1978 and 1980, he documents the so-called *architettura media* (middle-class architecture) of the "ugly" city's periphery, the privileged location of Spada's films. In this series of industrial landscapes, humans, as well as cars and other elements that might evoke the idea of movement intrinsic to a modern industrial city, are erased.

Finally, the void is also a distinctive feature of Antonioni's cinema, "whose ghost," wrote Italian critic Maurizio De Bonis, "hovers in every shot."[12] Let us think, for instance, about the memorable ending of *L'eclisse* (*The Eclipse*, 1962), set in the metaphysical streets of Rome's EUR, where empty streets and a mushroom-shaped water tower foreshadow an atomic conflagration and the extinction of humankind. A similar effect is achieved in *As the Shadow* by Spada's treatment of the urban landscape as "autonomous," to use Martin Lefebvre's term.[13] Building blocks or empty piazzas are interspersed with indoor sequences, suspending the diegesis and suggesting the separation of the individual from the external world where humankind seems to be extinct.[14]

Although Spada's films depict no apocalyptic scenarios, the insistence on urban voids confers on them a certain dystopian tone. In *Climate Trauma*, a study of futuristic dystopian films across genres, E. Ann Kaplan argues that exposure to media representations of natural catastrophes and other narratives of climate change is likely to generate in viewers a sense of doom and an excruciating uncertainty about the future. She defines such anxiety for future apocalyptic scenarios as "pretrauma."[15]

The deserted streets of Milan featured in Spada's films, while revisiting a twentieth-century visual tradition (from Mario Sironi to Antonioni and Basilico), are revealed to be disquietingly anticipatory, as they prefigure the empty streets of 2020, when the "pretrauma," to use Kaplan's term, became a trauma. Streets in Italian cities, and around the world, were emptied to contain the spread of the COVID-19 pandemic. Confinement in private spaces was imposed by law, and walking and proximity among humans was policed, for the health of the city was revealed as coextensive with the health of the city's inhabitants. While sitting in my apartment in New York City, I watched with astonishment the deserted piazzas of Italy through public webcams. Empty cities, the images of which invade the internet and museums, are now commemorative landscapes of loss.

Olga's disappearance propels Claudia on a journey through the city, along which she endeavors to literally make Olga visible by hanging flyers with her picture. At the same time, Claudia starts actively engaging and critically *seeing*

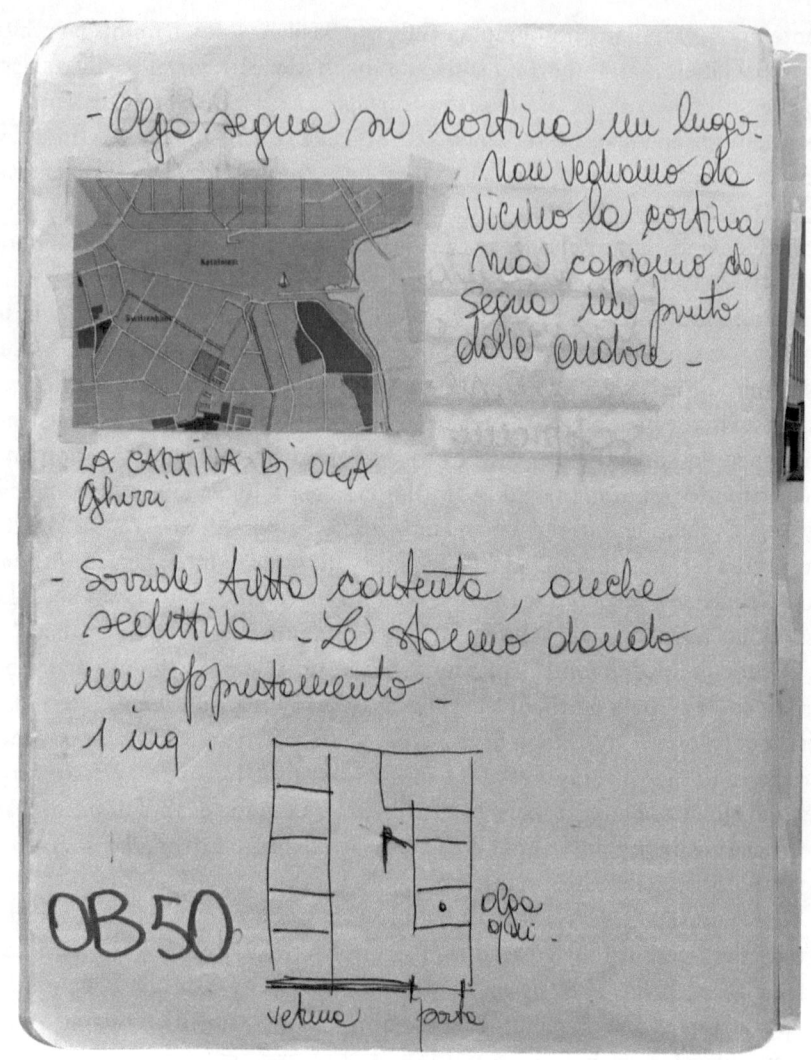

Figure 2.4. Film diary of *As the Shadow* (2006), directed by Marina Spada. Director's personal archive.

Milano est. giorno -

Olga guarda in macchina   g.st 18 ex 83
        1   2   ore 16
                              MERCOLEDÌ 13 AGOSTO
                              (82 A)

3 → solo
    muro sen
    edificio dietro

sguardo di
Olga in macchina.
Campo vuoto entra
in c. si guarda
attorno e poi
rivolge lo sguardo
in macchina -

↳ lungo →

CORRIDOIO OLGA -

1 INQUADRATURA) | LEI CHE GUARDA
                    E SI PERDE

Figure 2.5. Women's bodies in installments. Screen capture, *As the Shadow* (2006), directed by Marina Spada.

her surroundings. She is often framed standing while looking, images that reiterate the self-reflexive motif from the opening sequence and convey further reflections on women as signs in the streetscape.

Women as erotic objects are a consistent visual element of any urban landscape, but this film, while criticizing female objectification, proposes a recodification of the female body by reinscribing it into the landscape viewed by a critical, feminist gaze. As shown in figure 2.5, Claudia stares at a billboard truck parked in the middle of the street advertising some exotic vacation to be paid for in installments and exposing a woman in a "tempting" pose (the very presence of the truck in the middle of such a deserted street seems absurd since nobody is there to be seduced). This image (like others in the film) merges ideas of consumerist culture with the objectification of women's bodies, and all the while the truck is a signifier for consumption of fossil fuel, traffic, urban congestion, and pollution. The vacated streets featured in this film, as well as many other films discussed in this book, suggest the need to end an unsustainable way of living.

Claudia, who at the beginning of the film stands immobile while observing the city, at the end of the film leaves it. Having finally overcome her stasis, she undertakes, with Olga's suitcase, the reverse journey toward Ukraine, presumably to return Olga's belongings to her family and possibly to tell them the brief but impactful story of her in the Milanese landscape. At last she reaches a piazza traversed by people departing for and arriving from other countries. At this quintessential place of mobility, she reaches a point of connection.

As the Shadow, a film about women's invisibility and the way women's lives can be transformed by female solidarity and care, nearly remained unseen by the public. Despite having been well received at the Venice Film Festival, it did not obtain theatrical distribution, a common issue for independent films. It was thanks to a feminist initiative that *As the Shadow* found a broader audience beyond that of film festival denizens. In harmony with the film's story, the Libreria delle donne di Milano (Milan's Women Book Store), one of the major historical centers for the dissemination of feminist culture in Italy, successfully petitioned distribution companies to show *As the Shadow* in movie theaters in Milan, the city that shaped its own narrative.[16]

DOMESTIC DARKNESS AND LIGHT FROM THE VOID

A woman drives at night. It's raining. Headlights of cars traveling in the opposite direction are blinding, and her windshield fogs up. She is stopped by the police: the road is blocked, and she must take a detour. Soon she arrives at a modest country house. As she walks into dark rooms, she switches on the lights. Tools hanging on the wall tell us that a carpenter lives here. The house is empty and quiet, but a broadcast of a *Via crucis* procession is heard on the radio. Crosses and religious icons are all over the house. Cut. Another nocturnal shot: women walking in a way-of-the-cross procession. It's Easter time in a northern Italian village in the Po Valley.

The views from above that open *As the Shadow* and *Poetry You See Me* show the female protagonists in the act of looking. In contrast, in the opening sequence of *My Tomorrow* darkness indexes the character's reduced visibility. Interpreted as a self-reflexive device, the gesture of illuminating obscure spaces evokes both the act of impressing light on footage and the projection of the film on the screen. Still, this dimly lit sequence is charged with unambiguous Christian imagery of death and resurrection. Indeed, *My Tomorrow* is a mourning film that is also the story of a rebirth and restored vision.

Monica is an intelligent and attractive woman who works as a motivational trainer in a consulting firm. Apparently composed and self-confident, she is a melancholic person who leads a solitary life in Milan. She maintains a sexual relationship with her married boss and regularly visits her elderly and sick father in a rural village outside of Milan. After his death, Monica enters a period of profound crisis that eventually leads her to a life transformation. The relationship with her stepsister, long conflicted, falls apart, impeding Monica's

Figure 2.6. Monica's self-portrait. Screen capture, *My Tomorrow* (2011), directed by Marina Spada.

contact with her nephew, a fragile adolescent whom Monica loves dearly. Her lover, Vittorio, leaves her, and she realizes that the firm she works for is manipulating her. As a result, she decides to begin her life anew. Parallel to these events, Monica enrolls in photography lessons. In the end, after composing her self-portrait with the hills of the Po Valley in the background (the landscape of her childhood; fig. 2.6), she starts a new life elsewhere.

Leaving town is a common trope in city films; it suggests both that cities are perceived as unsustainable environments and more generally that displacement and relocation to a new landscape are considered vital to human existence. In the last shot of *As the Shadow*, while leaving the city Claudia stares at a field of dirt clods, a barren landscape seen along the road that replaces the cement and asphalt that occupy the screen for the entire film. In continuity with the previous film, *My Tomorrow* alternates between urban and rural landscapes (Milan, where Monica lives, and the country where she visits her sick father), suturing the two places and recognizing their mutual interdependence.

The story unfolds through a mobile geography. The frequent commute between Milan and the countryside village suggests (via editing) a geographical continuity between the built-up urban landscape of Milan, saturated with glass-and-steel buildings, and the hills of the Po Valley, spaced out by stands of birch trees that scroll outside the moving car windows along the road.

Rather than creating an opposition between nature and civilization, a common conceptualization of country versus city, this spatial organization, through voyages where the transition is seamless, serves to reinscribe nonhuman nature into the city and reminds us of our rural origins. However, the film also suggests that nonhuman nature is dead or moribund. A cherry tree has been chopped down; animals refuse their food. And framing strategies contribute to what Raymond Williams would call an "antipastoral": fields are photographed with static shots; slow camera movements linger on somber skies.[17] The silence, the melancholic music, and the sparse dialogue Monica entertains with her father suggest a sense of imminent end.

Along the same lines, the house appears dark and lifeless. This construction of both domestic space and nature works against gendered assumptions of both female affinity with nature and home as a woman's place. In *Space, Place, and Gender*, feminist geographer Doreen Massey explores the idea that spaces and places are defined in terms of social relationships and, therefore, are not only gendered but constitute the construction of gender itself. Discussing the equation nature/woman, as well as home/woman, Massey writes critically that in an androcentric culture, "woman stands as metaphor for nature . . . , for what has been lost (left behind), and that place called home is frequently personified by, and partakes of the same characteristics as those assigned to, Woman/Mother/Lover."[18] The film embraces Massey's rejection of those binaries by not making Monica at home in either place.

Domestic space, as represented in this film, speaks to the absence of an offscreen mother who is nevertheless enigmatically present. The mother-daughter conflict is central to the character's development and challenges the stereotypical figure of the self-sacrificing mother so deeply rooted in Italian culture; it also criticizes the pervasive demonization of troubled motherhood found in the media. The story of this mother remains untold and is unclear to the viewer, until the father's death makes space for Monica's grief over the loss of her mother to surface. It should be noted that all deaths in Spada's films are implied, not shown or mentioned, as if both words and images would fail to represent them.

Like Danco's *N-Able* (discussed in chap. 5), a strongly autobiographical film essay in which the loss of the mother opens and closes the narrative, the personal loss of the director's parents seems to be part of this story. During the burial scene, in fact, the name of the director's father, Carlo Spada, appears on a gravestone, and one of the film locations—as Spada shared in one of our conversations—is Filighera, near Pavia, her mother's hometown. While she repeatedly affirmed in public interviews that the story of *My Tomorrow* is not entirely autobiographical, the choice of personal locations appears as a moving iteration of the many authorial self-inscriptions scattered in these films, which revolve around the concept of void.

After her father's death, in an already empty house, where the sound of clacking heels echoes, Monica starts putting things away. At some point, she sits quietly, holding refined crystal glasses and mimicking the gesture of drinking, perhaps reminiscing about a childhood game. Then she gazes at a blurred photo of a woman holding a baby and some postcards. Her mother gradually emerges from these gestures and from the materiality of the objects she touches.

Later in the film, back in the city, Monica puts her mother's story into words. In a conversation with a lover, she reveals that as a child she was forced by her obsessively religious father to cultivate a profound resentment toward her mother, who had abandoned her family for an amorous adventure in Greece. "She had not seen anything, and she had not been anywhere in her life," Monica comments. A few years later, when the romance ended, she returned to her home village with an illegitimate child, but, in Monica's words, "nobody helped her." Implicit in Monica's account of her mother's life is that she suffered poverty and isolation as the consequences of a dissident choice: stepping outside the role prescribed to her by an oppressive Catholic environment.

A generation later, through education and mobility, a modern woman like Monica has gained the emancipation refused to her mother. Through living in the city, an environment less likely to exert the patriarchal control on women that a community in a smaller place often does, Monica is afforded the possibility of living an independent life, outside codified feminine roles. Yet, as represented in film, she is also isolated and estranged from the world and, to a certain extent, still disenfranchised by the logic of the neoliberal economy.[19]

As a motivational trainer, she leads a series of lectures about the concept of the "void" for a group of white-collar workers. She proposes that a "void" might not be conceived as a threatening, nonexistent space but rather as one that can be inhabited. This narrative thread offers multiple levels of reading: Monica, while preaching about the importance of conceiving emptiness as an opportunity to change, is attempting to embrace change herself. In addition, her reflections on the void can be intended as a commentary on Antonioni's cinematic lesson about space, which, as Spada's film diaries reveal, merges into the fictional matter, underpinning the narration (fig. 2.7).[20]

As David Forgacs writes, "Antonioni's way of dealing with physical locations was essentially to expand their importance relative to the role they had in conventional narrative films and even in some cases to reverse the priority operating in those films whereby people were assumed to be more important

Figure 2.7. Film diary of *My Tomorrow* (2011), directed by Marina Spada. Director's personal archive.

Figure 2.8. The city on the clock. Screen capture, *My Tomorrow* (2011), directed by Marina Spada.

than places."[21] Similarly, in Spada's cinema, buildings, empty streets, and piazzas do not need to contain characters to be framed by the camera. The lesson about the positive value of emptiness can be intended as an invitation to find new ways of looking at what fills the frame, and consider air, sky, and the city with its soundscapes as vibrant nonhuman characters, as well as to ponder on what transformations of places entail in ecological terms.

As we see repeatedly in the urban narratives presented in this book, women's nomadic identities are often aligned with the cities': their transformations, renewals, requalifications, and recoveries are intertwined. Images of construction sites, therefore, are signifiers of human and environmental states of becoming. *As the Shadow* and *My Tomorrow*, respectively shot in 2006 and 2010, capture the city of Milan during its first major urban renewal since the economic miracle, which ended by the mid-1960s. The first one, as mentioned, captures the soon-to-be-inhabited postindustrial Leoni district; the second frames the decade-long project of Porta Nuova to create a new business district—"the new Milan," as Spada called it.

During one of her urban peregrinations, Monica lingers around one of the Porta Nuova construction sites, observing from above the chasm in the earth, excavated to lay the foundation of a new building. Her pause along the way to observe the work makes us wonder: What are they building? As shown in

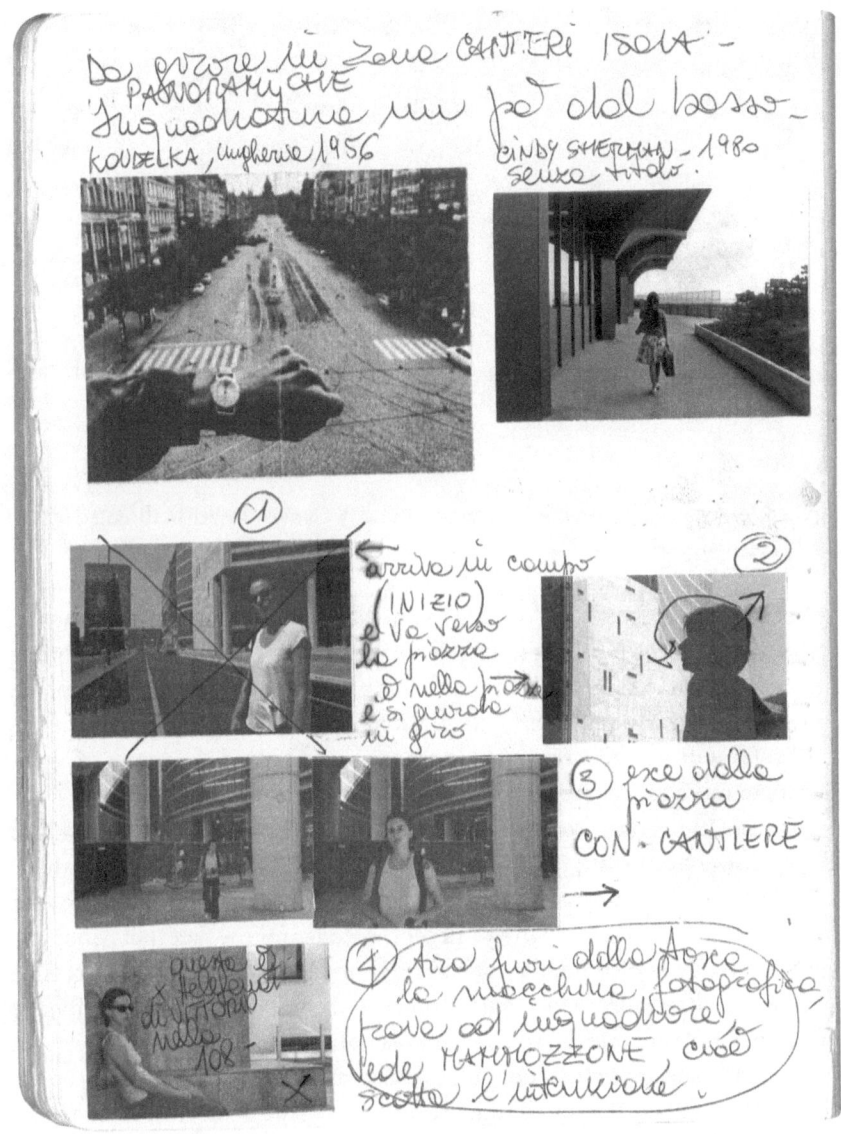

Figure 2.9. Film diary of *My Tomorrow* (2011), directed by Marina Spada. Director's personal archive.

Figure 2.10. A place for viewing. Screen capture, *My Tomorrow* (2011), directed by Marina Spada.

figure 2.8, Monica holds her camera in one hand, with the other showing her wristwatch over the building site.[22] Her walk, immersed in the overwhelming sounds of the city under construction, thus becomes a creative meditation on time, a potential critique of its further rationalization. The development of this new business district that presumably generates wealth and progress also opens the city to more speed, more transit, and more pollution.

Monica's "timely" photo of the city under construction heralds her decision to adopt a slower pace of life. She quits her job after realizing that her presentations to workers about the necessity of embracing change and the advantages of creating a clean slate are no more than a deceptive cover for the fact that neoliberal logic demands the disposability of labor. Having given herself the gift of time and now space away from the constrictions (and constructions) of the city, she repeats her mother's journey to Greece and finally comes to terms with her loss.

In Greece, she becomes a tour guide. What might seem to be an oddly uplifting twist to a gloomy film on the alienation of urban life is, on closer inspection, a subtle meditation on vision. *My Tomorrow* opens with a woman whose vision is impaired, driving in the dark—a woman whose eyes are fogged up. She is interrupted and deviated. She strains toward the light to see. Becoming a guide, Monica now helps people understand what they see; she turns into someone who unveils the hidden story of things. The film closes with the bright image of an amphitheater, literally a place for viewing in many directions (see fig. 2.10).

While the amphitheater surrounded by trees fades to black, the first verses from Antonia Pozzi's 1931 poem "Il mio domani," which inspired the film's title, appear on the screen: "Se chiudo gli occhi a pensare quale sarà il mio domani, vedo una larga strada che sale dal cuore di una città sconosciuta verso alberi alti d'un antico giardino." (If I close my eyes to think of how my tomorrow will be, I see a long road that rises from the hearth of an unknown city toward the tall trees of an ancient garden.)[23]

This, of course, is not merely a wish for a city with more green spaces. Gardens are places of a nature-culture continuum; they are human creations that "bridge nonhuman physical nature with the human capacity for reason and an aesthetic sensibility," as Monica Seger writes.[24] Gardens are also places that demand care, a slower pace, and observation. In his absorbing *Gardens*, Robert Pogue Harrison eloquently writes about the inability to see in a world saturated by images: "We live in an age, then, whose dominant perceptual framework makes it increasingly difficult to see what is right in front of us, leaving a great portion of the visible world out of the picture, as it were, even as it draws the eye to a plethora of pulsing images."[25] By gleaning and scrapbooking images from the work of artists who have thought deeply about the "lost art of seeing" in a contemporary world, and by suturing darkness and light; Italy and Greece; gardens, cities, and countryside, Spada's *My Tomorrow* offers a story of restored agency through the activation of a contemplative gaze and creates a vision of possibility.

POETRY YOU SEE ME: THE DIRECTOR, THE POETS, AND THE GHOST

A bird's-eye view on a square. On the left side, an equestrian statue and, at the top edge of the shot, a colonnade (see fig. 2.11). Silent crowds cross the piazza in all directions, and pigeons fly above, barely visible. Cut. A sequence of static cityscapes: buildings and roads traversed by cars and trains under a gray sky in flat light. The piazza is Milan's Cathedral Square, one of the rare identifiable piazzas featured in the films analyzed in this book. The cathedral, considered the most beautiful example of Gothic architecture in Italy and an icon of the city of Milan, remains off-screen, a framing choice that heralds a peripheral narrative.

A woman enters the scene and addresses the camera: "My words are images, images that keep me from feeling an outsider, and give me a reason to be in the world. I read poetry to understand my heart and the hearts of the others. Antonia Pozzi lived inside and outside her times. Her eyes open onto a world

Figure 2.11. Milan's Cathedral Square. Screen capture, *Poetry You See Me* (2009), directed by Marina Spada.

whose beauty and pain she captured. She was born and raised in Milan, like me. Antonia hasn't lived here for seventy years."

This is the opening sequence of *Poetry You See Me*, a film that unearths the work of poet and photographer Antonia Pozzi, who died by suicide in 1938 at the age of twenty-six and whose poetry lit the darkness at the end of *My Tomorrow*. Spada's film also highlights women's role in giving visibility to female artists from previous generations. Pozzi's hundreds of poems, letters, journals, and photos lay for decades in the "zones of repression and suppressed knowledge," where much of women's work is buried.[26] Consistent with Spada's diaries, the film might also be seen as a cinematic scrapbook of both Pozzi's life and legacy within and outside of the city. As the opening sequence described above communicates, *Poetry You See Me* is an autobiographical film in which Spada reflects "on the necessity of poetry" and on her own role as an artist who restores the legacy of a female poet.

Highly educated and cosmopolitan, a passionate mountain climber, and devoted to charity work, Pozzi began writing poetry and practicing photography at a young age (see fig. 2.12). Her upper-class family never encouraged her artistic inclinations, however. As Spada writes, "[She] was forced to conceal, behind a bourgeois façade, an intense passion that she could never quite reconcile with the constraints and conventions of the time."[27] In the early 1930s, Pozzi became part of a group of scholars who gathered around the philosopher

Figure 2.12. Antonia Pozzi. Screen capture, *Poetry You See Me* (2009), directed by Marina Spada.

Antonio Banfi. She was well respected as an intellectual but discouraged from pursuing poetry and advised by her family to "write as little as possible."[28] With the introduction of the Fascist racial laws in 1938, many of Pozzi's friends were forced to leave Italy, and she reportedly fell into a state of isolation that eventually drove her to suicide.

Despite her privilege, Pozzi's journey from the center to the periphery is no metaphor: she was born and raised in the center of Milan and rode her bicycle to the peripheral area of Chiaravalle, where she ingested an overdose of barbiturates and lay in the snow. Her end is tragically evoked in her most famous verse: "Per troppa vita che ho nel sangue, tremo nel vasto inverno" (For excess of life I have in my blood, I shiver in the immense winter). Found by a local farmer, she was taken to the hospital but died the day after, officially of pneumonia.

None of her work was published during her life, and it was later subject to censorship and critical neglect, especially the most sensual poems. In 1939, a selection of Pozzi's poems, *Parole* (Words), was published in severely truncated and censored forms supervised by her father, a lawyer well connected to the Fascist regime.[29] A decade later, an expanded, uncensored version was published by the prestigious literary press Mondadori with a preface by major poet Eugenio Montale, thus gaining official recognition. But it was not until the first decade of the twenty-first century that Pozzi began to receive broader

Figure 2.13. Marina Spada and her crew in Chiaravalle (2009). Photo by Renata Tardani. Director's personal archive.

critical attention, mostly thanks to the work of the scholar Graziella Barnabò and the curator of Pozzi's archive, Onorina Dino.[30] Spada's film contributes to this work of recovery and inspired other films on the figure of Pozzi as well as public initiatives in her honor.[31]

While maintaining a focus on Pozzi's work, Spada explores how her research on the poet is important to her and to their shared hometown, Milan, where her film registers the poet's absence. In following the void left by Pozzi's death and erasure, the director creates a contemporary framework that reenacts the remapping of the city she and a small crew engaged in during both the preparation and the shooting of the film (see fig. 2.13). As suggested by the scrapbooks, Spada stages her own filmmaking process on-screen as a way of shaping her own persona as a director.

To illustrate, Maria, Spada's fictional alter ego, wanders through her hometown of Milan, revisiting places where Pozzi lived and that supposedly inspired her poetry. Along the journey, she meets the H_5N_1, a group of young medical students and street poets to whom she introduces Pozzi's work.[32] Together they start haunting Pozzi's ghost, so to speak, retracing her itineraries and conversing about her poetry. The sensual "Cantico della mia nudità" (Song of My Nakedness), supposedly written during a tormented relationship Pozzi had with a schoolteacher, is heard over empty school desks at which Pozzi sat (see fig. 2.15). The filmmaker and the poets wander around the elegant residential district in which Pozzi was raised, Milan's old fairgrounds. They pass the Cathedral Square seen in the opening sequence and by the iconic theater La Scala that Pozzi regularly attended. Most of the time, the camera excludes the street level, framing from low angles edges of buildings, closed windows and gates, empty balconies. In this way, it creates a sense of suspended time and reiterates the idea of Pozzi's absence. Her story, the shots suggest, is now part of the hidden story of those places.

The idea of emptiness is also evoked by Pozzi's writing. One of the urban poets visits her home, now a museum in Pasturo, a mountain village near Lecco where Pozzi retreated to write (see fig. 2.16). Slow pan shots show the room and objects displayed on the desk, while we hear a passage from Pozzi's journal: "Sola, piccole cose mi scalpellano. Miserie mi corrodono. Quanto bene vorrei volere e non c'é nessuno. E se qualcuno venisse ormai sarebbe troppo tardi. Tutti sono lontani, perduti. In questa notte piena di echi come una caverna." (Alone, little things chip away at me. Miseries eat me alive. How much love I would give, but I have nobody. If someone would come, it would be too late, perhaps. Everyone is distant, lost in this night filled with echoes, like a cavern.)[33]

In another sequence, Maria and the poets travel to the peripheral Via dei Cinquecento on the southern edge of the city. There Pozzi would visit the infirm at the Casa degli sfrattati, a shelter for evicted people built after the demolition of slums in the late 1920s. The characters' wandering is accompanied by the reading of an entry from Pozzi's journal:

> Prima visita. Piano rialzato. Numero 28. Donna con sei bambini. Il marito è tornato un mese fa da Garbagnate. Guarito, dicono. Il che vuol dire pronto e spacciato per morire a casa sua. Lei ha la pleurite secca e un polmone già intaccato ma si ostina. Terrore dei corridoi, tutti identici, con le pareti di smalto sudice. Ogni venti metri una latrina e in mezzo file di porte uguali con piccoli numeri di ferro smaltato, come in un albergo di infimo ordine.

> First visit. Mezzanine. A woman with six children. Her husband came back from Garbagnate hospital, a month ago. 'Cured,' or so they say. Which means ready to die at home. She has dry pleurisy and her lungs are already shot, but she keeps going. Terrifying hallways, all identical, the varnished walls dripping, a latrine every twenty meters. Rows of identical doors in the middle with tiny enameled iron numbers, like at hotels of the lowest order. Behind every door, a family of five, of eight, ten, twelve. Children by the hundreds. Strange children who hardly make a sound.[34]

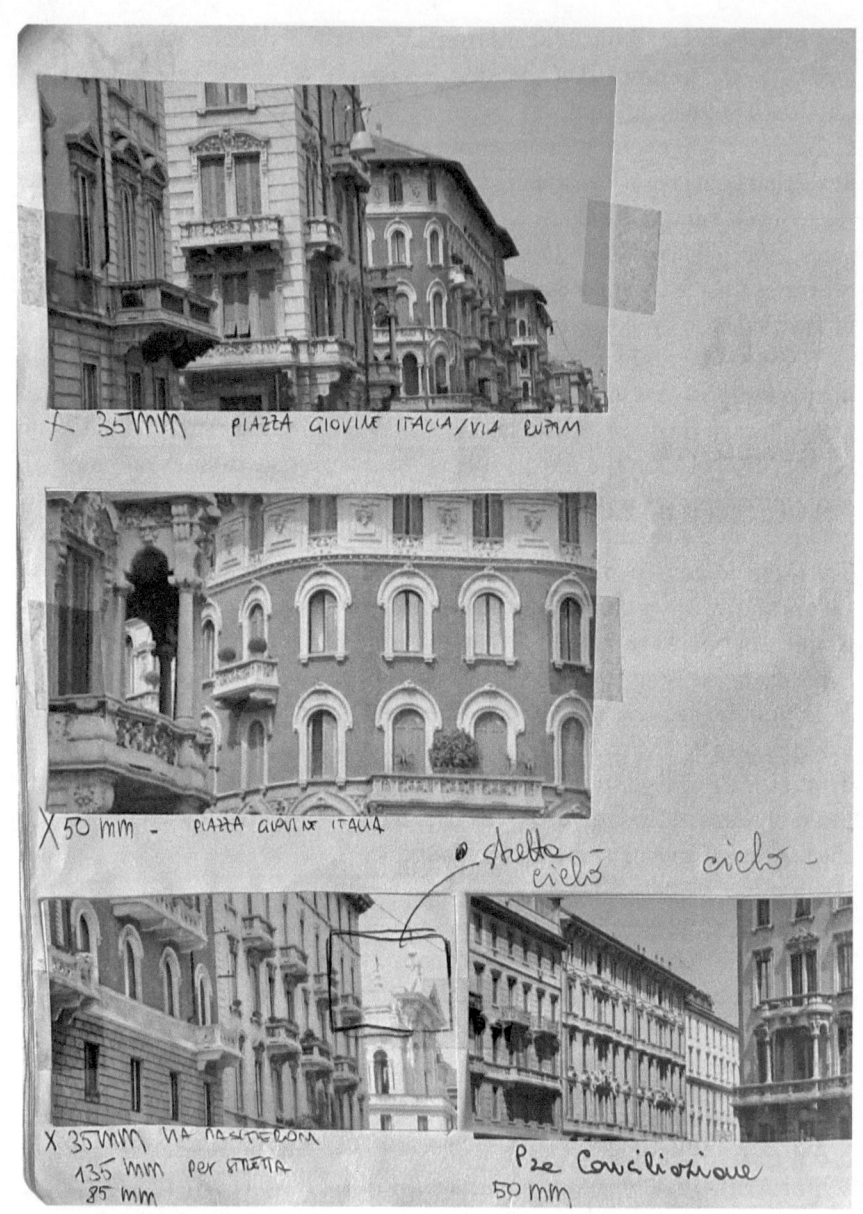

Figure 2.14. Film diary of *Poetry You See Me* (2009), directed by Marina Spada. Director's personal archive.

Figure 2.15. Film diary of *Poetry You See Me* (2009), directed by Marina Spada. Director's personal archive.

34c

anche
corello
nelle finestre -

luigi
ghirri -
STUDIO DI ALDO ROSSI
83/90

Figure 2.16. Film diary of *Poetry You See Me* (2009), directed by Marina Spada. Director's personal archive.

Here, there is an overlapping of temporalities. Whereas Pozzi vividly describes insalubrious, crowded spaces, the contemporary poets' walk unfolds along deserted streets, which suggests that the homeless have perished or have been, once again, displaced.

While revisiting the places of Pozzi's poetry, the film also shows the transformations of the urban fabric over time, the city's expansion, the road building, the construction of an underground transportation system, the elevation of tall buildings, and the covering of the water by concrete. This is most evident through the use of Pozzi's photos that feature bodies of water that no longer exist (see figs.2.18a and 2.18b). As John Foot writes in his urban history of the city, "Milan is a city built on *acqua* ... and traces of its watery past remained—dry docks, strange-shaped bars, bridges, floods, streets names, the smell."[35] The district Porto di Mare, as the character Maria recounts while walking, derives its name from a small lake that no longer exists. Similarly, most of the canals crossing the city were covered in the 1930s to create roads.

Pozzi's photos reveal to viewers Milan's "watery past." Interestingly, the photos are incorporated not only via editing but also in the actual filming, as the street poets are shown hanging reproductions of Pozzi's photos around the city. One of those pictures shows a long line of washerwomen kneeling along a canal, a reminder for both viewers and Milan's residents of the hard and humble jobs that unprivileged women did back then (and continue to do).

Poetry You See Me, like *Traveling with Cecilia*, discussed in chapter 1, "reclaims the archive" through the use of found footage.[36] As Laura Mulvey writes, "The compilation film has no inherent relation to women, but its formal properties fit well with stories that emerge out of silence and cultural marginalization, tentatively making the shift from an individual and private world into circulation in the public sphere."[37] *Poetry* gleans fragments of verses, pages of journals, photos, and home movies (most likely shot by Pozzi's father) to rewrite her story and make it visible in the city, in other words transforming it into a public experience rather than a private one.

The death of the artist, a vibrant and brilliant woman undone by her times, leaves a void in a city for all those who bother to notice, and through Spada's film, her verses become visible again, both materially and symbolically. In the final scene of *Poetry*, Pozzi's face, with her verses written next to it, appears on the sides of a streetcar moving through Milan. It is a reparative finale for all the years her work was neglected and a statement on the intent of the film. Making a documentary film on a modern poet not consecrated in the canon of Italian literature—and doing it by way of archival footage—is quite literally an act of "making the invisible visible" and even more so if we consider *Poetry*

Figure 2.17. Film diary of *Poetry You See Me* (2009), directed by Marina Spada. Director's personal archive.

56

2.18. Film diary of *Poetry You See Me* (2009), directed by Marina Spada. Director's personal archive.

64b

ultima

to be part of the feminist project of reinscribing women in art history as well as in film history.

Still, traces of Pozzi's life in the city are transitory, like the streetcar that travels through the neighborhoods and the flyers printed with Pozzi's verses that the H5N1 hang around town, inviting passersby to interrupt their preordered, repetitive paths. A woman director entrusted with the uncovering of Pozzi's life and work, Spada inscribes her own artistic experience within a place-centered artistic production that includes film, photography, and painting, all rooted in the city of Milan but also in a shared female genealogy, while advocating for other women artists' commitment to continue breaking the silence, restoring memories, and expanding knowledge.

NOTES

1. During the 1980s, Spada directed commercials and video portraits of Italian artists such as Pietro Lingeri, Fernanda Pivano, Arnaldo Pomodoro, Francesco Leonetti, Gabriele Basilico, and Mimmo Iodice. In 2000, she wrote her first feature film, *Forza cani* (Come on Dogs!). Denied funding from the Italian government, which is the primary financial source for film production in Italy, Spada fundraised 60 million lire on her own through the internet. This was the first time crowdfunding was used to finance an independent digital film in the country; in Spada's words, it was "an important step toward the democratization of Italian cinema." She teaches film direction and acting at the Film School Civica di Milano.

2. Marina Spada, interview by author, Zoom, July 20, 2020 (my translation).

3. The tower shown in the opening scene of *As the Shadow* was originally named Littoria Tower. Built during the Fascist period, it was closed for decades until it was restored by the liquor company Branca, an example of how consumerist culture is engrained in the urban fabric. At the time of the film's shooting in 2005, the tower had been recently reopened.

4. Alaimo, "Insurgent Vulnerability and the Carbon Footprint of Gender," 28.

5. See Past, *Italian Ecocinema Beyond the Human*, 191.

6. Bernadette Luciano and Susanna Scarparo explore how the Italian cinematic tradition has been embraced and transformed in Italian women's films in their book *Reframing Italy*.

7. Luciano and Scarparo, "Gendering Mobility and Migration in Contemporary Italian Cinema," 171.

8. Di Bianco, "Interview with Marina Spada," 243.

9. Marina Spada, interview by author, Zoom, July 20, 2020 (my translation).

10. It should be recognized that the urban renewal of the Leoni district speaks to an ongoing process of gentrification. This area was a working-class

neighborhood gentrified by beautiful apartments built for the bourgeoisie—the only people who are allowed to have a new park.

11. I borrow this expression from Gandhy, "The Cinematic Void," 322.
12. De Bonis, "Il mio domani."
13. Lefebvre, "Between Setting and Landscape in the Cinema," 23.
14. Pier Paolo Pasolini used a similar editing strategy in his *Mamma Roma* (1962), where the Roman cityscape is bestowed with a destructive power. A shot featuring the Church of Saint John Bosco, built in a rationalist style, abruptly appears during the tragic ending, linking the death of the young subproletarian to the city and its new peripheries.
15. See Kaplan, *Climate Trauma*.
16. Modini, "Perché desidero che tutte/i vedano il film *Come l'ombra* di Marina Spada."
17. Williams, *The Country and the City*, 13.
18. Massey, *Space, Place, and Gender*, 10.
19. See Wilson, *The Sphinx in the City*, 7.
20. The story of the mother who abandoned her family is inspired by Antonioni's 1957 *Il grido*. The director's notes read, "The father walks. Monica enters the frame and walks slowly, at distance. Long preceding tracking shot. After the dialogue, walking faster than the camera, they surpass it, leaving the scene empty." The camera stops over a long take of the fields (my translation). This is an analysis of the camera works from Antonioni's film.
21. Forgacs, "Antonioni: Space, Place, Sexuality," 103.
22. This deliberately symbolic shot is the remake of a photo by Joseph Koudelka, who captured an empty Prague right before the 1968 Soviet intervention in Czechoslovakia. The same page from the diary of *My Tomorrow*, figure 2.9, shows that Cindy Sherman's work was also a visual reference for the walking sequence.
23. Translation in the DVD of the film, Kairos Film, 2011.
24. Seger, *Landscapes in Between*, 38.
25. Harrison, *Gardens*, 116.
26. Bruno and Nadotti, *Off Screen*, 152.
27. Artist's statement in *Poetry You See Me*'s press book. The film was presented at the 2009 Venice Film Festival in the section "Giornate degli Autori" (Days of the Authors).
28. The character of Maria reads pages from Pozzi's journals, in which the poet reports to be advised against writing.
29. According to Spada, Pozzi's *Parole*, the first selection of poems published in 1939, was focused on Pozzi's love for nature. This, in my opinion, is a subtle form of censorship that perpetuates women's association with nature.
30. Graziella Bernabò is the author of Pozzi's biography, *Per troppa vita che ho nel sangue*.

31. Since *Poetry You See Me,* two other films have been devoted to Pozzi: Ferdinando Cito Filomarino's feature film *Antonia* (2013) and the documentary film *Il cielo in me: Vita irrimediabile di una poetessa* (The Sky in Me: The Irreparable Life of a Poet, 2014) directed by Sabrina Bonaiti and Marco Ongania.
32. The group of street poets cast in the film is called H5N1 (bird flu).
33. Translation from the English-subtitled version of the film.
34. Translation from the English-subtitled version of the film.
35. Foot, *Milan since the Miracle,* 8.
36. See Callahan, *Reclaiming the Archive.*
37. Mulvey, *Afterimages,* 142.

Fegatello: *Ophelia Does Not Drown*

MIXING EXTRACTS FROM ARCHIVAL FOOTAGE from the 1930s to the 1970s with video art performances often featuring the director herself, Francesca Fini's *Ofelia non annega* (Ophelia Does Not Drown, 2016) surrealistically reinvents the tragic ending of the Shakespearean heroine while contributing to a feminist reinterpretation of the sociological and historical documentary films from the Istituto Luce, the former producer and distributor of documentary films founded in Italy during the fascist era.

"Ofelia," states the artist, "is not the fragile teenager in love with Hamlet, but many women of different colors, features, and ages. Our Ophelia is not lost in the woods of Denmark, but in the countryside of the Lazio region, from the Gazometro (an iron structure once used to store the capital's gas supply, now an industrial relic) to the junkyard in Cisterna di Latina, from the arid limestone caves of Riano Flaminio to the wonderful futuristic Villa Perugini in Fregene, passing through a thrilling scenic ride on a tourist bus in Rome."[1] Ophelia is a survivor among Italian ruins.

At the heart of the film and its inspiration is the commemoration of an incident, known as the Tragedy of Savoia Street, that occurred in 1951 in Rome. Over one hundred women competing for a typist's position crowded the stairs of a dilapidated building, which collapsed under their weight. Seventy women were injured, and one died.[2] Juxtaposing the black-and-white images of the newsreel and other documentaries showing women interacting with various machines with Fini's own chromatically vivid performances, *Ofelia Does Not Drown* suggests that technology both liberated and enslaved women's bodies.

Performance art becomes a ritual of mourning when we see Fini walking on the street where the accident occurred and, right after, into a white space

Figure 2.19. The artist's hands rewriting Ophelia's ending. Screen capture, *Ophelia Does Not Drown* (2016), directed by Francesca Fini.

where she pours her blood into the ribbon of an old Olivetti typewriter to type and retype the title of her film: *Ofelia non annega* or *Ophelia Does Not Drown*.

NOTES

1. Artist's statement. https://www.francescafini.com/about-me-1.
2. This incident inspired the 1951 film *Roma ore 11* (Rome 11:00) by Giuseppe De Santis.

THREE

MOTHERS AND DAUGHTERS: STORIES OF SURVIVAL AND CARE

The White Space, I Like to Work

> We know more about the air we breathe, the sea we travel, than about the nature and meaning of motherhood.
>
> —Adrienne Rich, *Of Woman Born*, 1976

ON A SUMMER DAY IN 2014, director Francesca Comencini welcomed me into her luminous house near Corso Trieste in Rome for a conversation about her urban filmmaking. Motivated by an interest in the process women go through to become directors and how that path often merges with autobiographical narrative matter, I asked her about her beginnings in the mid-1980s.

As discussed in my preface "Women Make Movies in Italy," access to the Italian film industry is more challenging for a woman than for a man, but this was not the case for Francesca Comencini, "figlia d'arte" (daughter of an artist) of Luigi Comencini, one of the masters of popular Italian cinema. However, while admitting that having grown up on her father's sets gave her enormous advantages, she revealed that while she was helped on one hand, she was hindered on the other. "My father never wanted me to be and never accepted that I was a filmmaker," she said. "I made my first film *Pianoforte* against my father. It was an autobiographical film, and for my father cinema was something else. It was a film of rebellion. In a sense, it placed me right from the start in a logic of discontinuity with my origins."[1] She continued forcefully: "The beginning for me was not about 'making movies,' it was about telling my story. I didn't have to start from the ground up, but I was very young, without sufficient preparation, and I started in a very instinctive and desperate way. I made my first film to survive. I needed to tell a story that was very traumatic, a story of drug addiction and death. My own. This is something that happens for all of my films: I decide to make a film only when it feels necessary."[2]

After *Pianoforte*—a film that in vivid terms Comencini defines as "a pregnancy" —with shoestring budgets and a minuscule, sometimes one-woman crew, she started "taking possession of the medium" and shaping an idea of cinema that engages in "an intense relationship with reality."[3] Like Spada and many other women directors, Comencini contributed, at least at the beginning of her career, "to remembering and reinventing women's history"—in her case, through a documentary film on a figure she calls a "literary mother," Elsa Morante.[4] The latter led to other documentary film projects on social and political matters. *Carlo Giuliani, ragazzo* (Carlo Giuliani, a Boy, 2002) reconstructs the last living moments of the victim of a police crackdown on protesters of the G8 Summit in Genoa in 2001 through his mother's memories and videos shot by protesters featured in the film; *Firenze il nostro domani* (Florence, Our Tomorrow, 2003)—a collective film—documents the four-day European Social Forum held in Florence in 2002; *Le ragazze di San Gregorio* (The Girls of San Gregorio, 2009) collects women's testimonies amid the rubble of the massive 2009 earthquake in the region of Abruzzo. As they often do, these works of *cinema d'impegno* (committed cinema) reveal from the titles that Comencini privileges place-centered stories and women's lived experiences, especially in urban contexts.

Elaborating on the centrality of the city to her directorial efforts, she shared that, due to traumatic events she experienced in her hometown, Rome, she relocated at a young age to Paris and lived there for twenty years. This relocation made her acutely aware of emotional geography. "Consciously, from *Shakespeare a Palermo* to *Un giorno speciale*, each of my films is a film on the city," she said. "For this reason, I find your book project important. That's my way of making films: I put the intimate story of a character, mostly female characters, in relation to the social and political apparatus that determines her emotions. The city is the more visible apparatus for a character in a film. Indeed, the city determines your emotions, the geography of your love, your loneliness, your maternity. The streets of a city, the geography of a city, shape the story I'm narrating, and this begins during the process of writing and then continues with the filming process."[5]

These days Comencini is an established filmmaker, known to larger audiences as one of the directors of *Gomorrah*, the popular TV crime series set in Naples, directed by a team of filmmakers, of which Comencini is the only woman. No longer constrained by small budgets and working within the narrative structure of the TV series, she continues to focus on women in the city, and, in many episodes of *Gomorrah*, she investigates the involvement of the criminal organization Camorra in environmental crimes and women's relationship to male power.

In this chapter, though, I examine two films from Comencini's early cinematic production: *Lo spazio bianco* (*The White Space*, 2009) and *Mi piace lavorare—Mobbing* (*I Like to Work—Harassment*, 2003).[6] I privilege these films from Comencini's extensive women-centered urban filmography because they tackle in compelling and innovative ways a central theme of feminist filmmaking: the experience of motherhood in contemporary Italian society.

Motherhood has a rich history in Italian cinema. In their 2017 edited volume *Italian Motherhood on Screen*, Maria Elena D'Amelio and Giovanna Faleschini Lerner examine a body of contemporary films and web series that "consider the specificity of experiences of the maternal" in Italy. Drawing from key feminist film studies such as Lucy Fisher's *Cinematernity: Film, Motherhood, Genre*, they probe how, in contemporary Italian society, the idea of motherhood and its very experience have been affected and transformed by "the perceived crisis of the family, the economic crisis, and the crisis of national identity, provoked by the forces of globalization and migration, secularization, and the instability of the labor markets." This crisis, insofar as it pervades all aspects of human and nonhuman life, in addition to being "social, political, and philosophical," is also an ecological crisis.[7]

While Comencini's films rightly have received significant critical attention within Italian screen studies, her women-place-centered films have not been read from an ecocritical perspective. Unlike Barbanente and Mangini's documentary film *Traveling with Cecilia* (chap. 1), a film that—by highlighting the entanglement of poverty, environmental degradation, and pollution-induced illnesses—articulates an explicit call for environmental justice, Comencini's films, similarly to Spada's, might not appear to be environmentally conscious. The unambiguous signifiers of ecological crises—the visibly polluted bodies of water and skies filled with black smoke from industrial plants as seen in *Traveling with Cecilia*, or the littered streets and the dry bed of a river turned into a dumpsite of Alice Rohrwacher's *Corpo Celeste* (2011) in chapter 4—remain mostly unseen or unspoken in the Naples of *The White Space* and in the Rome of *I Like to Work*. However, if the ecocinematic approach can be about probing the cinematic framings and bringing into view what remains off-screen, or just evoked or hinted at, my analysis aims to foreground feminist urban ecologies. The ecological dimension of Comencini's films, though, does not reside only in the interplay of women and the environments they live in.

The White Space and *I Like to Work* are stories of single motherhood that articulate a discourse on the different dimensions of care, intended both as predisposition (caring for) and the practice of care (taking care of someone or something). Care intended as an inclination, as Joan Tronto elucidates in *Moral Boundaries*, involves, first, "the recognition that care is necessary" and then the "acceptance of some form of burden." Care, Tronto elaborates, "can be fraught with conflict when care givers will find that their needs to care for themselves come in conflict with the care they must give to others, or that they are responsible to take care of a number of other persons or things whose needs are in conflict with each other."[8] Care as a practice consists, most commonly, in childrearing or other labors of care for other vulnerable beings. Care work, theorists of political ecology Wendy Harcourt and Christine Bauhardt point out, "is characterized by its time intensity, the continual requirements of the dependents and the inability of the carer to postpone the care needs."[9] Despite its necessity, this kind of labor is devalued in capitalist society and assumed to be the responsibility of women or other marginal social subjects.

The White Space, set in Naples, addresses the emotional conflict caused by maternal ambivalence—the coexistence of feelings of love and rejection for the child—the social isolation in which motherhood is often experienced and that Tronto describes as the conflict of care.[10] A teacher in her forties unexpectedly becomes pregnant and gives birth to a premature baby. Suspended in the anxiety of waiting for the baby to live or die, she explores feelings of ambivalence, fear, and hope in a deserted city. As she gradually connects with a community of mothers and her students, she comes to embrace motherhood (i.e., her responsibility of care). The second film, set in Rome, explores women's struggle to reconcile motherhood and paid work, especially outside the heterosexual nuclear family structure and the violence the neoliberal economy inflicts on women's bodies. It is the story of a single mother who, already struggling to support her ten-year-old daughter and sick, elderly father, becomes a victim of workplace harassment. While her life is limited to repetitive itineraries and the hostile spaces of the office, her daughter, in her absence, engages with a multiethnic city.

These are both "necessary" (to recall Comencini's term) stories of survival and care that unfold in urban environments, which, much like the subjects who inhabit them, are themselves surviving and transforming. I argue that showing how women take up the burden of care, one that takes time and requires "solicitude, carefulness, thought, [and] concern," these films contribute to an understanding of how care is vital to the survival of humans, nonhumans, and places.[11]

The analysis sets off by looking at a key scene from *The White Space*: an unsteady aerial view of Naples, framing (once again) a cement-congested cityscape and a woman standing in a deserted piazza. I discuss the significances of Comencini's dystopian Naples, considering the city's decades-long waste crisis.

I suggest that Comencini's empty and clean city is a signifier of the separation from the world that the protagonist experiences in her single motherhood but also a defiant reimagining of the city. Engaging with the concept of maternal ambivalence and Adriana Cavarero's notion of maternal inclination (in line with Tronto's idea of care), I observe how the protagonist's gradual embrace of motherhood in a precarious world is articulated in spatial terms.

The section on *I Like to Work—Harassment* opens with a definition of workplace harassment and its gender implications and provides a brief production history of the film and its Roman setting. I discuss the different relationships that mother and daughter have with the city: the mother's is affected by the aggressive demands of her work, the daughter's by the open engagement with a multiethnic city in the absence of her mother. My film analysis aims to demonstrate how the neoliberal economy, with its demands for acceleration, is not only violent against women but also causes crises of care that can be overcome by seeking justice against forms of oppression deeply rooted in sexism and by welcoming the idea of an inclusive city as well as an expanded notion of family.

Embracing the feminist ecocritical ethics of care, I propose conceiving of (maternal) care in ecological terms, as a leaning toward the human and nonhuman world, as a response to ecocrises. Finally, inscribing myself into the narrative of this chapter, I share how Comencini's stories of survival resonated with my own story of survival and impacted my understanding of the urgency of care.

LO SPAZIO BIANCO (*THE WHITE SPACE*, 2009): TIME, CARE, AND A SANITIZED CITY

A woman wearing a hospital gown stands on the roof of a building. She gazes absentmindedly at her surroundings while anxiously smoking (see fig. 3.1). A handheld camera follows her, recording an unstable cityscape cluttered with cupolas, bell towers, the sloping roofs of an old quarter mixed with modern apartment buildings piled on top of one another; a few skyscrapers stick out far on the horizon, and a volcano dominates the background, piercing a cloudy sky. This is Naples's tragically beautiful cityscape. Cut.

Now the woman is walking through a semideserted, airy piazza with a man. He walks ahead of her while a group of people (seemingly tourists) passing in single file crosses the piazza and separates the couple. She loses sight of him while standing alone in the piazza with an incredulous and anxious expression on her face. The camera now frames her from above in a tilt shot, against the cobblestones, while she holds in her hands the sonogram image of a fetus (see

Figure 3.1. Anxious city viewing. Screen capture, *The White Space* (2009), directed by Francesca Comencini.

Figure 3.2. An urban pregnancy. Screen capture, *The White Space* (2009), directed by Francesca Comencini.

fig. 3.2). Cut. Back to the terrace, where the woman continues to smoke her cigarette, immersed in her memories and gazing at the cityscape.

The above-described scene from Comencini's *The White Space*, appearing roughly thirty minutes from the beginning of the film, portrays the female protagonist, Maria, standing on the rooftop terrace of the hospital where she has just given birth, recalling the day she learned she was pregnant. An independent, strong, single woman in her forties, who teaches literacy to underprivileged adult students while enjoying an active social life in Naples, Maria unexpectedly becomes pregnant after a brief relationship. She soon realizes that she is going to be a single mother. Feeling overwhelmed by the responsibility of taking care of a child, one day she collapses on the street in the sixth month of her pregnancy, goes into labor, and, after being taken to the hospital, gives birth to a premature baby girl. Fearing the prospect that the child might die, or survive with impairments, she spends long hours in a hospital waiting in limbo, watching over her baby in an incubator and contemplating the city from above.[12]

Just as the opening scenes of *Traveling with Cecilia* and *As the Shadow* position women as observers and storytellers, the above-described scene is pregnant with meanings, so to speak, that enunciate the complex themes and emotions of the film: a city, a woman's body, motherhood, survival, care, anxiety, hope, and uncertainty.

While views from above might suggest an objectification of the external world and a desire for control, the handheld camera swiveling around the character and displaying a shifting visual field communicates a sense of precariousness, not just for the woman who has recently given birth but also for the whole urban environment itself.[13] Maria, immersed in a scene of contrasts, wears a hospital gown, a garment that supposedly protects her from contamination, while she pollutes her own body by smoking.

In the immediate background, there is the messiness of the cityscape, a cacophony of human construction that is itself challenged further by the looming presence of Mount Vesuvius, one of Italy's active volcanoes. Vesuvius's threat of eruption casts a shadow on the human and nonhuman world in Naples and imbues them with a sense of instability and vulnerability; it challenges human attempts at domination over nature.[14]

As mentioned, this "precarious" landscape is sutured, via editing, with a flashback that is anticipatory of the future of the character's life and the development of the story, almost like a prophetic daydream. Maria initially walks with a man and then remains alone. The spatial separation of the couple clearly alludes to the man's disengagement and his refusal of the paternal role, and more broadly to a breaking of the traditional heteronormative family most commonly represented in film and media.[15]

Fittingly, single motherhood as represented in the image I entitle "An Urban Pregnancy" is placed in a piazza, or *agora*, the heart of the *polis* where, in ancient Greece, citizens would gather in assembly. From a feminist ecocritical perspective, such a framing choice challenges the ancient, deep-rooted chains of patriarchal associations between women, procreation, and nature—one that ecofeminism itself ironically reinforced at its inception in the mid-1970s—and reconfigures motherhood as "a naturalcultural process."[16] In this light, this is a claim for a motherhood that belongs to the *polis*.

The piazza, however, is empty. Glimpses of a colonnade render the film's Neapolitan location recognizable (at least to my eyes): Piazza del Plebiscito, Naples's largest and most beautiful piazza, the vibrant site of encounter for this Mediterranean city's inhabitants and tourists. Over a decade since its release, *The White Space* is still striking for its uncommon and somehow controversial representation of the city: a quiet and semideserted Naples, covered by a leaden sky.[17]

Through the frequent views from above like the one described earlier, and deliberately emptied public spaces, this city of one million inhabitants (or three million, including the sprawling metropolitan area), otherwise known for its operatic and all-too-often menacing life, is freed from its typical exegetic chaos. Comencini's representational approach is interpreted by Claudia Karagoz in her essay "Motherhood Revisited" as a failure of the film in rendering the city's, and its inhabitants', vitality. While it is true that Comencini's film "leaves Naples and its people largely unrepresented," or at least fails to portray many aspects of their struggles, the monumental Naples of *The White Space* forcefully functions as an extension of the character's solipsistic self.[18]

Still, such a void needs to be interrogated. What is erased? What is Maria not seeing? What are we not seeing? What is concealed? A "sanitized" Naples appears particularly puzzling considering the city's persistent troubles with waste.[19] Since 1994, the region of Campania, and particularly the city of Naples, have been dealing with a waste management crisis, which reached its "spectacular" peak in 2008.[20] Well documented by the media, this crisis produced, in Serenella Iovino's words, "the world-infamous image of a beautiful and ancient city literally swallowed by its own trash."[21] Most troublingly, while the piles of uncollected garbage were "offensive to eyes and nose," as Elena Past put it, they represented "the most visible face of a much larger, often invisible, toxic crisis that threatens Naples and Campania."[22] The region, in fact, and particularly an area between Naples and the city of Caserta, is plagued by an alarming number of illegal dumpsites filled with toxic waste partially buried in the soil and partially disposed of through recurrent illegal fires, which earned this area the label "Land of Fires."[23] In 2013, in an attempt to stop these environmental abuses, the government installed numerous cameras in the area, supposedly monitored by the police. A reportage conducted by the TV program *Le iene* in November 2020 shows how the dumping and illegal fires continue regardless of the cameras recording these crimes. Shockingly, those cameras are often unmonitored (nobody is looking) or self-erase when their memory storage reaches capacity.

The evidence of these environmental crimes remains unseen, but the global success of Roberto Saviano's book *Gomorrah*, as well as Matteo Garrone's film adaptation and the five seasons of the internationally acclaimed TV drama series of the same name, plus numerous documentary films on the issue of toxic waste, reinforced in the collective imaginary what Past calls the image of a "dirty Naples," in which criminality, drugs, toxicity, and environmental degradation dominate the city's life.[24] Released in 2009, Comencini's *The White Space* was shot immediately after (or perhaps even in the midst of) the crescendo of the waste management crisis, most of which remains completely off-screen.

While keeping things "out of sight" might contribute to reinforcing what Rob Nixon calls "geographies of concealment," the empty Naples proposed by Comencini can be interpreted as a defiant reimagining of the city.[25] A woman, soon to be a mother, stands alone in an empty, unsoiled, and unlittered piazza. As Millicent Marcus confirms in her chapter "Unnatural Child Birth," "the image of Naples, which has been exerted as a kind of protagonist throughout the film, is freed from its iconic connection with easy fertility, traditional family structure, and general socio-economic backwardness."[26] This framing choice alludes to the social isolation in which women often experience motherhood while asserting that the political dimension of motherhood ultimately codes the city, despite its messiness and precariousness, as a generative space.

Comencini does not ignore the crisis in Naples, however; she simply treats it laterally. Under attentive examination, a fleeting yet significant reference to Naples's ecological crises can be gleaned from a dialogue between Maria and one of her students. In one scene, after leaving the hospital while her baby is still in the incubator, the protagonist ventures to an unknown peripheral part of the city to visit Luisa, a former student who terminated her studies. Luisa warmly welcomes Maria to her tidy, middle-class apartment and asks her to take her shoes off and keep her eyes shut. Taken to the balcony, Maria realizes that Luisa, to enjoy a micro-dose of nature, installed artificial grass on the concrete floor of her balcony, turning it into a minuscule meadow overseeing Vesuvius. More unsettled than delighted, as Luisa was expecting, Maria gazes at the volcano against the backdrop of buildings and interrupted construction, which speaks to the city's incessant sprawl and erasure of green spaces (see fig. 3.3).[27]

Asked why she has stopped coming to school, Luisa explains that she is struggling financially. In order to pay for the significant municipal trash fees that were due at the same time as her daughter's university tuition, she was forced to borrow money from an old acquaintance, a loan shark. And to repay him (at an exorbitant interest rate), she had to take a second job, leaving no time for evening classes. Luisa's story, which she tells succinctly and without

Figure 3.3. Mount Vesuvius and the continuous city. Screen capture, *The White Space* (2009), directed by Francesca Comencini.

drama, suddenly reminds viewers of the "ancient city literally swallowed by its own trash," to recall Iovino's words. Furthermore, it reveals the not-so-apparent concatenation of environmental and social issues, the enmeshment of legality (official fees, public sanitation) and illegality (loan sharking, illicit dumping, which, while not explicit, would be understood at the time as part of the public debate). This fleeting conversation connects, in the same brief scene, the volcano, the concrete, the invisible yet ever-present garbage, a woman's struggle to sustain her family and give her daughter a chance for an education while abandoning her own, and finally the precarious life of Maria's child. Apparently changing the subject of the conversation, her mind returning to her daughter in the hospital, Maria abruptly asks, "Why does this baby not breathe?" and continues, "I want Irene to live, but sometimes, I don't know if that is what I want."

Here, Maria is expressing her maternal ambivalence, love mixed with anxiety, guilt, and shame. However, the conversation about garbage and the bleak view over the volcano outside the window—strong reminders of the insalubrious world in which the baby is learning to breathe—suggest that Maria's anxiety around her daughter's survival is not unconnected from the predicaments of ecological crises.

Ultimately, by portraying a moment of empathy among mothers, this delicate scene shows how Maria—previously shown standing erect and autonomous, albeit unstable, on the hospital's roof, as well as in the piazza—is gradually accepting motherhood. As Marcus writes: "Maria... will evolve from a state of shock, confusion and ambivalence to one of growing preparedness and confidence in her own maternal strength."[28] She becomes what prominent feminist philosopher Adriana Cavarero would call "an inclined I."[29]

In her book *Inclinations: A Critique of Rectitude*, Cavarero elaborates on Hannah Arendt's reflections on the significance of inclination: "Every inclination turns outward, it leans out of the self in the direction of whatever may affect me from the outside world." Inclination, as Cavarero speculates in dialogue with Emmanuel Levinas and echoing Judith Butler's idea of precarious life, is a critical tool "to rethink a subjectivity marked by exposure, vulnerability, and dependence."[30]

As Bernadette Luciano and Susanna Scarparo observe in their article "Maternal Ambivalence in Contemporary Italian Cinema," Cavarero configures the maternal experience in relational terms, as an inclination, not intended as a natural predisposition but as the deliberate choice to lean toward the other in the act of care.

The concept of "maternal inclination," according to Cavarero, is visually illustrated by Leonardo da Vinci's painting *Sant'Anna, la Madonna e il bambino con l'agnello* (*The Virgin and Child with St. Anne*, 1503–1519).[31] Diverging from a traditional iconography of the dyad mother and child, da Vinci's painting shows the Virgin Mary sitting on her mother's lap while leaning toward the Christ child, who, in turn, is holding a lamb, a symbol of vulnerability. The disposition of the bodies and their interrelated gazes (St. Anne is looking at her daughter, who looks at the child, while the lamb is looking at all of them) expresses the leaning out of the self that maternal care entails. As Cavarero poetically suggests, "The mother here is inclined over her child who, as an emblem of dependent and vulnerable creature, attracts her in a forward motion, in a protrusion beside herself that endangers her balance."[32] St. Anne sustains Mary's effort and supports her.

Similarly, Comencini's Maria is sustained along her path toward maternal experience by a group of mothers whose premature babies are in the same hospital. Initially incredulous, shocked, and impatient (that is, refusing to accept her condition as a patient), she is reluctant to connect with them. But as she finds her way to motherhood and allows herself to break the isolation in which she has barricaded herself (of which the empty city is a signifier), she daydreams about the mothers dancing in their hospital gowns in the neonatal intensive care unit. While Maria is not yet imagining herself as part of the choreography, this scene represents a turning point in her participation in hospital life and in her interactions with the other mothers. Comencini's maternal dance, as imagined by an ambivalent mother like Maria, is reminiscent of the concept of maternal inclination, here literally exemplified by the corporeal poses of the characters. The rotating movement of the camera suggests a change of perspective. The mothers move slowly while caressing, embracing, and supporting each other, until, as shown in figure 3.4, they all bear the youngest of the group. A scene of great

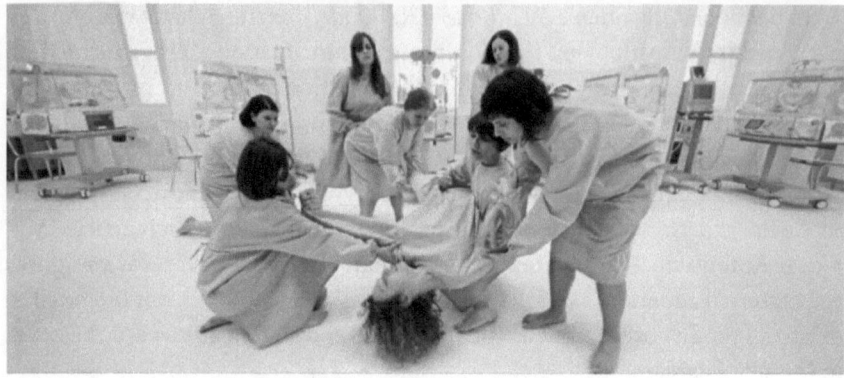

Figure 3.4. Maternal dance. Screen capture, *The White Space* (2009), directed by Francesca Comencini.

poetic impact and tenderness, it reconfigures motherhood and mothering as a shared endeavor by a community of mothers and as an act of reciprocal care.[33]

Recalling what Luciano and Scarparo write about Cristina Comencini's (Francesca's sister) *Quando la notte* (*When the Night*, 2011) and Alina Marazzi's *Tutto parla di te* (*All About You*, 2012), two contemporary Italian films tackling the complex issue of maternal ambivalence, *The White Space* also invites us "to reflect on the crucial role that women play or can play in supporting each other through the difficult choice: to care or not to care for the child."[34]

A similar supporting role is also played in the film by Maria's students, a nomadic community of learners. The evening classes she teaches are not given a set location by the city administration; they take place periodically in different areas of the city and spaces—at first in a dilapidated building with windows facing the sea, then in a seemingly royal palace, later in a kindergarten. This additional plot line allows the protagonist—as well as the spectator—to undertake a voyage into the city (another form of flânerie), creating spatial and conceptual continuities and blurring the boundaries of the city's dichotomies: beauty versus ugliness, center versus periphery, mobility versus immobility, known versus unknown spaces. The final location of the itinerant school, a location "from where"—Maria's friend and colleague comments—"they won't be kicked out," is a former suburban abattoir, as the sign "macello" outside the door reveals.

Social hierarchies are replicated through space. The unprivileged Neapolitan students are moved to the edges of the city—like the slaughterhouses that, since the early nineteenth century, have relocated outside the city for sanitary reasons and to be kept out of sight. Slaughterhouses, nevertheless, wherever

Figure 3.5. Deserted Naples. Screen capture, *The White Space* (2009), directed by Francesca Comencini.

they are placed, are sites for the production of meat for human consumption and places of animals' suffering and death that a repurposing of the material space can only partially erase.[35]

Furthermore, this thought-provoking plot detail seems to suggest that the inclination toward the other that allows Maria to accept the role of motherhood might be understood in posthuman terms. After all, the conditions of exposure, vulnerability, and dependence that Cavarero imagines as constituents of an altruistic subject are conditions humans share with the material and nonhuman world.[36] By appropriating the confines of a decommissioned slaughterhouse, *macello* in Italian, they are, in a way, transubstantiating the mess—also a synonym for *macello*—of urban chaos into something hopeful and new.

The ideas of learning, a new life, and a new city beautifully come together in the final sequence of the film. While students are taking their final exam to get the *licenza media* (middle school diploma), Maria receives a call from the hospital that her daughter, now considered out of danger, is breathing on her own.[37] As she rushes out of the building and starts walking toward the hospital, a spectacular crane shot frames her in an aerial view along Via Toledo, a street that Stendhal described as "the busiest, most joyous thoroughfare in the entire universe."[38] The scene is edited so that it connects, step by step, various moments of Maria's life by alternating between her present, fast-paced, liberating stride and flashbacks to the languid, fatiguing period of her pregnancy. Maria's walking, in fact, reactivates the memory of her slow pace three months earlier, when on the same path she experienced labor pain. Buildings are then shown from a low, distorting angle, perceived from Maria's point of view, from the ground up.

Figure 3.6. Neapolis' new citizen. Screen capture, *The White Space* (2009), directed by Francesca Comencini.

The camera continues to pan upward in an expansive crane shot, progressively showing a larger and larger part of the city, which again is unrealistically empty (see fig. 3.5). It is not a realistic locale, but a place created by Maria's consciousness. It is also *Neapolis*, the New Town, where a new citizen, Irene, is born. The infant's face, previously shapeless behind the glass and among the tubes, now fills the frame, emerging within a wide screen shot and in the mother's hands.

MI PIACE LAVORARE—MOBBING (I LIKE TO WORK—HARASSMENT, 2003): TIME, CARE, AND A PARENT-POLIS

While *The White Space* explores the path to motherhood through a woman's pregnancy and gradual inclination toward maternal care, *I Like to Work* interrogates the challenges faced by women in reconciling their roles as mothers and members of the workforce. According to theorists in the field of feminist political ecology, child and elder care are considered "unproductive" within a capitalist and patriarchal system, with these tasks assumed to be women's innate responsibility. As Wendy Harcourt and Christine Bauhardt's analysis of the unrecognized value of care work in a capitalist economy puts it, "Empirically, and globally, this work is mostly done by women and it is socially considered to be 'women's work.'"[39] Often unable to reconcile the necessities of childcare and housework with paid employment, and in light of market demands for flexibility, women become more vulnerable laboring bodies and are therefore more exposed to the risk of being "mobbed."[40]

Comencini's film addresses the largely unrepresented, yet alarmingly widespread, phenomenon of emotional abuse in the workplace commonly known as bullying or harassment and its specific gender implications, a phenomenon known in Italy as "mobbing." Along with Silvia Ferreri's documentary *Uno virgola due* (One Point Two, 2007), *I Like to Work*, over a decade from its release, is the only Italian film that treats this issue. Mobbing is a form of psychological violence intentionally perpetrated on an individual worker by one or more colleagues, for an extended period, with the purpose of expelling that worker from the workplace.[41] Such a ruthless strategy of moral aggression is often adopted by management in companies that, due to corporate restructuring or merging with other companies, need to reduce the number of their employees but cannot do so because of state regulation or union protections. Workers considered "redundant" are deliberately humiliated, isolated, and led to believe that they are inadequate until they are forced to resign.[42] Scientific studies demonstrate that this form of bullying heavily impacts workers' mental health, inducing anxiety, depression, insomnia, and suicidal drive; it might have an impact on cardiovascular pathologies and diabetes.[43] Not recognized in the Italian civil and penal code as a crime, mobbing is difficult to identify and prevent also due to the victims' reluctance to call it out.

In 2000, the Chamber of Labor of Rome started a series of antimobbing educational programs. The CGIL Union (Confederazione Generale Italiana del Lavoro) set up help desks where workers could consult with psychologists and occupational doctors to establish if they were targets of workplace harassment and eventually seek the union's assistance to take legal actions against their companies. The overwhelming number of requests for help that such desks received revealed how widespread and acute the issue was throughout the country.[44]

The absence of an antimobbing law is a significant obstacle to the prevention of this form of social oppression. To aggravate the situation, a legislative decree introduced by the Berlusconi government and known as the "Legge Biagi" (February 14, 2003. N.30) allowed for the possibility of a "flexible" job market through the creation of short-term labor contracts. In theory, the liberalization of labor created job opportunities for underemployed groups, especially young people, and possibly women too. While allegedly rendering employment more flexible, this legislative scenario privileges companies at the expense of workers' rights, with labor flexibility translated into workers' precariousness, and it facilitates an increase in cases of harassment, especially toward women.[45]

Comencini's interest in this form of social exploitation was welcomed by the CGIL Union, which actively took part in the realization of the film project, granting the filmmaker access to documentation, providing locations,

Figure 3.7. Morgana in the multiethnic city. Screen capture, *I Like to Work* (2003), directed by Francesca Comencini.

collaborating on scripts, and even allowing its members to be cast in secondary roles. In preparation for the film, Comencini, who had much training as a documentary filmmaker, shot a series of video portraits of actual mobbing victims whose stories formed the basis of her script. To demonstrate how gender issues aggravated the effects of harassment, Comencini decided to convey all the stories of her film through a central female character.

Anna is a single mother living in Rome. Her life is limited to office and home, to which she arrives exhausted every night. When Anna's company merges with a larger one, she—who in addition to being a single mother is burdened with caring for her sick, elderly father—is considered "inflexible" by her manager and, therefore, "in excess." To elude the laws protecting women workers, her company adopts the strategy of mobbing to force her to resign. In her absence, her young daughter, Morgana, takes care of herself: she does her homework, shops for groceries, and walks around the Esquilino neighborhood where they live.

Located around the portico-lined perimeter of the largest square in Rome, Piazza Vittorio, built after Italy's unification and named after King Vittorio Emanuele II, Esquilino is the Eternal City's most vibrant multiethnic neighborhood.[46] Inhabited since the 1980s by a diverse concentration of immigrants, it harbors religious, cultural, linguistic, and gastronomic hybridities in what Teresa Fiore defines as "a postnational scenario of multiethnic coexistence."[47]

In this lively area, to fill the void of her mother's absence and escape solitude, Morgana becomes a child flaneuse, actively exploring the city (see fig. 3.7). While Anna engages in hardly any social relationships outside of her office and

Figure 3.8. Walking home. Screen capture, *I Like to Work* (2003), directed by Francesca Comencini.

in several episodes demonstrates ambivalence toward people not ethnically Italians, practicing a certain social separation, Morgana interacts with street musicians and befriends the children of immigrant families. The multiethnic neighborhood of Piazza Vittorio offers Morgana relationships outside the domestic space and substitutes for her dysfunctional family, becoming almost like a "parent-city."[48]

While Morgana experiences the openness of Piazza Vittorio, intended both in social and spatial terms, Anna's mobility in the city is restricted to preordered and repetitive daily itineraries between her house and the office. She sends her daughter to school, descends into the subway, and returns when the teeming streets are quiet at night, always transiting under the porticos or along other confined spaces. Comencini's framing strategies, as shown in figures 3.8 and 3.9, highlight how cloistered Anna's life is.

Indoor spaces, the office, its corridors, and its restrooms, where extensive portions of the film take place, also suggest a sense of entrapment. As the story of harassment unfolds, Anna is removed from her usual responsibilities and assigned tedious tasks; she is progressively isolated and becomes the object of scorn by colleagues. The continuous vexations weaken her psychologically and physically. Her body shrinks, and her pale face fades against the white wall.

A particularly poignant scene illustrates the gendered dimensions of workplace harassment—the corporeal violence that neoliberalism inflicts on

Figure 3.9. Walking to work. Screen capture, *I Like to Work* (2003), directed by Francesca Comencini.

women's bodies—while also calling for solidarity among women. After discovering she has been excluded from a work meeting, Anna retreats into the restroom, where she meets her only sympathetic colleague, a woman who is also seeking refuge from the hostile work environment. The latter is the mother of a newborn infant, recently returned to work after a very brief maternity leave. Prevented from going home to breastfeed her baby during her office shift, her breast starts leaking and her clothes are spotted with milk. Anna, who understands her sense of shame, gives her colleague her own shirt so that she can attend a meeting.

In a later scene, we see the same woman hastily pumping milk from her breast and then dumping it into the sink to continue to work. The power of these scenes goes well beyond the obvious suggestion that offices should be equipped with spaces for nursing mothers or that breastfeeding might be incompatible with the demands of "flexible" time regiments of the office. More damningly, they illustrate how capitalism inhibits maternal care, which is, as psychoanalyst Massimo Recalcati observes, "in open conflict with the maniacal acceleration of time."[49] Moreover, in both scenes, this woman shows a sense of despair and shame, as if her nourishing maternal liquid was a dysfunction of her unruly body and thus superfluous material to be discarded as waste, like any corporeal excrement might be flushed away. Significantly, it is in the restroom, when the hostility is about to reach a point of physical aggression by a group of male employees, that Anna, fearing for her safety, collapses.

After a brief period of medical leave, during which the daughter is forced to assume a parental role and is burdened with care, Anna returns to her

Figure 3.10. A fading woman and a Xerox machine. Screen capture, *I Like to Work* (2003), directed by Francesca Comencini.

workplace, where the abuse continues. During a climactic harassment scene toward the end of the film, Anna is asked to sign her letter of "voluntary" resignation. According to the harassing human resources officer, Anna is to blame for her isolation. He affirms that, despite her good qualities, she is not adequate to the rhythms of the company. "Perhaps a smaller company would be more suitable for you?" he asks with a patronizing tone. As Anna sits in silence, the manager becomes more explicitly aggressive: "What happened to you so far is nothing compared to what will happen if you do not resign. We can be evil. You cannot continue to handle your personal issues with all the frustrations that you have to put up with here. You'll return home with serious problems. And what will you tell your daughter, who has only you?" With composed indignation, Anna refuses to sign and leaves the office to care for her daughter.

Here Comencini's film further elaborates on the issue of time and care. Being kept beyond usual office hours, Anna realizes that she missed an appointment with her daughter, who, that evening, has a ballet recital. She rushes from the building, and when she does not find Morgana either at home or at the dance studio, she starts frantically searching for her in the neighborhood. At the same time, Morgana, dressed in her ballet costume, wanders the streets in search of her mother. Parallel scene editing illustrates the simultaneity and the concatenation of the two situations and conceptually ties together the issues of gendered harassment with a crisis of care: while Anna is being harassed in the office, her daughter is alone in the city's streets, unprotected.

Figure 3.11. A mother in need of care. Screen capture, *I Like to Work* (2003), directed by Francesca Comencini.

As the mother-daughter search for one another continues, a city congested by traffic comes into view. The hectic movement of the handheld camera, positioned from what would be the low angle of Morgana's line of sight, her figure glimpsed among cars in streets scarcely illuminated, emphasizes the child's vulnerability, and the menacing soundtrack foreshadows a tragic ending for her. What in previous scenes was presented as a friendly city for the young flaneuse, who in absence of her mother would wander around connecting with other children and street artists in the multiethnic neighborhood of Piazza Vittorio, a sort of "parent-city," to repeat, now turns into an unhealthy, threatening space, perilous for walkers and especially for children.

The "petro-aesthetic" of this scene with its unending, cacophonous vehicular traffic, preceded by the scene of the aggression explicitly framed in discriminatory gendered terms, reveals the intersection of gender and ecological issues.[50] The capitalist logic is all about increasing speed and efficiency and utilizing technologies to this end. In contemporary times, these technologies rely largely on extracted sources of energy, especially petroleum and coal, both highly polluting with damaging environmental and social consequences. Care for humans, as Recalcati wrote, especially for children, does not, cannot, follow the same schedule. Childrearing is an inherently slow process. Organic nurture and growth in a healthy manner takes time and is therefore in conflict with the speed and efficiency demanded by capitalist production during this period of neoliberalism.

Figure 3.12. Mother and daughter leaving the city. Screen capture, *I Like to Work* (2003), directed by Francesca Comencini.

In the end, Anna finds her child safe in the house of a family from North Africa who runs the grocery store where Morgana shops. While the presence of immigrants, although sympathetically represented, is too fleeting and silent to convey a critique of Italy's recurrent manifestations of intolerance and racism, the scene gestures toward the idea of an inclusive city where non-native inhabitants and marginal citizens play a salvific role for contemporary Italian society.[51]

Finally, mindful of her responsibilities as caretaker, Anna, who seeks the help of a female union representative, gathers the strength to oppose her oppressors and seek justice by suing her company.

A last glimpse of the colonnade of Piazza Vittorio in daylight is shown at the end of the film, when mother and daughter are seen joyfully walking with suitcases, about to leave the city for good. As Luciano and Scarparo noticed in their analysis of *I Like to Work*, this finale, with the child taking the parent by the hand while walking away, is reminiscent of Vittorio De Sica's *Ladri di biciclette* (*Bicycle Thieves*, 1948). However, contrary to the inconclusive nature of neorealist films that—as Zavattini writes—"[do] not offer solutions," in Comencini's film Anna and Morgana leave the city with an indemnity check in hand and a new job awaiting.[52] This ending is an optimistic one, but it is necessary to the social and political intent of the film that urges women to fight against this form of oppression. Writing about this minor film—reiterating its message—also contributes to that fight.

Comencini's films compellingly address aspects of the experience of motherhood in contemporary society scarcely represented on the screen: the emotional conflict of maternal ambivalence, the social isolation in which motherhood is often experienced, the challenges of motherhood outside the family structure, women's struggle to reconcile motherhood and paid work, and the violence of a neoliberal economy on women's bodies. All these issues are related to the burden of care.

In Italian, the English term *care* translates as *cura*, which comes directly from the Latin. A potent word that holds a host of different meanings, it also means *cure* (i.e., the medical treatment that aims to heal an ill or injured organism, eventually restoring health) as well as *concern, affliction, torment,* and *anxiety.* As both *The White Space* and *I Like to Work* demonstrate, cura requires an inclination: "leaning toward the other,"[53] vigilance and devotion, commitment, empathy. Care takes time.

Conceived in ecological terms, as Tronto eloquently put it, care is "a practice aimed at maintaining, continuing, or repairing the world,"[54] and therefore constitutes a feminist ecocritical antidote and actual method of planetary survival. Its adoption as a response to ecocrises is urgent. The irony is that we have an ecological emergency that demands urgent action very much in line with neoliberal notions of time. However, the care that is required to address ecocrises, like motherhood, necessarily takes time, as well as an understanding of the vital function of care.

Harcourt and Bauhardt ask a question that is at the core of the feminist ecological agenda: "How can we learn to care for each other and nonhuman others in increasingly unequal, politically toxic and deteriorating natural environments?"[55] Comencini's films of mothers and daughters in the city, and ecocinema more broadly, contribute to building a feminist ecological culture that "can provide the population with critical instruments necessary to develop their own 'strategy of survival' both environmentally and politically" and eventually learn to care.[56]

This chapter, as all the other chapters in this book, opened with an encounter with the director, whose own story of survival, and her interest in motherhood, resonated with me in a visceral way. When I first became acquainted with Comencini's films, and particularly with *The White Space*, I had just gone through breast cancer treatment. My fertility being inhibited by the medical treatment, motherhood was neither a possibility nor a priority; surviving was.

I understood, profoundly, both the urgency of care and the experience of waiting, the suspension of life that one experiences in a hospital, where supposedly everyone works to preserve life. I also recognized as my own Maria's initial reluctance to connect with other patients, and I imagined myself, as she, dancing in a surgical gown with other women and gradually leaning toward others, even while concerned with self-preservation. Examining these films as a longtime breast cancer survivor and ecocritical scholar meant reconfiguring their and my own meanings. Not only was it the medical care I received—the timely surgical removal of my cancer and the salvific poisoning of my body that followed—that kept me alive; films and writing about them also helped me to survive, to regain a new self, an ecological self, a new sense of place, of being in the world and being part of the world, and, above all, of caring.

NOTES

1. Francesca Comencini, interview by author, Rome, July 14, 2014 (my translation).

2. Comencini, interview.

3. Comencini, interview.

4. Luciano and Scarparo, "Reinventing Our Mothers," 83. In this chapter, the authors provide an analysis of several women-directed films devoted to the world's most influential female historical figures: Stefania Sandrelli's *Christine Cristina* (2009) on Christine de Pisan, author of *Le livre de la cité des dames* (*The Book of the City of Ladies*, 1431); Antonietta De Lillo's *Il resto di niente* (The Remains of Nothing, 2004) on the life of Eleonora Pimental de Fonseca, a Portuguese revolutionary involved in the short-lived Neapolitan Republic of 1799; and Susanna Nicchiarelli's *Cosmonauta* (Cosmonaut, 2009) on Valentina Tereshkova, the first woman to orbit the Earth in 1963. The chapter also examines contemporary documentary films revisiting the women's liberation movement in Italy.

5. Francesca Comencini, interview by author, Rome, July 14, 2014 (my translation).

6. *The White Space* is available on DVD (European region) with English subtitles; *I Like to Work* was published by Ediesse along with the book *Il lavoro molesto: Il mobbing. Cos'è e come prevenirlo* by Daniele Ranieri. Unfortunately, this edition is not subtitled in English. A Spanish subtitled version of this film is available on YouTube.

7. Faleschini Lerner and D'Amelio, introduction to *Italian Motherhood on Screen*, 4, 6, 6, 7.

8. Tronto, *Moral Boundaries*, 103, 109.

9. Bauhardt and Harcourt, "Introduction: Conversations on Care in Feminist Political Economy and Ecology," 3.

10. Tronto, *Moral Boundaries*, 109.

11. Lewis and Short, *A Latin Dictionary*, 500.

12. The Neapolitan setting, Millicent Marcus explains, situates *The White Space* within a larger cinematic practice that associates pregnancy and the pregnant body with the city. Comencini challenges this pattern by representing the city as empty, lacking vitality (here, vitality meaning liveliness and fertility), and precarious. Marcus elaborates: "In Comencini's film, instead, a street in the old city becomes the setting for Maria's collapse and the prolongation of her pregnancy by artificial means in the neonatal intensive care unit of a Neapolitan hospital. The iconic link between the city and the pregnant body becomes denaturalized—technology intrudes to challenge the stereotypical association of Naples with easy and abundant procreativity." "Unnatural Child Birth," 197.

13. This uncertainty, of both mother and *polis*, is described by Marcus as a "precarious pregnancy," which alludes to the artificiality and possibility of ex-utero pregnancy in Naples. Marcus, 198.

14. Piero Bevilacqua writes that the presence of four active volcanos in Italy (Vesuvius, Etna, Stromboli, and Vulcano) and the recurrence of earthquakes in volcanic areas, along with other natural forces like watercourses, confers the landscape with a certain "instability." "The Distinctive Character of Italian Environmental History," 16.

15. Marcus interprets the title *The White Space* as a reference to the possibility inherent in motherhood, health technology, adult education, empty urbanism, and nontraditional family structures displayed in the film: "*Lo spazio bianco*, then, is the space of possibility and hope afforded by the technology of artificial gestation on the one hand, and by the freedom from the strictures of the conventional love plot on the other." "Unnatural Child Birth," 198.

16. Wichterich, "Transnational Reconfigurations of Re/production and the Female Body," 211.

17. In her book *I pori di Napoli*, Roberta Tabanelli writes that in the 1990s Neapolitan directors such as Mario Martone, Antonio Capuano, Pappi Corsicato, and Antonietta De Lillo initiated an antifolkloric renovation of Naples's image, deliberately avoiding the postcard "Napoli pino-sul-golfo" (Naples, the Pine-on-the-Bay), eliminating the sun while also introducing its growing hinterland to the screen. Although not being part of the so-called *scuola napoletana* (Neapolitan school), Comencini also avoids adhering to the common, iconic image of the sunny city and frames Naples in novel ways. *I "pori" di Napoli*, 11.

18. Karagoz, "Motherhood Revisited in Francesca Comencini's *Lo spazio bianco*," 106.

19. Karagoz, 106.

20. Past, "Documenting Ecomafia," 81.

21. Iovino, "Naples 2008," 335.

22. Past examines the issue of waste's invisibility in "Documenting Ecomafia," 82.

23. The term ecomafia was first used by the leading Italian environmental organization Legambiente in its 2004 white paper. Ecomafia is the involvement of criminal organizations in the illegal disposal of toxic waste and urban speculation. Such irreversible poisoning of the soil, water, and air is the cause of alarming rates of cancer pathologies among the inhabitants of the area. See Corona, *A Short Environmental History of Italy*, 105.

24. The most sensational documentary on the subject is *Biutiful Cauntri* (*Beautiful Country*, Esmeralda Calabria, Andrea D'Ambrosio, and Peppe Ruggiero, 2007). See also *La bambina deve prendere aria* (The Baby Needs Fresh Air, Barbara Rossi Prudente, 2008), *Una montagna di balle* (A Pile of Garbage, Nicola Angrisano, 2009), *Campania infelix* (Unhappy Campania, Ivana Corsale, 2010), as well as mainstream film melodrama such as Diego Olivares's *Veleno* (Poison, 2017). For an analysis of these documentary films, see Angelone, "Talking Trash" and Past, "Documenting Ecomafia," 62.

25. Nixon, *Slow Violence and the Environmentalism of the Poor*, 47.

26. Marcus, "Unnatural Child Birth," 207.

27. Luisa's artificial turf grass, an attempt to bring the outside in, reflects the natural-manmade, inside-outside backwardness explored primarily through Irene's incubation and ex-utero development: "The categories of inside and outside have undergone a monstrous inversion. Blood vessels have been replaced with synthetic tubes, the placenta by a network of electrodes whose signal are translated into numbers to be broadcast on monitors for public consumption." Marcus, "Unnatural Child Birth," 201.

28. Marcus, "Unnatural Child Birth," 198.

29. Cavarero, *Inclinations*, 6.

30. Cavarero, 5–6, 99.

31. Cavarero, 97.

32. Cavarero, 99.

33. Though the artificiality of the incubator, which Marcus describes as "transparent, porous, and synthetic," physically inhibits Maria from fully posturing herself as the inclined mother, an ethos of maternal care is fostered within the community of mothers who support and incline toward each other. "Unnatural Child Birth," 201.

34. Luciano and Scarparo, "Maternal Ambivalence in Contemporary Italian Cinema," 54.

35. Inviting us to think about the metaphorical significance of the slaughterhouse, Matteo Gilebbi reminds us, in his poignant analysis of Ivano Ferrari's poetry, that the "term *macello* in Italian, means slaughterhouse but also 'mess' 'disaster,' 'massacre,' 'chaos.'" "Becoming Human in the Slaughterhouse," 10; See also "Witnessing the Slaughter," 48.

36. Cavarero, *Inclinations*, 97–106.

37. Marcus contends that the exam is also a moment of white space. Maria encourages a student of hers to write a "presente nuovo" when he is stuck, and, in doing so, "liberates him from the spatial strictures of conventional essay form and allows him to write his own text for a 'presente nuovo.'" "Unnatural Child Birth," 199.

38. Stendhal, *Rome, Naples, and Florence*, 350.

39. Harcourt and Bauhardt, "Introduction," 4.

40. Helbert, "Australian Women in Mining," 232.

41. Ranieri, *Il lavoro molesto*, 42.

42. Ranieri, 10.

43. A 2020 study by psychologists Liliana Dassisti and colleagues that surveys the literature on the subject asserts that women are more often the target of workplace harassment. "Donne e uomini, autori e vittime di mobbing in Italia."

44. Ranieri, *Il lavoro molesto*, 79–83.

45. Galetto et al., "Feminist Activism and Practice."

46. Built in Piedmontese style to resemble a northern city between 1880 and 1882 by architect Gaetano Koch, Esquilino constituted part of the urban development, following the unification of the country, to house the new northern bureaucratic class after the relocation of the capital from Florence to Rome.

47. Fiore, *Pre-Occupied Spaces*, 78.

48. In 2006, after the release of Comencini's *I Like to Work*, Piazza Vittorio became a cinematic and literary *topos* thanks to the success of Agostino Ferrante's documentary film *L'orchestra di Piazza Vittorio* (*The Orchestra of Piazza Vittorio*, 2006) and Amara Lakhous's novel *Scontro di civiltà per un ascensore a piazza Vittorio* (*Clash of Civilizations Over an Elevator in Piazza Vittorio*, 2008). The latter was adapted into a 2010 film of the same title, directed by Isotta Toso. In all these works the narration is set in the multiethnic neighborhood of Esquilino (where Piazza Vittorio is located) in the heart of Rome, whose urban landscape has been profoundly transformed over the last couple of decades by waves of migrants. See Di Bianco, "La funzione salvifica dell'immigrato," 118–21.

49. Recalcati, *Le mani della madre*, 16, quoted in Faleschini Lerner, "Cybermoms and Postfeminism in Italian Web Series," 149.

50. Wilson, Carlson, and Szeman, "Introduction: On Petrocultures," 6.

51. Di Bianco, "La funzione salvifica dell'immigrato," 118–21.

52. Zavattini, "Some Ideas on the Cinema," 51.

53. Cavarero, *Inclinations*, 5.

54. Tronto, *Moral Boundaries*, 104.

55. Harcourt and Bauhardt, "Introduction: Conversations on Care," 2.

56. Iovino, "Naples 2008," 342.

Fegatello: *All About You*

AMONG THE MULTIPLE FACETS OF the experience of motherhood, affirming, prosaic, or tormenting, postpartum depression is frequently met with silence. All too often, it remains ignored or undiagnosed due to the general expectation that "it will pass." Yet its effects can be profound, leading to troubled, sometimes tragic mother-child relationships. Alina Marazzi's *Tutto parla di te* (*All About You*, 2012) investigates the transformations of identity women experience with motherhood, and it breaks the silence on the issue of postpartum depression.

Pauline, a woman in her sixties, returns to her hometown of Turin to conduct research on young, distressed mothers in a *casa delle donne* (women's support center). There, she takes an interest in Emma, a dancer who feels alienated from her newborn child. Staying in her childhood home, Pauline recovers her own painful memories: when she was a child, her mother had intentionally set her house on fire and killed her baby brother. Seeing in Emma the helpless mother she once had, Pauline decides to help.

In the scene depicted in figure 3.13, a sleep-deprived Emma walks away from her child, whose incessant crying, along with the city's din, overwhelms her. Luckily, she finds refuge in the *casa delle donne*—a safe space for women in the city. Found in various cities in Italy, these women's houses have historically been places that disseminate feminist culture and offer assistance to women victims of abuse. In *All About You*, the center is represented as a space where sisterhood prevails, where vulnerabilities can be revealed and motherhood becomes a shared responsibility.

Employing an innovative hybrid cinematic language that mixes fiction, stop motion animation, found footage, and photography, and relies on artistic

Figure 3.13. Emma walks away. Screen capture, *All About You* (2012), directed by Alina Marazzi.

collaboration among women, *All About You* is the fourth of Marazzi's tetralogy about "female subjectivity, motherhood, and memory," a small but powerful body of films that generated a fruitful debate in feminist film studies and, hopefully, paved the way to overtly feminist filmmaking practice in Italy.[1]

NOTES

1. The three other works are *Un'ora sola ti vorrei* (*For One More Hour with You*, 2002), a portrait of the director's lost mother, made almost entirely from home movies; *Per sempre* (*Forever*, 2005), a documentary about cloistered nuns; and *Vogliamo anche le rose* (*We Want Roses Too*, 2007), which revisits the women's liberation movement in Italy using archival footage and women's diaries. The definition of her work as a tetralogy of "female subjectivity, motherhood, and memory" is the director's.

In my essay "Women's *Archiveology*, Lost Mother Found Footage," I provide a more extensive analysis of the use of mixed media and found footage in Marazzi's *All About You*. See Di Bianco, "Women's *Archiveology*," 285–306.

FOUR

COMING OF AGE IN THE CITY: GARBAGE, CORPSES, AND MIRACLES

Corpo Celeste, Domenica, Lost Kisses

IN 2011, HAVING JUST SEEN the dark but hopeful film *Corpo Celeste* (2011) by the young director Alice Rohrwacher, I reached out to its production company, Tempesta Film, to learn more about it. Located in Bologna, rather than the sometimes less than welcoming center of Italy's film industry in Rome, the staff at Tempesta made themselves available to help and quickly connected me with the director.

Since I was living in Astoria, Queens, and she in Berlin, my dialogue with Rohrwacher started remotely on Skype (with her young daughter occasionally interrupting us) and continued in person on multiple occasions years later in New York City, always early in the morning. "When noon comes, I get desperate as I feel the day slipping away," she said once to justify the request to meet before eight o'clock. Such a comment made me especially appreciate the time she took to discuss many aspects of her work: the gradual gestation of her film projects, her need to seek refuge from the often-harsh logic and mechanisms of the film industry, her slow approach to filmmaking, and the desire to work with recurrent collaborators, predominantly women.

Despite her collaborative approach to cinema, Rohrwacher, like Cecilia Mangini, is reluctant to be labeled as a "woman director," as if it was "something extraordinary," and is uncomfortable with the idea of a "womanish" interpretation of her work.[1] While I quite personally understand a woman's fear of her work being diminished on account of her gender, the ideas that Rohrwacher articulated about the female gaze confirm my sense that a feminist interpretation can help unpack her work:

> The female gaze does exist; it is multi-faceted and highly variegated. The female gaze doesn't belong only to women, just as the male gaze doesn't

belong only to men. However, I think that the women's gaze on places is special. Women have a different perception of places, houses, horizons. If I think of films directed by women, I can see that space itself is always an important character that determines the development of the story. In my case, the city was the first character. I knew from the beginning that I wanted to work in that city, with the people I met there.[2]

Not surprisingly, the entirety of Rohrwacher's small but compelling cinematic production is constructed on relationships between humans, nonhumans, and the environment, both urban and rural, overcoming the time-worn separation of these two realms. Her first short film is a segment of the collective film *Checosamanca* (What Is Missing, 2006), the story of a boy, a river, and its detritus. With the support of producer Carlo Cresto-Dina, she developed that short into her first feature, *Corpo Celeste*, about a thirteen-year-old girl who relocates to Reggio Calabria with her family after living in Switzerland for ten years. Her subsequent film *Le meraviglie* (*The Wonders*, 2014) is a partially autobiographical story of a family of beekeepers, and *Lazzaro felice* (*Happy as Lazzaro*, 2018) follows a community of sharecroppers displaced to the periphery of a city.[3]

Embracing the legacy of neorealist cinema, in all these films, Rohrwacher places children at the center of her stories. This is indeed a prominent trend in contemporary Italian cinema. As Danielle Hipkins writes, "If filmmakers seek new ways in which to imagine, to frame and to interpret our world, then the child, with all her connotations of perception without preconception, offers the ideal vehicle through which to seek out that renewed vision."[4] In Rohrwacher's films children or adolescents are "witnesses of adult weakness or ineptitude . . . observers of a society that is out of control," as well as observers of irremediably transformed landscapes and places.

Wandering Women, as demonstrated in the previous chapters and *fegatelli*, is largely about filmmakers who work—or have worked for an extensive part of their career—on the margins of the film industry and who remain invisible in the international film landscape. Over the past decade, however, Rohrwacher has become one of the most sophisticated and thought-provoking Italian auteurs from a new generation of women directors to come to the attention of international film critics, audiences, and scholars. Not coincidentally, as mentioned in the introduction, Mark Cousins includes her in his encyclopedic *Women Make Film: A Road Movie through Cinema* (2018).[5]

This acknowledgment has greater implications than the simple recognition of the significance of Rohrwacher's work. Considering that her films are explicitly ecologically minded, they bring issues that might otherwise be of interest only to already ecologically sensitive viewers to the attention of larger audiences. But, also, by cracking the veneer of invisibility under which Italian women filmmakers suffer, Rohrwacher paves the way for other (women) filmmakers to undertake film projects with ecological or other ethical dimensions. Her work invites film scholars and, hopefully, curious audiences to consider films that had far less visibility and limited circulation.

This chapter, which focuses mainly on Rohrwacher's *Corpo Celeste*, suggests that Rohrwacher's work offers a fruitful framework for the analysis of Wilma Labate's *Domenica* (2001) and Roberta Torre's *I baci mai dati* (Lost Kisses, 2010). The latter two, films that circulated less internationally, while not conveying environmental concerns as explicitly as Rohrwacher, provide further compelling examples of the ways women frame the world, its "places, houses, horizons," through the eyes of female children.[6]

Corpo Celeste, *Domenica*, and *Lost Kisses* are three coming-of-age stories set in the impoverished southern cities of Reggio Calabria, Naples, and Librino (near Catania), following lonely female children and adolescents from troubled or entirely absent families. The sense of disorientation, typical of the transition from childhood to womanhood, is conveyed through the characters' dynamic relationships with their surroundings and through a symbolic use of the city view.

These female adolescents embark on journeys of self-discovery while wandering through desolate, anonymous peripheries. I argue that their walks, which nourish their personal maturation and self-awareness, and the anthropogenic landscapes these walks bring into view, expose the inadequacy of the (collapsing) structures that family, state, and church provide for building life-sustaining communities. As in the films discussed in previous chapters featuring adult women, the act of seeing signifies not only a form of female empowerment and a modality of asserting female authorship but also the ability to see beauty in wounded places, acknowledging the predicaments of struggling communities of people and imagining possible futures.

I further assert that in these films, urban wandering entails a quest for nature, which is hidden or even erased from the socially disadvantaged environments that the films showcase. Significantly, the routes of Marta (*Corpo Celeste*), Mimì (*Domenica*), and Manuela (*Lost Kisses*), the films' main characters, all lead to the sea. While proposing a critique of the contemporary city as a toxic environment and a place of patriarchal violence, each director, to a different extent, attempts to overcome the tired dichotomy between nature and culture by reincorporating nature into the city. The protagonists' quest to see nature—that is, to reach the sea—empowers them within the seemingly denatured city.

The treatment of each of these films opens with the usual view from above and an analysis of the landscapes of the Anthropocene they display, followed by reflections on the cinematic representation of the places where events unfold: Reggio Calabria, Naples, and Librino (Catania). The section on *Corpo Celeste*, the most overtly ecologically minded of the three films, concentrates on two key aspects of the Anthropocene narrative: cement and refuse as material objects and as signifiers. The analysis of *Domenica*, while also considering the cementification of the landscape, deals primarily with the issue of violence against female bodies, but also with the trope of what is unseen. The third case study of the chapter, *Lost Kisses*, also focuses on the debasement of female bodies and explores issues concerning the male gaze. In the close readings of these three films, I examine the spatial practice of walking as a form of introspection, alienation from established structures such as the family and the church, but also as a practice for restoring life in forgotten places and things. Finally, I suggest, by adopting Serenella Iovino's concept of narrative "re-habitation," that women's ecocinema, which often recycles and reconfigures male narratives, and engages in stories of girls who although growing up in endangered urban environments, are able to envision futures of possibilities.

ALICE ROHRWACHER'S *CORPO CELESTE*: WALKING THROUGH WASTE

A girl rushes up the dimly lit stairs of an unfinished building. As she quickly exits the scene, and we hear the off-screen sound of a door opening, lights illuminate the walls. The camera lingers over them for a few moments. Bricks have been laid with minimal amounts of mortar, just enough to make them stick. There is no harmony of materials. Terra-cotta bricks are set against cinder blocks, and the joints between them suffer from the same careless work as the walls themselves. A weathered wood structure crosses the frame vertically and diagonally. It seems like scaffolding or some provisional handrail. Electric cables hang from the wall, partially covered by protective vinyl housing, partly not.

This transient, apparently uninteresting image that connects indoor and outdoor spaces might easily pass unobserved. Lacking aesthetic appeal, it might be registered as the "empty" frame left by the passage of the human actor. Or, as Monica Seger defines it, "The interstice is the unaccounted-for-in-between."[7] However, the precarious walls shown in figure 4.1, upon attentive examination,

Figure 4.1. Precarious walls. Screen capture, *Corpo Celeste* (2011), directed by Alice Rohrwacher.

eloquently introduce the Anthropocene landscape that is shown in the rest of the sequence through the inquisitive eyes of a thirteen-year-old girl, Marta.

Marta returned to Italy with her mother and sister after ten years in Switzerland. To help integrate her into the new community, Marta's mother enrolls her in catechism lessons to prepare for her confirmation. She starts attending the local church, populated by bored adolescents and other tragic characters, such as Santa, the fanatical catechism teacher, and Don Mario, a priest who hopes to advance his clerical career through local political connections. Marta, who is experiencing puberty, engages in narcissistic observations of her own body in front of the mirror and appears alienated from her family as well as from the bored adolescents she meets in the church. Although supported by a single mother—who is caring, though worn out by work—she experiences a form of solitude magnified by her desire for introspection. Feeling disoriented and perplexed by her religion, Marta stands on the roof of the unfinished building where she lives, contemplating a sprawling city in which the sea extends far across the horizon, just out of reach of the viewers' gaze.

In the first of the various views from above of *Corpo Celeste* (fig. 4.2), Marta's blurred silhouette on the left edge of the frame meshes with rows of *palazzi* (buildings), some still under construction. As the camera pans, replicating the trajectory of the girl's gaze, it shows more unfinished buildings, the remains of a stone wall, a stretch of grass on which a meager flock of sheep grazes in the proximity of a highway, the improbable residue of a pastoral tradition.

Figure 4.2. Marta discovers the sprawling city. Screen capture, *Corpo Celeste* (2011), directed by Alice Rohrwacher.

A soundscape of traffic and construction complements the view, evoking more building and asphalt. The camera continues to pan until it spots a group of kids traveling in an old Ape 50 (utility van) along a dirt road adjacent to the highway. They stop and load into it a broken armchair, abandoned on the roadside, amid weeds, truck tires, and other refuse.

The anonymous, heavily cemented cityscape, followed by an interstitial pasture, a roadscape, and dumpsite, belongs to Reggio Calabria, a rarely represented southern city that suffers from deep economic and cultural underdevelopment as well as urban degradation. In the last fifty years, a study conducted by urbanists L. Fiorini, F. Zullo, A. Marucci, and B. Romano attests that the southern regions of Campania, Basilicata, Puglia, and Calabria have been subject to a constant consumption of soil "caused precisely by the proliferation of such 'urbanized areas' that replace the natural and semi-natural soil sectors with artificial materials, such as concrete, aggregates and asphalt, creating non-reversible conditions for removing the surface layer of non-renewable soil resource."[8]

The alleged slowness and immobility of the south of Italy, so rooted in the collective imaginary, is challenged by the speed of such "uncontrolled urban sprawl."[9] While the phenomenon applies to the entire country, as the various overwhelmingly built cityscapes I have been meditating on throughout this book demonstrate, "the most serious phenomenon concerns Calabria, with almost 40% of the coastline consumed by the building activity at a rate of well over half a hectare per day for half a century."[10] The precarious walls of Marta's new home, and the portion of the city she contemplates from its roof, show the landscape produced by this construction frenzy.

In our first interview, Rohrwacher spoke about the choice to set her film in Reggio Calabria, a city where she had lived in her twenties and that "marked her": "We expressed the urgency to speak in no uncertain terms about the cultural genocide of a community. I wanted to tell a story through the lens of a place, a place that could also be abstract in a way."[11] Indeed, *Corpo Celeste*, despite being a place-centered narrative, strips the Italian landscape of commonly identified landmarks. The film depicts the periphery of a world rather than a specific Italian city. To this purpose, she excludes Reggio's seafront from her representation, described by the poet Gabriele D'Annunzio as "il chilometro più bello d'Italia" (Italy's most beautiful kilometer); the art nouveau buildings of the city center and the archaeological sites from the Greco-Roman age remain off-screen, thus depriving the city of its historical-geographical dimensions. In this way, while rooted in a concrete place, Rohrwacher's film is less local and more global. Further elaborating on the film's location, she said,

> I was motivated by rage. Eight hundred meters of seafront are not enough to make a beautiful city. Everyone uses those few kilometers of sea to show that Reggio Calabria is a beautiful city. (Probably beautiful is not even the right word.) The neat side of the city has become a cop-out to avoid seeing the rest. My idea was to produce a narrative about the city that could include its defects, to make a "flawed film," so to speak, without representing something that is already known, or something that would satisfy any preconceived notions of the south. I know many of the marvelous things of the city and the region. Because I love these beautiful things, and I respect them, I don't want to show them. I show only what I hope can be changed; I show what I hope people can see, anything that can open a debate.[12]

While pleasing representations of Italy's "great beauty" persist both in Italian and international cinema, as Rohrwacher alludes, a decade after the release of *Corpo Celeste* images of dirty Italian cities, "beautiful and ancient cit(ies) literally swallowed by their own trash," to recall Iovino's words, are also sadly widespread.[13] Unlike the Naples of Comencini's *The White Space*, Reggio Calabria is represented as a garbage dump.[14] Trash is strewn everywhere: under the highway overpass where a religious procession takes place in the opening scene, in the streets along which Marta continuously walks; it is an integral part of the overconstructed landscape that Marta observes, as well as of the set design. Most poignantly, it accumulates in a dry riverbed—which Rohrwacher calls "a scar on the belly of the city."[15]

As Robert Stam writes, waste has a highly symbolic value, with its own hidden transcripts: "Garbage defines and illuminates the world; the trash can, to recycle Leon Trotsky's aphorism, is history. Garbage offers a database of material culture off of which one can read social customs or values."[16] In Rohrwacher's film, accumulation of garbage is evidence of local urban decay while signaling an ecological disaster that goes beyond the borders of the city—a disaster perpetrated by individuals and industry. In *Corpo Celeste*, refuse transcends its materiality and becomes a signifier of the country's environmental crisis as well as of the deterioration of its values.

To fully understand the multiple significances of garbage as a distinctive element of an anthropogenic landscape, it is necessary to take a closer look at the opening sequence in which Reggio's religious community is introduced and then to follow Marta's perambulations through the city. The film opens with nocturnal shots—a self-reflexive device that replicates the act of impressing light on film footage that Rohrwacher employs in all her films—traffic noise and voices singing religious chants in the background.[17] As the scene slowly lights up at sunrise, the camera shows a group of people gathered around the statue of a Madonna in a grim spot under a highway overpass. A fair-skinned blonde girl—Marta—looks around, bewildered and curious (the nape of her neck or profile is often included on the frame's border). A priest announces to the crowd that in an exceptional turn of events, the bishop will participate in the procession, and they will welcome him "with [all] the warmth and joy of which [their] community is capable." To add to the atmosphere of absurdity, two disquieting, giant papier-mâché puppets (a folkloric tradition of Calabria and Sicily) start dancing when a marching band breaks the silence. Simultaneously, a voice from a billboard-covered truck advertises the candidacy of a local politician, promising a bright, improbable future.

While focusing on Marta's solitude and sense of alienation from this community, Rohrwacher uses this provincial parish to highlight Italy's cultural backwardness, its indifference and resignation, racism, and ultimately its violence.[18] Despite the central role the church plays in *Corpo Celeste*, Rohrwacher repeatedly stated that she did not intend to make an anticlerical film but rather "a coming-of-age story, narrated through the magnifying glass of the church. The church is one of those few institutions still standing for the community; however, it lacks real questions, any real wondering. It is always about giving answers, a ceremony that lacks a rite."[19] Nevertheless, a critique of the church as an inadequate guiding institution for a depressed place like Reggio Calabria does emerge through the film's portrayal of ecclesiastic involvement in local political elections. Moreover, the preparation for a religious ceremony—one that Don Mario wants to be a "big

Figure 4.3. Marta walks through waste. Screen capture, *Corpo Celeste* (2011), directed by Alice Rohrwacher.

event"—involves a series of games, quizzes, and songs that seem to be modeled more after "trash television" culture rather than anything spiritual.[20]

While the spiritual dimension lacks meaning, what seems inherently meaningless, like garbage, regardless of its form, actually carries meaning. Refuse is the inevitable remains of human activities in figure 4.3—a quotation of Béla Tarr's *Sátántangó* (1994)—where Marta walks down a street after an open-air market has closed and the wind theatrically scatters paper, pieces of cardboard, plastic bags, and bottles. Ultimately, this is the nadir of a consumerist society. The dump-city becomes a metaphor for Italy itself, thereby extending Rohrwacher's film beyond the geographical confines of Reggio Calabria.

Waste is also associated with and made from human flesh. In a rare occasion in which the family is reunited around a meal, Marta's aunt proudly declares she only buys fish from the Atlantic, not the Mediterranean, where fish eat the corpses of drowned migrants.

Marta's aunt evokes floating cadavers although they are not shown in this scene. As Julia Kristeva writes, "The corpse is the most sickening of waste. [It] is the utmost of abjection. It is death infecting life. Abject. It is something rejected from which one does not part, from which one does not protect oneself as from an object."[21] If abjection, as Kristeva suggests, is a "failure to make sense" the subject experiences when there is no separation from the object, then the corpse of the migrant becomes hyperabject as the embodiment of otherness. By associating human bodies with waste, the scene encapsulates Italy's collective anxiety about the refugee crisis while conceptually linking racism to environmental ruin, as part of the same exploitative and discriminatory culture, a discourse that Rohrwacher develops later in *Happy as Lazzaro*.

Along the same lines, a sense of abjection repeatedly emerges in the film around nonhuman animals, who are objects of cruelty and eventually turned into waste. When Marta discovers kittens amid a pile of junk in the back of a sacristy, one of the "believers" follows the orders of the catechism teacher and throws them into a plastic bag, bashes them against a concrete rise, and hurls them into the river bed, along with other refuse.[22] The horror of this episode—the wanton cruelty to nonhuman creation, the violent hypocrisy of a church representative entrusted to teach supposed Christian values of love and compassion—is magnified when seen through the eyes of a child. The experience so sickens Marta she literally flees the church, also foreshadowing the spiritual departure to come.

The sense of abjection, or fear of potentially polluting bodies, returns once again in a scene that remarkably brings together women's bodies, spirituality, and the earth. Marta's furious walk leads her along a highway. Don Mario, who sees Marta while driving, pulls over and convinces her to join him on a "special mission" in his natal village of Roghudi. There, they will visit an abandoned church that houses an antique crucifix that Don Mario wishes to install in his Reggio parish in place of the unpopular, neon-lit rood currently in place.

Along the way, Don Mario stops in sparse restaurants and community centers in the province of Reggio Calabria to collect signatures for the upcoming political election. Sitting with Marta in a restaurant, he notices with apparent embarrassment that Marta's trousers are spotted with menstrual blood. He severely scolds her for being "dirty." Don Mario's reaction, which hardly hides his repulsion for a woman's bodily fluids, arouses a sense of shame in Marta, who flees in panic. This fundamental episode in a woman's life (central to a female coming-of-age story)—is depicted quietly, with a few rapid, silent, but intense shots that illustrate well how menstruation has been for centuries perceived in patriarchal society, and continues to be perceived, as "a negative event in need of hygiene" rather than "a natural part of a woman's lifecycle" to be celebrated.[23] Marta is seen in close-up, hiding in the bathroom while a woman (the restaurant's owner) behind the door tells her—in an unconvincing tone—that "it is a beautiful thing, even if it doesn't look like it." The language used by this woman, calling menstruation "the thing"—as if it was a mysterious, unnamable phenomenon—signals how women internalize the concept of menstrual blood as impure, something that caused Don Mario's sense of repulsion.

Marta's passage into womanhood becomes a solemn moment in the film (thus symbolically celebrated) as Marta and Don Mario resume the journey and arrive in Roghudi, a marvelous ghost town. Located at the foot of the massif Aspromonte, Roghudi is an ancient village of Hellenic origins (its name in ancient Greek means "cliff," "full of crevices," or "harsh"), once a Griko-speaking community of about a thousand souls.[24] Arduous life conditions determined by geographical asperity, isolation, and the limited sources of sustenance (mainly agriculture and pastoralism) triggered, at the beginning of the twentieth century, a gradual process of emigration. Depopulation was accelerated by a series of natural disasters such as earthquakes, landslides, and floods that earned the village the fame of being "the unhappiest village in Italy, perhaps the world."[25] Old Roghudi was abandoned in 1973, and a decade later a New Roghudi was constructed about forty kilometers from the old village.

In *Corpo Celeste*, Rohrwacher does not indulge in framing the romantic postcard-like view of the village perched on the slope of the mountain but rather shows its collapsing remains through Marta's bewildered eyes as she silently wanders among rubble and the cracked shells of empty houses. The ghost town, undeniably permeated with charm and mystery, is also loaded with a sense of solastalgia, defined by environmental philosopher Glenn A. Albrecht as "the ongoing loss of solace and the sense of desolation connected to the present state of one's home and territory," the kind of earth emotions generated by "cultures being lost and home environments irreversibly transformed."[26]

In the abandoned church, Marta encounters the village's remaining inhabitant, an elderly, blind priest imbued with defiant wisdom. Marta's questions about Christ are answered with a spiritual clarity that she has never encountered, amplifying a radical version of Christ as a rebel, a social misfit who ran from place to place articulating truths that were incomprehensible to nearly all. In a gesture of spiritual and physical affection, Marta draws her hand along the carved body of Christ, simultaneously caressing it with love while also removing the dust coating it. The camera lingers on her hands on the body of Jesus, producing an unsettling moment. When I asked Rohrwacher about her intent in shooting this scene, she answered,

> That scene is the reason the film's title is *Corpo Celeste*, the heavenly body that everyone talks about, the one that is always far away, unreachable. When the catechism teacher reads the texts, she always says, "You have to think that the body of Jesus is not like yours; it is instead a heavenly body, perfect, distant."

It is quite the opposite; we can touch it. The heavenly body is the planet. I wanted to shoot a scene in which Marta finally touches something, a body. Because until that moment, Marta never touches anything. I wanted it to be a sensuous scene, let's say. That sensuousness came out as I was shooting. After all, when a body touches another body, it's always sensuous in that it engages the senses, not [necessarily] in an erotic way.[27]

The encounter with the material yet heavenly body of Jesus will prompt Marta to leave the church once again. After returning from Roghudi, she prepares for her confirmation, one that will supposedly integrate her into the Roman Catholic Church and the local community. She walks away during the ceremony, however, remaining an outsider. Through parallel editing (alternating scenes that happen simultaneously in different locations) that breaks every logic of spatiotemporal continuity, Marta suddenly enters a culvert and slowly walks through it. While the scene recalls the tragic finale of Robert Bresson's *Mouchette* (1967), in which the protagonist drowns herself in a lake, Marta instead finds her way through this water-filled tunnel to a sea repeatedly mentioned in the film as far away and impossible to reach on foot (fig. 4.4).[28]

Once on the shore, Marta finally understands what children, occasionally seen throughout the film, were doing with the garbage they collected from the riverbed. Arranged on a beach scattered with detritus are pieces of furniture, doors, windows, and other unidentifiable discharged objects. Reggio's children—a variation of the rag pickers or urban nomads whom Walter Benjamin saw as the last incarnation of the flaneur—were resurrecting the garbage as objects of transcendent beauty.

The landscape shown in the final scene is a new one that child scavengers had redesigned: one that reincorporates nature in the city and the city's waste into nature. What was previously identified as "garbage" is liberated from the polluting stain of rubbish as repurposed art, illustrating the underlying ethos of the film—namely, that despite the garbage swallowing (this largely overlooked portion of) Italy, there is a chance for regeneration given the will and the imagination to do so.

Like the puppets Otello and Iago from Pasolini's *Che cosa sono le nuvole?* (What Are the Clouds?, 1968), who admire the clouds while lying on a pile of garbage, Marta looks through those objects with amazement, discovering what Pasolini called "la straziante meravigliosa bellezza del creato" (the heartbreaking wonder of creation).[29] She exults in a "spaesamento" (literally meaning "to be without land") combined with the marvel of one who realizes the miracle of the earth suspended in the universe.[30]

Figure 4.4. Marta looks at a trashscape. Screen capture, *Corpo Celeste* (2011), directed by Alice Rohrwacher.

WILMA LABATE'S *DOMENICA*: THE CORPSE, THE CITY, AND THE FEMALE STREET URCHIN

Wilma Labate began her filmmaking career in the mid-1980s and directed her first feature film, *Ambrogio*, in 1992. Set in the late 1950s, *Ambrogio* is the story of a woman who seeks a career as a sea captain but cannot find a shipboard job despite graduating from a nautical institute. "That was my story as a woman filmmaker," said Labate in an interview I conducted with her in 2014. "A male profession that was, and still is, hard for a woman."[31] She eventually became an established filmmaker in Italy; and yet, her professional success might have come earlier had she abandoned the political themes of her films. Labate struggled to obtain film production funds from the start, but the endeavor was especially difficult when she tried to raise money for her second film project on the topic of terrorism in Italy. While she was offered the chance to direct several comedies, she was explicitly discouraged, as a woman, from pursuing such a "political" project.[32] Nevertheless, she succeeded in directing *La mia generazione* (My Generation, 1996), for which she earned significant critical visibility and popular success; she has continued to make such political films up to the present.[33] These include collective projects such as *Un altro mondo è possibile* (Another World Is Possible, 2001), on the antiglobalization protesters at the G8 Summit held in Genoa in 2001; *Lettere dalla Palestina* (Letters from Palestine, 2003), on the condition of Palestinians in the Israeli-occupied territories; and her own, fictional feature *Signorina Effe* (Miss F, 2007), a love story set in Turin against the backdrop of a thirty-five-day strike by Fiat workers in 1980. Over the past few years, she directed two compelling documentaries: *Qualcosa di noi* (Something About Us, 2014) and *Arrivederci Saigon* (Goodbye Saigon, 2018). The former places a sex worker in intimate dialogue with a group of young artists and writers; the latter is about an Italian women's soul band, affiliated with the Communist Party, that toured in Vietnam in the 1970s. Most recently, Labate directed another female coming-of-age story set in the periphery of Trieste, *La ragazza ha volato* (The Girl Has Flown, 2021).

Though many of Labate's films provide critical commentary on women's experiences in contemporary Italian society, given the focus of this book and this chapter, I concentrate on *Domenica* (2001), a female coming-of-age story set in Naples that deals with the fraught and, in Italy, rarely treated topic of rape, and even more challenging, the rape of a child. Twelve-year-old Domenica, nicknamed Mimì, lives in an orphanage. One day, police detective Sciarra arrives and asks her to identify a corpse. In a series of flashbacks, it is revealed the body might be that of the man who had raped Mimì sometime before. According to the police, the alleged rapist threw himself from a police station window during an interrogation.[34] Mimì's identification of the body is essential to closing her rape case. Reluctantly, Mimì agrees to go with Sciarra. Terrified of seeing a cadaver, however, she delays their arrival at the morgue through a series of contrived detours. Sciarra—who is dying of kidney cancer and is on his last day on the job—cannot postpone the identification.

The film unfolds through the streets of Naples over the course of an entire day. Consistent with the nomadic narratives I engage, *Domenica* establishes a complete identification between the young female protagonist and the body of the city, extending the physical and psychological violence endured by the former to the physical, urban environment.

A series of hazy, densely built cityspaces that frame different areas of Naples opens the film. As we observed in the view from above of Comencini's *The White Space*, also set in Naples, cupolas, bell towers, the sloping roofs of an ancient city, and a group of skyscrapers (Centro Direzionale, i.e., the Business District) are packed into the same congested vista. Masses of modern apartment buildings piled on top of one another depict the chaotic continuity of construction from different epochs and ceaseless urban expansion.

Figure 4.5. Domenica's cityscape. Screen capture, *Domenica* (2001), directed by Wilma Labate.

What follows is a fixed aerial view of Naples's harbor district, which at the time of *Domenica*'s shooting was a neglected part of the city, "impregnated with centuries of history that holds a tragic beauty," as Labate described it.[35] Contrary to the traditional function of the harbor as a point of transit, Labate's opening cityscape suggests a sense of immobility (fig. 4.5). The camera is still; the traffic, shot at a distance, moves almost imperceptibly. Opening credits unfold and the film title appears on the screen over a melancholic musical opening. The protagonist's name—written with a child's script—is inscribed into the urban landscape (fig. 4.5), thereby asserting the child's belonging to the city but also extending the vulnerability of the child to the city. The rape of her body parallels the rape of the city, which is, recalling Iovino's words, "systematically disfigured by building developers."[36]

In *Domenica*, Naples appears mostly tranquil, at times somber, and informed by a sort of melancholia that she calls *orfanite* (orphanhood). Labate coined *orfanite* to name a sense of loneliness and abandonment incarnated not only by the protagonist but by Naples itself: a city-orphan of the nation. Such *orfanite* recalls the *solastagia* of Reggio Calabria depicted in Rohrwacher's *Corpo Celeste*—that is, a sadness caused by environmental destruction. Although not as fully articulated in Labate's film as in Rohrwacher's, the opening sequence, the attention to the cityscape throughout the film, and the choice to leave the sea off-screen convey an environmental critique that intersects with the feminist discourse on women's bodies.[37]

The violated body of the city will be juxtaposed to a cadaver: "death infecting life."[38] After the somber city view at its opening, the film moves abruptly indoors to a morgue, where Sciarra stands in front of a corpse covered by a white sheet. As will be revealed later in the film, this is supposedly the body of Domenica's (i.e., Mimì's) rapist. The violence one might infer by the sight of an anonymous, veiled corpse emphasizes a sense of death and abjection that permeates the entire film. Moreover, the scene creates a *mise en abyme* of the act of looking.[39] Viewers look at Sciarra, contemplating his own death as he looks at the body.

Labate adopts a narrative strategy that harkens back to the original notion of drama and Greek tragedy, in which violence is never depicted on stage. The child's rape is an obscene/unrepresentable event that precedes the beginning of the film. The face of the rapist is never shown, which transmits to the spectator Mimì's fear and "anxiety of seeing." Drawing from Stephen Heath's speculation on what is off-screen, Kaja Silverman writes, "The narrative moves forward and acts upon the viewer only through the constant intimation of something which has not yet been fully seen, understood, revealed; in short, it relies upon the inscription of lack."[40] Similarly, the viewer in *Domenica* is sutured into the narration by a corpse that remains off-screen for the duration of the film (only to be exonerated by the victim at the end). Yet, as the narrative unfolds, that corpse and its relationship with other alive and agonizing bodies—Mimì's, Sciarra's, and the city's—is often evoked.

Labate's camera intentionally replicates an aggressive male gaze on the female body. When Mimì is introduced to the audience at the beginning of the film, her body is framed in a way that alludes to her rape. The child is shown as she rises from bed at the orphanage, preparing for her daily ramble through the city. After framing her in close-up while she washes her face, the camera pans down her legs, lingering on her childish body, particularly on her lower abdomen. This latter image, which Labate sustains at an uncomfortable length for the viewer, is both moving and disturbing. On the one hand, it shows the fragility of a child, unprotected and exposed to the risks of the city; on the other, by reproducing a predatory gaze over the female body, it reminds us of her experience of rape in the city.

While proposing a dramatic cinematic representation of Naples, Labate draws from Neapolitan popular culture by locating the so-called *scugnizzo*, the street urchin, at the narrative center. Giuliana Bruno rightly points out that the Neapolitan street-child (traditionally an illegitimate child of the lower class) was a recurrent character in popular literary genres such as the feuilleton and later became the hero of a subgenre of Elvira Notari's silent melodramas from the 1920s—"the Gennariello films."[41] The figure of the street urchin would later be reelaborated by Pasolini in his early novels, such as *Ragazzi di vita* (*The Street Kids*, 1955) and *Una vita violenta* (*Violent Life*, 1959), as well as in his early films, such as *Accattone* (1960) and *Mamma Roma* (1962), in which the Roman *scugnizzo* represents the last guardian of an "uncorrupted" subproletariat.

In his study of the Neapolitan school, Marlow-Mann observes that "the *scugnizzo* is portrayed in equivocally positive terms as someone who has suffered but who maintains the joy of life stereotypically associated with Neapolitans."[42] Labate proposes an uncommon female version of the *scugnizzo* who maintains the vitality and playfulness of the typical street urchin despite having suffered the most atrocious violence that can be inflicted on a child, that of sexual abuse.[43]

In treating such a complex theme, Labate utilizes cinematic and literary references that extend beyond Italian culture. *Domenica*, in fact, is loosely adapted from a Spanish novel by Juan Marsé, *Ronda del Guinardò* (1984), set in Barcelona during the Franco dictatorship. While maintaining the same plot, Labate eliminates the novel's specific historical-political dimension and relocates the story to contemporary Naples. Second, it is inspired by Robert Bresson's *Mouchette* (1967), in which the protagonist, like Domenica, has been raped. But, while Bresson's protagonist commits suicide, "Labate transforms [her protagonist] into a survivor."[44]

Like Marta from *Corpo Celeste*, Mimì, as an orphan, or even worse, as a child abandoned by a mother who is "somewhere in the city," brings testimony to the dissolution of the family that is reiterated by the recurrent presence of other lonely children in the orphanage and throughout the city.

Labate highlights the role of two other primary institutions: the Catholic Church and the state. Unlike in *Corpo Celeste* and *Lost Kisses*, where it is harshly criticized or even mocked, the church is represented positively in *Domenica*. As Labate said ironically, "All that the left did not take care of was covered by the church."[45] The parish church is a shelter for unwanted children as well as a theater where children like Domenica can recuperate their natural playfulness.

Conversely, the state, embodied by the tragic character of Sciarra, entrancingly interpreted by popular actor Claudio Amendola, is a dying father, sick with cancer—a corrupting body. This sense of inadequacy is exemplified through Sciarra's relationship with the city and his limited mobility within it. With respect to Italian regional cultural identity, Sciarra (from Rome) is considered a stranger in Naples, an outsider who does not even speak the language

Figure 4.6. Mimì walks ahead. Screen capture, *Domenica* (2001), directed by Wilma Labate.

(i.e., Neapolitan dialect) and is unfamiliar with the city terrain. Despite his paternal role, Sciarra is unable to lead or protect Domenica, who, in turn, despite her fragile position as a female child, is granted agency and thus leads the tour in the city. She is often framed from a low angle, which gives her authority, while Sciarra walks behind her, dragging himself (see fig. 4.6).

The film often shifts between Mimì and Sciarra's point of view; accordingly, the city assumes different connotations. In his limited mobility, Sciarra perceives the city as dangerous and warns Domenica of possible risks, while the girl is completely at ease in the city, either in threatening empty streets or streets congested by traffic. Whereas Sciarra is an outsider (about to leave Naples), Domenica is completely integrated into the urban fabric: she interacts with its inhabitants from different social classes and ethnicities and even takes part in its economy by raising funds for her orphanage. Ultimately, as shown in the various stops along the path to the morgue, the city is a substitute for Domenica's nonexistent family. Naples, like Rome for Morgana in Comencini's *I Like to Work* (chap. 3), is a "parent-city."

Domenica's city stroll also displays the peculiar social geography of Naples. As many space theorists and feminist geographers such as Gillian Rose, Doreen Massey, and Edward Soja have argued, the urban spatial configuration of center-periphery reproduces the social division between upper and lower class. Although this division might hold for many, if not most, European cities, it does not apply to Naples, where popular districts such as Rione Sanitá, Quartieri Spagnoli, and L'Avvocata are located in the center, and palaces are surrounded by lower-income housing.[46] In *Domenica*, this spatial proximity appears when the protagonist attends a countess's wake and later visits a disabled child from a poor family who lives on the same street. Incidentally, Mimì refuses to look at the countess's body at the wake, a detail that recalls the corpse left off-screen at the beginning of the film and maintains narrative tension along the journey.

While trying to postpone the identification—that is, looking at the corpse of her supposed rapist—Mimì breaks free from Sciarra in order to exercise her own "to-be-looked-at-ness," a female attribute apparently learned from the fashion magazine she reads.[47] She meets a group of boys for some "business." After receiving payment, she leafs through a magazine, letting them glimpse at her panties. The camera alternates between the audience's supposed point of view and the boys' point of view. It zooms in on Domenica's skinny legs and then frames the boys (in close-up) masturbating. This scene replicates and simultaneously parodies what Laura Mulvey defines as the "pleasurable structures of looking in the conventional cinematic situation."[48] The scene playfully reproduces the cinematic situation in which women function as erotic spectacles for male pleasure. Here though, Mimì controls, regulates, and exploits the gaze of male children.

Moving from the consenting object of the gaze, Mimì becomes an active looker when the characters finally arrive at the morgue and she is faced with the identification. Sciarra and Mimì stand in front of the table upon which the shroud-covered corpse lies (fig. 4.7). Mimì stands with obvious discomfort, holding in vomit at the coming spectacle of her abuser. Sciarra partially lifts the white sheet, and Mimì, after gazing at the body for a few pregnant seconds, declares, "It's not him," before fleeing the room. In her absence, Sciarra takes a long look at the corpse himself, noticing deep bruises around the neck that indicate to him a case of police brutality and understands that the man had been strangled while in custody and that the police are trying to disguise their murder as a suicide. Had Mimì identified the body as that of her rapist, the case would have been closed. The police officers responsible for the death of the man on the table would go unindicted, and Mimì's actual rapist would remain free.

By demonstrating the complicity of police in leaving Mimì's violation unpunished, Labate implicitly comments on (and protests against) Italy's long history of unpunished rape.[49] As Antonella Vitale documents, reforms of the penal codes regarding sexual violence in Italy took place thanks to the courage of rape survivors who endured painful legal battles and the efforts of the women's liberation movement, particularly over the 1980s and 1990s. Until then, the fascist

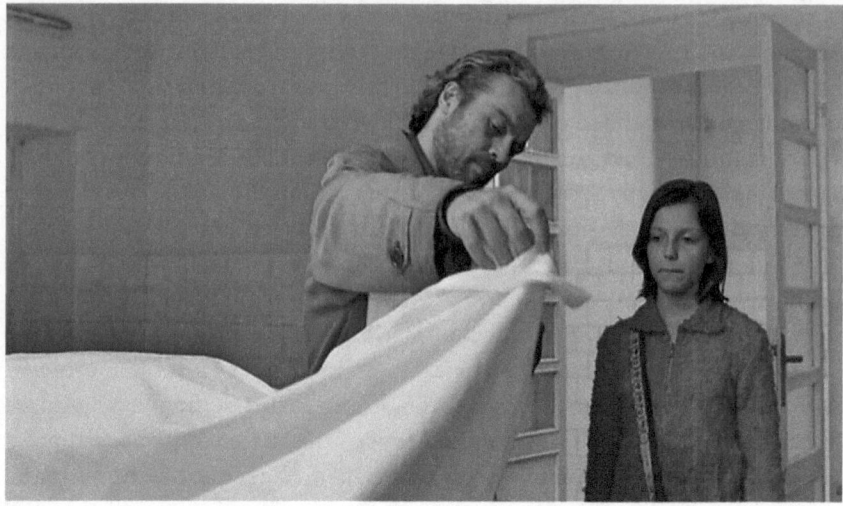

Figure 4.7. Looking at a corpse. Screen capture, *Domenica* (2001), directed by Wilma Labate.

code of honor was in force, which entailed that a victim of rape could be forced to marry her rapist to repair the honor of the family. It was only in 1981 that honor codes were abolished and only in 1996 that rape, until then considered a crime against public morality, was recognized as a crime against an individual. The latter, as Vitale writes, was "the most monumental transformation in the Italian rape laws," insofar as it "establishes the status of a woman as a full human being rather than an object or property of her father or husband."[50]

Feminist filmmaking also contributed to "such monumental transformation."[51] In 1978, six filmmakers from the feminist film collective of Rome—Maria Grazia Belmonti, Anna Carini, Paola De Martiis, Annabella Miscuglio, Rony Daopoulo, and Loredana Rotondo—recorded on video a rape trial. The victim was a young woman, Fiorella, who had been kidnapped and gang raped by four men in a house near Latina, in Latium. The documentary dramatically demonstrates the vicious misogyny at play in the courtroom, where the victim is aggressively interrogated and her morals questioned to demonstrate that she "provoked" the aggression. *Trial for Rape* was broadcasted by RAI television twice in 1979, both times drawing millions of viewers, and stirred a powerful public reckoning with structural misogyny, violence against women, and the impunity that perpetrators of rape culture had in Italian society.

Labate's film, notwithstanding the radically different aesthetic and narrative approaches, also contributes to exposing patriarchal violence and "raise(s) unresolved and at times disturbing questions about the future of women in a national space that is still determined by patriarchal institutions and rituals."[52] Going beyond the Italian cultural context, by inscribing the female body in the urban landscape and by visually aligning human and nonhuman suffering and resilience, the film embraces the ecofeminist foundational idea that abusive environmental practices, the debasement of women's bodies, poverty, and social inequality are part of the same oppressive culture.

Mimì's resilience, her ability to survive in the city and be a vital component of it, resists and challenges such a culture. Similar to *Corpo Celeste*, Domenica's journey through the city ends up at the sea, left off-screen for the entire duration of the film, an exclusion that recalls Ortese's book *Il mare non bagna Napoli* (literally, "the sea does not reach Naples")—nor does it reach Reggio Calabria or Librino. In short, the natural beauty of the place does not alleviate human sorrow. The sea is a conduit of relief for Sciarra, as he departs the city by boat. But it is also a source of love for Mimì, who expresses the hope that her lost mother will return to her from the sea.

The journey through the body of the city offers neither revelation nor resolution. As the ship leaves the harbor, a familiar metaphor for the existential journey continuing, we exit the cityscape with a sense of hopeful solastalgia for Domenica's unfulfilled desire for maternal love but also with her resilience and courage as she looks at the sea ahead of her.

A personal story Labate shared reveals to me that the vision of the sea, its discovery, is indeed Labate's origin story as a filmmaker. After graduating with a degree in philosophy in the early 1980s, she got a job as a researcher for a documentary film on psychiatric health care. Having completed her research, and intrigued by the world of film with which she had come into contact, she asked the production company if she could assist the director during the shooting:

> Part of what was being filmed was a psychiatrist's experiment of taking patients on an excursion from a mental hospital in Rome, called Santa Maria della Pietà. It was the patients' first time out in twenty-five years! Everyone traveled by bus to a place called Zoo Safari and then to a litter-strewn beach in Fiumicino (near Rome). I had no specific role other than helping the director and accompanying the patients. I was very young at the time, and seeing psychiatric patients for the first time, I must confess that I was a bit scared. There were about thirty patients; some of them told me they were around thirty-five years old, but to me they looked seventy. The trip was tense and exciting at the same time. They "went crazy" with joy and curiosity. But the most moving part of the trip for me was the stop at the beach, which was absolutely ugly. It was winter, after all. Many of these patients were seeing

the sea for the first time and were completely enthralled; they undressed and threw themselves into the water. I was absolutely amazed and decided then, with complete conviction and a hint of madness, that I wanted to be a filmmaker.[53]

ROBERTA TORRE'S *LOST KISSES*: MIRACLES IN THE NEW TOWN

The act of seeing, and more specifically the visual appropriation of the cityscape, is a central motif of all the films analyzed in this study. The opening sequence of Roberta Torre's *Lost Kisses* carries out this function, providing another example of authorial self-inscription, albeit in a dreamlike, comedic manner. The deep breathing of someone asleep is heard in the background while the opening credits appear on a black screen, followed by the blurred image of a minor public square seen from a high angle, presumably the point of view of someone looking from above through a curtain. As the veil is removed, it shows a crowd gathered around a Madonna statue that has just been unveiled. A priest is astonished at the sight of the statue, as is the rest of the crowd. The breathing continues, the only sound heard in the scene (fig. 4.8). The camera pans to include an adolescent girl, Manuela, sitting on a scooter and zooms in to her looking straight into the camera with a pensive expression, simultaneously directing her gaze toward her community and toward the audience (fig. 4.9).

In Torre's own words, *Lost Kisses* is "a story of giants: the individual, the Madonna, the miracle or the desire for a miracle."[54] Manuela is a fourteen-year-old girl living in Librino, a lower class residential area on the outskirts of Catania. She works at a hair salon and spends her free time traveling around the blighted urban area on her scooter. In uneventful Librino, a Madonna statue has been erected recently in the central piazza but is found decapitated just a few days after the inauguration. Manuela, who earlier saw some local children accidentally knock its head off with a soccer ball while playing, then hiding the head in a basement, later claims that the Madonna herself told her where the head was hidden. When the statue's head is recovered following Manuela's directions, Librino's community pronounces it a miracle. Manuela's mother, Rita, frustrated with her husband's financial shortcomings, jumps into the lucrative business of miracles. Transformed into a saint by her mother and the local priest Don Livio, Manuela is nearly forced into performing other "miracles."

Lost Kisses is Torre's fifth feature film. A Milanese who adopted Palermo as her hometown, she has set nearly all her films in Sicily, a place she lyrically defines as "a wonderland, an inextinguishable reservoir of faces, extraordinary,

Figure 4.8. Librino's believers. Screen capture, *Lost Kisses* (2010), directed by Roberta Torre.

ancient faces, natural actors, with an unusual corporality."⁵⁵ As Aine O'Healy observes, "Torre's statements about her experience in Sicily are often tinged with romantic invocations of exoticism and exceptional vitality."⁵⁶ This hyperbolic vision is very much in line with Torre's idea of cinema, defined by several critics as "baroque" or as a "postmodern pastiche," mainly characterized by visual excess, kitsch settings and costumes, and a taste for the absurd and the bizarre.⁵⁷

She debuted with a musical on the Mafia, *Tano da morire* (To Die for Tano, 1997), and later directed another musical, *Sud side stori* (2000), a comical reinterpretation of Leonard Bernstein's *West Side Story*. She later directed *Angela* (2002), a more sober melodramatic love story that highlights women's relationships to male power, specifically organized crime. In 2006, she directed *Mare nero* (Dark Sea), a detective story set in the underground world of swingers and red-light district bars in Rome. While over the last decade she worked predominately in theater directing musicals and operas, most recently she directed *Riccardo va all'inferno* (Bloody Richard, 2017), a visionary cinematic reinterpretation of Shakespeare's *Richard III* set in Rome, which adds to the current trend of Mafia mockeries that Torre herself initiated with *Tano*.

Figure 4.9. Manuela. Screen capture, *Lost Kisses* (2010), directed by Roberta Torre.

All of Torre's films, including her documentaries and short films, feature peripheral urban settings.[58] When asked about her idea of place-centered storytelling, Torre answered, "The contemporary city is always the container of my stories. . . . I redeem dreadful stories and landscapes of urban decay with the human adventure, which never ceases to amaze and reveal its poetry."[59] While conferring to cinema (and particularly a comedy like *Lost Kisses*) the power of "redeeming degraded urban landscapes" might sound overly optimistic, by setting her films in the margins of the city while rendering the stories of ordinary people extraordinary, Torre admittedly demonstrates that filmmaking, and more specifically ecocinema, can contribute to restore a sense of place and social hope. Indeed, Torre's penchant for marginal subjects and forgotten places resonates with Iovino's idea of "narrative re-habitation": an ecocritical project of "retrieving the stories of places, but above all imagining, through these stories, new 'endings' for places and their inhabitants."[60]

Lost Kisses is set in Librino, a town that, "born from a great utopia, became a ghetto."[61] Planned in the 1970s by the Japanese architect Kenzo Tange, Librino was originally thought of as a "new town"—a so-called *città giardino* (Garden City). The initial project included large areas of greenery and infrastructure that would have rendered it a model satellite town to Catania.[62] Tange's original masterplan was never carried out, however, and today Librino is a densely populated urban area, sadly known for drug trafficking and other criminal activity, and is often in the national news for its homicide rate.

Torre does not focus on crime and only fleetingly alludes to the use of drugs among young people. Instead, with comic and sometimes tender and melancholic tones, she tells a female urban coming-of-age story, investigating how the desolation of the urban landscape enhances the sense of disorientation, desire for exploration, and self-discovery typical of adolescence. Torre follows Manuela's scooter rides in long camera car shots, in a postmodern version of flânerie. Long blocks of flats, shown from Manuela's moving and distorted perspective, scroll across the screen, while fragments of her life are interjected in a long pan shot: a man (her father) sits at a slot machine; a woman in a revealing outfit (her mother) irons apprehensively. These human presences appear abruptly, almost like hallucinations, and do not seem to belong to the landscape. Background music with radio interferences of an Arabic chant evokes a Sicilian past erased from the present landscape.

In a discussion of Palermo's image in the films of absurdist directors Ciprì and Maresco, film scholar Abele Longo notices how the city appears "unfurnished and dilapidated." As he puts it, "It is precisely the absence of any distinguishable signs which leaves Palermo lost in time and space."[63] Drawing from John Foot's analysis of Silvio Soldini's representation of Milan, Longo points out that urban landscapes deprived of landmarks are a recurrent characteristic of contemporary Italian cinema, signifying a loss of identity.

Torre's vision of Librino, not as dark as Ciprì and Maresco's Palermo, plays with the undistinguished nature of the landscape. By adding human elements that "redeem dreadful panoramas," she narratively reinhabits the place, to recall Iovino's concept. Humans, while looking out of place and dwarfed in the frame, render that landscape implausible but poetic. For instance, as shown in figure 4.10, fishermen hold a net in a deserted piazza against the backdrop of apartment blocks, signaling the proximity of the sea and inviting viewers to reimagine the view (though Librino is not on the coast) as a place with its own identity.

In the same spirit, and in line with the pastiche aesthetic of her first films, Torre integrates a convincing Foucauldian *heterotopia* into Librino: the hair salon where Manuela works. In Foucault's words, "Heterotopias are sites that have a general relation of direct or inverted analogy with the real space of society.... Their role is to create a space that is other, another real space, as perfect, as meticulous, as well arranged as ours is messy, ill constructed, and jumbled."[64] In contrast to the bleak cement and asphalt scenery shown along Manuela's scooter ride, the hair salon, a location evocative of Pedro Almodóvar's palette,

Figure 4.10. Implausible landscapes. Screen capture, *Lost Kisses* (2010), directed by Roberta Torre.

is imbued with a surreal atmosphere. In this place, orchestrated by Viola—an extravagant hair stylist and optimistic fortune-teller—the women of the neighborhood are transformed into creatures of "unusual corporality," as Torre describes them, wearing pop art outfits and ostentatious hairstyles (fig. 4.11).

In Torre's aesthetic of exaggeration one can perceive the legacy of Fellini, whose films were populated by *maggiorate fisiche* (physically developed) women who were purely performative. Paolo Bertetto notes this dynamic in Fellini's cinema: "The logic of his representation is excess. The Felliniesque woman is never simply described or narrated, she is always staged. Makeup, costumes, acting, and the diegetic inscription, intentionally highlight the *mise-en-scène*. There is nothing in Fellini's women that can be placed on the level of reality. Everything is thought, designed, and built to reach a scenic and cinematic effect."[65]

Bertetto's description of Fellini's modality of women's representation applies to nearly every female character in *Lost Kisses*. Apart from Manuela, Librino's women act and speak in chorus and are therefore more a symbolic presence than real women. By surrounding Manuela with this spectacle of women, Torre takes part, with playful tones, in the women filmmakers' critique of the contemporary idea of the female body dictated and/or reinforced by the media. This discourse is also conveyed through the repeated insertion throughout the film of animation sequences showing collages of women's faces made of fragments of different female bodies assembled together asymmetrically (fig. 4.12).

Figure 4.11. Unusual corporalities. Screen capture, *Lost Kisses* (2010), directed by Roberta Torre.

Figure 4.12. Asymmetrical woman. Screen capture, *Lost Kisses* (2010), directed by Roberta Torre.

Representation of women's bodies in film has been, and continues to be, a central concern in feminist film scholarship. In her foundational essay, "Woman's Stake: Filming the Female Body," Mary Ann Doane argues, "Contemporary filmmaking addresses itself to the activity of uncoding, decoding, deconstructing the given images. It is a project of de-familiarization whose aim is not necessarily that of seeing the female body differently, but of exposing the habitual meaning/values attached to femininity as cultural constructions."[66]

Making these collages float on screen, recurrently suspending the narration, Torre reaches the effect described by Doane of questioning beauty standards while also communicating the sense of confusion and disorientation that Manuela experiences in her search for female identity models. Despite the exaggerated notions of female beauty at the salon in which she works, as well as the example of her heavily made-up and provocatively dressed mother, Manuela presents herself in a way that downplays gender identity, boyish and girlish at once. At the same time, she lives in disoriented Librino, a town conceived through idealistic intentions that has descended into malaise. Salvation, for many, can only come through divine intervention by which Manuela has become the medium.

Pressured into the duty of performing miracles, Manuela seeks relief through her scootered ambles through the periphery of an already peripheral settlement. Escaping the urban decay of Librino, and the fatiguing entreaties of her neighbors, Manuela reaches the sea. There, she naps on a beach, and in her dreams, she envisions corpulent women crocheting (fig. 4.13). With their huge hair, they are reminiscent of the Medusa's head, the Greek gorgon symbol of castration that Torre already employed in *To Die for Tano*.[67] With calm expressions on their faces as they proceed with their handiwork, however, they seem a benign domestic version of the terrifying mythological figure.

These female creatures embody a model of femininity that Manuela simultaneously feels repelled by and attracted to, a model also embodied by her mother, Rita. As Ann E. Kaplan writes in her essay "The Case of the Missing Mother," mothers are represented through codified types in popular culture: "the good mother," "the bad mother/witch," "the heroic mother," and "the silly/weak/vain mother." "Found most often in comedies, [the latter] is ridiculed by husband and children alike, and generally scorned and disparaged."[68] Rita represents this latter type. Brilliantly and theatrically played by Angela Finocchiaro, the hyperfeminine Rita offers a derisive critique (which does not conceal some misogynistic tones) of the working-class housewife who, although frustrated by her role as the "angel of the house," is unable to embark on a path of emancipation.

Like Labate—but using comic and grotesque tones—Torre also critiques the institution of the family, showing how it has lost its guiding social role. In Labate's film, the church functions as a substitute for the family, whereas in *Lost Kisses*, as in Rohrwacher's *Corpo Celeste*, it is too inadequate to take up

Figure 4.13. Medusa women crocheting. Screen capture, *Lost Kisses* (2010), directed by Roberta Torre.

this role as it is depleted of any sense of spirituality. Like Rohrwacher but with different tones, Torre uses the church to deride the contemporary obsession with body image and the desire to be part of a media spectacle. This obsession even figures in the space of the church itself. In one scene, Don Livio, Librino's priest, is seen running on a treadmill placed in his sacristy—an ecclesiastical substitute for the salon—addressing a Madonna statue and praying, "I don't do it for vanity; I want to be God's athlete." The priest, as an alleged aesthete who wants to bring "art" to Librino, is also in charge of refashioning Manuela into a saint and orchestrates, with Rita, the business of miracles.

Reminiscent of Fellini's *La Dolce Vita*, Torre sardonically represents the commercial speculations that so often arise from so-called supernatural manifestations that tend to exploit people's desperation for the miraculous, and it shows "a society out of control" through Manuela's gaze.[69] As noted previously, when it is announced on TV that a girl from Librino speaks directly with the Madonna, the entire town shows up at her door, asking for a miracle. In a series of shot-countershots, Manuela is framed sitting at a desk, receiving her neighbors' visits. The characters follow one another, asking for divine intervention to fulfill their desires and aspirations. Mixing comic and dramatic tones, these cameos depict a society both afflicted by economic recession and seduced by the myth of show business to escape social invisibility. One supplicant wants to leave Librino for Rome (which is identified with Cinecittà), where he can be part of the cast of *The Big Brother* reality show, the ultimate way of being "visible." For another, the miracle is simply finding a supermarket or factory job.

In this sequence, overloaded by cleverly mixed cinematic references, Torre pays homage to the fathers of Italian cinema and to its neorealist tradition. Among the "believers" is a young man who appears standing in a piazza at the start of the film, holding a net with a small group of people (fig. 4.10). These fishermen, a peculiar presence in an urban context, appear to be a contemporary version of the inhabitants of Acitrezza, portrayed by Luchino Visconti in *La Terra Trema* (1948). In *Lost Kisses*, one of the fishermen asks for the Madonna's help to retrieve his stolen net, without which he cannot work. The episode itself recalls one in Vittorio De Sica's *Ladri di biciclette* (*Bicycle Thieves*, 1948) in which Antonio Ricci and his son ask a fortune-teller for help in recovering his stolen bicycle.

Refusing to take further part in the swindle organized by her mother, Manuela confesses that she never spoke to the Madonna. But, at the moment she is about to quit her career as a saint, a miracle actually occurs. A blind girl who repeatedly visited Manuela regains her sight. The miracle is attributed to Manuela, and explicit reference is made to the tale of Jesus and the man of Bethsaida mentioned in the Gospels. In addition, in one of the encounters with Manuela, the blind girl reveals that as a child she had lost her sight when she witnessed her father's murder.

Although arguably oversentimental and lacking the comic verve of the rest of the film, this finale reiterates the idea presented in the opening scene (and recurrently throughout the body of films examined in *Wandering Women*): the female appropriation of the gaze. As Linda Williams observes in her essay "When the Woman Looks," the figure of the blind heroine is very popular in melodrama and classic narrative cinema: "Blindness in this context signifies a perfect absence of desire, allowing the look of the male protagonist to regard the woman at the requisite safe distance necessary to the voyeur's pleasure, with no danger that she will return that look and in so doing express desire of her own."[70] In other words, for Williams, who draws from Metz and Mulvey's speculations about cinema as a form of voyeurism, the lack of vision signifies the ultimate lack of agency. Even though Williams is more concerned here with issues of female spectatorship than female authorship, her speculations on female failure of vision relate well to Torre's finale, and to a certain extent to *Corpo Celeste* and *Domenica*. This consolatory finale in which the community of Librino rejoices in the miracle of the blind girl—a young woman restoring the sight of another young woman—can be read as a moment of female empowerment and an assertion of female authorship. Ultimately, it demonstrates the ethical dimension of women's ecocinema as a critical tool to "restore the imagination of a place" and "invent new endings for inhabitants and places."[71]

In these three films, the symbolic use of the city view, along with the act of preadults strolling through the city, assumes multiple significations, even if it is analogous in part to those in films featuring adult females. The characters' city meanderings are prompted by their lack of place in society, a condition that Turner defines as a "liminal state," a state of transition from childhood to adulthood, or—in the case of the female adolescents of these films—from girlhood to womanhood.[72] This liminal state, as I demonstrated in the analysis of the films of Marina Spada and Francesca Comencini (and as I shall discuss in the concluding chapter on Eleonora Danco's *N-Able*) is a condition characterized by an identity in formation and dangerously transforming landscapes. It is from the margins of the city, of the world, and the cinema that they reshape a narrative about the world we inhabit.

Corpo Celeste, *Domenica*, and *Lost Kisses*, along with all the films directed by the women filmmakers considered in this study, confirm a trend in women's filmmaking of placing and investigating female subjectivity in urban contexts and choosing the city as a privileged setting to narrate contemporary Italian society and its ecological crises.

By placing children or adolescents at the center of their narration, and by adopting the narrative strategy of the journey in the city, Labate, Torre, and Rohrwacher continue, expand, and "reframe," as Scarparo and Luciano argue, a male-dominated cinematic tradition, that of neorealism as well as of auteurs' cinema from the 1960s that often represented children as salvific figures and the future of the nation. Women's ecocinema, which often recycles and reconfigures male narratives, engages in stories of girls who are precariously growing up in the Anthropocene to quicken our understanding of the urgency of the ecological crisis. Marta, Mimì, and Manuela, with their ability to perceive the sacredness of the planet, their resilience after experiencing violence, and their ability to "restore the sight" while bringing communities together, are an "ideal vehicle through which to seek out a renewed vision" of the world and imagine futures of possibility, maybe dystopian, uncertain, or even happy, but futures nonetheless.

NOTES

1. Di Bianco, "Interview with Alice Rohrwacher," 251.
2. Di Bianco, 252.
3. In 2020, Rohrwacher realized with JR, a French artist famous for his displays of gigantic faces in public places (including a film he did with Agnès Varda titled *Faces, Places*), *Omelia Contadina* (Funeral Homely). The latter is in Rohrwacher's words "un'azione cinemografica" (a cinematic action), a form of art intervention that would symbolically hold a funeral to peasant agriculture while pronouncing a *j'accuse* against the agroindustry that depletes and pollutes the earth, as well as the corruption and inaction of government.
4. Pitt and Hipkins, eds., *New Visions of the Child in Italian Cinema*, 1.
5. *Corpo Celeste* (2011) was awarded the David di Donatello (the Italian Oscar) in 2012, and *Le meraviglie* (*The Wonders*) won the Grand Prix at the 2014 Cannes Film Festival; *Lazzaro felice* (*Happy as Lazzaro*) won Best Script at Cannes 2018. Rohrwacher was the Film Society at Lincoln Center's 2016 Filmmaker in Residence.
6. Di Bianco, "Interview with Alice Rohrwacher," 252.
7. Seger, *Landscapes in Between*, 4.
8. Fiorini et al., "Land Take and Landscape Loss," 46.
9. See Cesaretti, *Elemental Narratives*, in particular the chapter titled "Concrete and Asphalt Geographies of Environmental Disruption in Modern Italy."
10. Fiorini et al., "Land Take and Landscape Loss," 50.
11. Di Bianco, "Interview with Alice Rohrwacher," 249.
12. Di Bianco, 252.
13. Iovino, "Naples 2008," 335.
14. Iovino, 335.
15. Alice Rohrwacher, interview by author, Rome, 2012 (my translation).
16. Stam, "Palimpsestic Aesthetics," 76.
17. In "Ecocinema *Ars et Praxis*," I provide a detailed commentary on Rohrwacher's self-reflective device of beginning films with dark or dimly lit scenes.
18. Many Italian film critics saw in *Corpo Celeste* a merciless portrait of contemporary Italy and the effects of decades of severe economic crisis, as well as a harsh critique of the church. See Ferzetti, "Alice nel paese della televisione"; Maltese, "Cresima show"; Piccino, "Marta ragazzina arrabbiata in cerca d'indipendenza."
19. Di Bianco, "Interview with Alice Rohrwacher," 249.
20. A critique of television entertainment returns in *The Wonders*, Rohrwacher's second feature film. The latter is about the life of a family

of beekeepers (supposedly farmers by political choice) whose survival is threatened by the new sanitary standards for agriculture as well as by the media's commodification of food and traditions. Significantly, in this film, a television show "celebrating" local food traditions takes place in an Etruscan tomb, suggesting that television represents the death of Italian culture.

21. Kristeva, *Powers of Horror*, 232.

22. The central role given to various forms of waste inscribes *Corpo Celeste* in a body of contemporary Italian films that deal with the garbage management crisis and the illegal disposal of toxic waste, such as *Biutiful cauntri* (Esmeralda Calabria, Andrea D'Ambrosio, and Peppe Ruggiero, 2007), *La bambina deve prendere aria* (A Child Must Have Fresh Air, Barbara Rossi Prudente, 2008), and *Campania infelix* (Unhappy Campagna, Ivana Corsale, 2011). For a treatment of these documentary films, see Past, "Documenting Ecomafia."

23. Gaybor, "Menstrual Politics in Argentina and Diverse Assemblages of Care," 230.

24. The village was home to 1,488 inhabitants at the beginning of the twentieth century, according to the census of 1911. Di Figlia, "Places in the Memory: Abandoned Villages in Italy," 52.

25. Di Figlia, 52.

26. Albrecht, *Earth Emotions*, 41.

27. Di Bianco, "Interview with Alice Rohrwacher," 250.

28. Wilma Labate's *Domenica* was inspired by Bresson's *Mouchette*.

29. "Straziante meravigliosa bellezza del creato" (the heartbreaking wonder of creation) is the last line pronounced by the character of Iago (played by Totò) in the finale of Pasolini's *Che cosa sono le nuvole* (What Are the Clouds?), an episode from *Capriccio all'italiana* (Caprice Italian Style, 1968).

30. This wonderment is described in the incipit of Anna Maria Ortese's memoir *Corpo celeste*, which Rohrwacher cites as the film's inspiration.

31. Wilma Labate, interview by author, Rome, July 2014 (my translation).

32. Labate recounts that a woman producer to whom she pitched the film project told her in very crude terms, "I am not going to produce this film for you because I believe that, to make a film like this, one needs a 'cock,' not [be] a woman." Wilma Labate, interview by author, Rome, July 2014 (my translation). To be sure, the furious debates at the time around the proposed *indulto* (legal pardon) for crimes of terrorism might have made funding any film on the subject difficult.

33. Luciano and Scarparo, *Reframing Italy*, 39.

34. The accident of the man falling from a window during a police interrogation is possibly a reference to the anarchist Giuseppe Pinelli's alleged suicide in 1969. This tragic episode was investigated by Elio Petri in the

documentary film *Documenti su Giuseppe Pinelli* (Documents on Giuseppe Pinelli, 1970) and represented in Marco Tullio Giordana's *Romanzo di una strage* (*Piazza Fontana: The Italian Conspiracy*, 2012).

35. Wilma Labate, interview by author, Rome, July 2014 (my translation).

36. Iovino, "Naples 2008," 336.

37. As discussed in the analysis of Comencini's *The White Space* (chap. 3), cities like Naples "suffer from overrepresentation." As Giuliana Bruno writes (referring to Naples and New York), "Shot over and over again, these cities have become themselves an image, imagery, a picture postcard." Bruno, *Streetwalking on a Ruined Map*, 47. In line with Bruno's argument, on the first day of shooting, Labate playfully announced to the crew that "any framing of the sea or of the city's iconic Aleppo pines was strictly forbidden." Wilma Labate, interview by author, Rome, July 2014 (my translation). Indeed, Labate's *Domenica* eschews any stereotypical representation of Naples, breaking with the city's lovable, musical image. In *The New Neapolitan Cinema*, Alex Marlow-Mann rightly places Labate in the group of filmmakers who contributed to Naples's cultural renaissance and the defolklorization of its image. See Marlow-Mann, *New Neapolitan Cinema*, 2.

38. Kristeva, 4.

39. Kristeva, 232.

40. Silverman, *The Subject of Semiotics*, 213.

41. Bruno, *Streetwalking on a Ruined Map*, 187.

42. Marlow-Mann, *The New Neapolitan Cinema*, 93.

43. In addition to *La pelle*, among the films directed by women and dealing with women's bodies in relation to Naples, it is worth mentioning Lina Wertmuller's *Un complicato intrigo di donne, vicoli e delitti* (A Complicated Intrigue of Women, Alleys, and Crimes, 1985). In this film, which concerns women's empowerment over and against the Mafia, the gender division is articulated through the city space.

44. Luciano and Scarparo, *Reframing Italy*, 39. Since the film's young hero is a rape survivor who wanders the streets of Naples (as opposed to being a "streetwalker," with all its implications), *Domenica* relates to Liliana Cavani's remarkable film *La pelle* (*The Skin*, 1981, adapted from Curzio Malaparte's novel, 1949). Ruth Glynn writes of the latter film: "The female body—its perceived weakness and vulnerability to penetration—serves as the prime metaphor for the humiliations and abjection wrought upon the Italy nation-state under Allied occupation." "Engendering Occupation," 348.
Although *Domenica* is set in Naples of the twenty-first century, the city is still the locus of the patriarchal violence seen in a drama placed in the 1940s.

45. Wilma Labate, interview by author, Rome, July 2014 (my translation).

46. See De Seta, *Napoli*. In Randi's *Into Paradiso* (2010), immigrants, who are generally located at the margins of the city, live in "Avvocata," a neighborhood

in the center of Naples. Urban space is articulated through horizontal layers. Whereas the roofs belong to the immigrants, the street level remains controlled by the mobsters.

47. Mulvey, "Visual Pleasure and Narrative Cinema," 11.

48. Mulvey, 10.

49. See Vitale, "The Body of Law: Redefining Rape in Italy." Vitale documents reforms of the penal codes regarding sexual violence that took place over the 1980s and 1990s. Until then, the fascist code of honor was in force, which entailed that a victim of rape could be forced to marry her rapist to repair the honor of the family.

50. Vitale, 258.

51. Vitale, 258.

52. Luciano and Scarparo, *Reframing Italy*, 46.

53. Wilma Labate, interview by author, Rome, July 2014.

54. Roberta Torre, "Intervista per Antonio Vitti," http://www.robertatorre.com/about/Preview/about.html.

55. Conti and Fonio, *I baci mai dati e altre storie*, 77 (my translation).

56. O'Healy, "Anthropological Anxieties," 87.

57. Marcus, "Postmodern Pastiche, the *Sceneggiata*, and the View of the Mafia from Below in Roberta Torre's *To Die for Tano*," 234.

58. Among her city short and documentary films: *Angelesse* (1991), *Palermo bandita* (1996), *Il Tiburtino terzo* (2009), and *La notte quando morì Pasolini* (2009).

59. Conti and Fonio, *I baci mai dati e altre storie*, 28–29 (my translation).

60. In 2019, Antonio Presti, president of the local Fondazione Fiumara D'arte, created a massive photo installation involving local photographers, cultural associations, schools, and the people of Librino, called *The Canticle of Librino*. It is composed of 1,200 gigantic portraits of *librinoti* (citizens of Librino) on whose faces are impressed words from Saint Francis's "Canticle of the Creature," one of the first example of ecopoetry in vernacular Italian celebrating the sacredness of the nonhuman world and our kindship with it. This work of street art is a compelling example of what Iovino calls "narrative re-inhabitation."

61. Conti and Fonio, *I baci mai dati e altre storie*, 28–29 (my translation).

62. In urban planning a "satellite town" is a town on the edge of a larger metropolitan area. Kenzo Tange is known for the reconstruction of Hiroshima. In addition to Librino, he also designed Naples's service center Centro Direzionale di Napoli (1995) and the district Quartiere Affari e San Francesco in San Donato milanese. The latter was also conceived as a satellite town to Milan and remained incomplete (1990–1999). The green areas were never developed. See Bettinotti, ed., *Kenzo Tange*.

63. Longo, "Palermo in the Films of Ciprì and Maresco," 189.

64. Foucault, "Of Other Spaces," 24.
65. Bertetto, "Dall'ossessione alla rimozione," 119–20.
66. Doane, "Woman's Stake," 24.
67. See Creed, *The Monstrous-Feminine*.
68. Kaplan, "The Case of the Missing Mother," 468.
69. O'Healy, "Are the Children Watching Us?" 121.
70. Williams, "When the Woman Looks," 17–18.
71. Iovino, "Restoring the Imagination of Place," 106.
72. Nicoletta Marini-Maio, drawing from anthropologists Victor Turner and Arnold Van Gennep, refers to the theory of liminality in her essay "The Children Are Still Watching Us," 151.

Fegatello: *The Macaluso Sisters*

SEVEN YEARS AFTER HER FIRST film, *Via castellana bandiera* (*A Street in Palermo*, 2013), theater director and writer Emma Dante directed the screen adaptation of her critically acclaimed play *Le sorelle Macaluso* (*The Macaluso Sisters*, 2020). The result was a tender film about life and death, loss, grief, time, and sisterhood.

Five orphaned young sisters live in a dusty apartment facing the sea on the outskirts of Palermo, Sicily. They make a living breeding doves and renting them for lavish weddings. Pinuccia enjoys the admiration of suitors for her sensual beauty; Maria dreams of becoming a dancer; the calm Katia loves food; the introverted Lia loves books; the youngest, the sweet five-year-old Antonella, loves Barbie dolls, chocolate, and entertaining the doves with a music box that plays Eric Satie's *Gymnopédie No. 1*.

One summer day, they journey from their neighborhood to the village of Mondello and sneak into its historic bathing club, Charleston. What was a day of joyful frolics turns tragic as the young Antonella dies after slipping from a ladder leading up to one of the club's private decks. This loss marks the end of their youth and of any chance for future happiness. Katia eventually leaves and marries. The others continue living in the apartment, imprisoned by their sense of guilt and resentment. Maria, who gave up the dream of being a dancer, dies consumed by sorrow and stomach cancer. The older Pinuccia, who had continued in her maternal role for a time, leaves soon after. Lia, who blames herself for the accident, remains until the film's end surrounded by the ghosts of her lost sisters.

While *The Macaluso Sisters* centers on the very human sentiment of grief and how it can shape one's existence, the film is also interwoven with powerful

Figure 4.14. Mourning doves. Screen capture, *The Macaluso Sisters* (2020), directed by Emma Dante.

posthuman dimensions. Nonhuman characters are employed for entertainment and companionship, and nature erupts in liminal urban spaces. Vegetation grows wildly along the Oreto River; the sea grows visually closer and closer, seemingly trying to reappropriate spaces taken by the city, or as Dante eloquently said, "down-sizing our arrogance and our encumbrance."[1] The doves, once a source of livelihood for the sisters, are beautifully framed throughout the film: they whirl in the sky above the building and wander around in empty rooms. No longer rented to others to celebrate the happy occasions now incomprehensible to the sorrowful sisters, they continue to cohabit the space and mourn with the Macalusos until the end.

NOTE

1. Emma Dante, "Le sorelle Macaluso: Intervista ad Emma Dante," interview by Chiara Borroni, *Cineforum*, December 18, 2020, https://www.cineforum.it/intervista/Intervista-a-Emma-Dante-Le-sorelle-Macaluso.

FIVE

A PSYCHOGEOLOGY OF THE CITY

N-Able

Io con il lavoro che faccio conosco bene l'isolamento. La drammaturgia è una condizione solitaria ma era una forza sapere che il mondo fuori agiva e io ero chiusa in casa a scrivere. Ora che è una condizione comune, giustamente necessaria, io che ho sempre fatto il contrario, nei primi giorni non sono riuscita a riempire la pagina, il computer mi guardava muto, poi per fortuna ho reagito, e ho scoperto che mi dava gioia il silenzio esterno, l'assenza dei rumori dei motorini che qui a San Lorenzo tutti accendevano e spegnevano di continuo. Mi manca il rapporto fisico con la strada, che vivo come uno stato di veglia. Ho sempre avuto bisogno della strada. Adesso con il virus la strada è nemica, è un luogo che sbilancia.[1]

—Eleonora Danco, 2020

I know isolation well because of my job. Dramaturgy is a solitary condition, but it gave me strength to know that the world outside was acting while I was inside writing. Now that it is a common condition, a necessary one, I, who had always done the opposite of what the world did, in the first days could not write a page. My computer would stare at me, mute. Then, luckily, I reacted, and I found joy in the outside silence, the absence of noise coming from the engines of *motorini* being turned on and off continually here in the neighborhood of San Lorenzo. I miss the physical relationship with the street, which I live as a condition of awakening. I always needed the street. Now with the virus it is an enemy, it is an unsettling place. (my translation)

In 2015, at the Open Roads: New Italian Cinema festival in New York, I saw a spellbinding film: *N-Capace* (N-Able, 2014), directed by Eleonora Danco, an established actor and playwright in her first experience as film director. Known for an "electric theater" that captures audiences with "screams, raving movements, and heads banged against the wall," Danco created a film of equal energy, comic verve, dramatic intensity, and visionary power.² Performing in the role of the protagonist, Anima in Pena (Lost Soul), she frantically walks, rolls on the ground, screams, and wields a pickax to destroy what she deems necessary. *N-Able* is a film about "the undecipherability of life" that resists any classification of genre.³

In his memoir *H.C. for Life, That Is to Say*, Jacques Derrida writes that after reading Hélène Cixous's *Le prenóm de Dieu* (1967) he asked himself, "What is this? What is happening here? What is happening to me? What genre? Who could ever read this? Me? So, I'll have to come back to it."⁴ I asked myself these questions after seeing *N-Able* for the first time, and I felt the desire to see it again, eager to discover what it might reveal at each screening. Derrida defined Cixous's book as an "Unidentifiable Literary Object," an expression that critics would adopt (in different variations) to label contemporary literary works that are hard to classify in terms of genre.⁵ Danco's film might be defined as a UCO, Unidentifiable Cinematic Object, or what influential film critic Adriano Aprà calls a film "fuori norma," translatable as outside the norm, open format, but also in violation of regulations.⁶

If there is a genre in which a misfit like *N-Able* might be placed, it is that of the essay film, which has countless subjective variations. It is dialogic, open (in the sense Umberto Eco intended the open work), lacks narrative closure; it is fragmentary, self-reflexive, playful, and political insofar as it expresses dissent and articulates "a form of potential subversion and assertion of the self into the polis."⁷ The investigation of the truth (or what is believed to be true) and the display of the filmmaking process itself is often a central part of the narrative. *N-Able* presents all these features as well as a compelling hybridity of cinematic language: it brilliantly mixes interviews, performance art, and theater tableaux while drawing from visual art and the cinema of the past, from Giorgio De Chirico to Luis Buñuel, Federico Fellini, Agnès Varda, and Pier Paolo Pasolini.⁸ Such hybridity is appropriate for a film that investigates (similarly to all the films of *Wandering Women* but with different aesthetics) a condition of liminality and nonbelonging.

Paradoxically, *N-Able* is a homecoming story. Ten years after the death of her mother, Lost Soul returns to the coastal town of Terracina, where she grew up. There, she engages in an intimate dialogue with her father, local seniors, and adolescents about their beliefs, desires, and the expectations they hold for their own lives, all the while engaging in apparently aimless and playful wandering. Haunted by doubts, consumed by memories, and enraged by the uncontrollable changes happening all around her, the peripatetic protagonist wanders between the seaside and the city of Rome, where she lives as an adult, without any sense of spatiotemporal coherence. Indeed, *N-Able*'s roaming narrative makes organizing the narrative of this chapter especially challenging.

I analyze *N-Able* through the concept of psychogeography, "the art of moving through space according to feelings and effects rather than ordinary purposes," and its related concept of *dérive* (drifting), the practice of spontaneously inhabiting space and shaping the topography of a place according to one's emotions, introduced by the Parisian Situationists of the mid-1950s.[9]

After outlining the key concepts that resonate with Danco's ways of experiencing and individualizing the city, I engage with a series of tableaux from the film, so-called memory installations, reenactments of childhood memories, and other forms of exhibition in the public space.[10] I assert that these are performances of authorship, symbolic gestures of appropriation and reimagining of places, as well as protests against urban deterioration through a call to protect the beauty of ancient artifacts and places. Removing the separation between public and private space and performing her role as actor and director, Lost Soul, the tormented protagonist of *N-Able*, claims her place in the world and her role as enunciator of the story.

As we shall see, psychogeography, a concept that resists "definition through a shifting series of interwoven themes and [is] constantly reshaped by its practitioners," expands to another realm in Danco, that of psychogeology, conveyed literally and symbolically through the vertical spatial trajectory of the film, descending from the top of a hill (the "view from above," as seen in other chapters) to the bottom of a quarry, the limestone bedrock of the city. Digging into both earth and soul in order to understand the "undecipherability of life," Danco builds a psychogeology of the city. Likewise, employing an ecocinematic approach, I dig into the affective landscapes in which the protagonist places herself, unearthing both their symbolic and material significances to foreground off-screen urban ecologies.

Consistent with *Wandering Women*'s project, my feminist ecocritical analysis is informed by my dialogue with the director, whose vision, accounts of creative process, inspirations, places, biographical details, and complicated production history informed and enriched my own vision. After the screening that left Lincoln Center's audience bewildered, Danco and I started an informal conversation that she decided to continue the following day at MoMA, where she was interested in seeing Robert Rauschenberg's paintings, whose material stratifications would later inspire her show *dEVERSIVO* (2017). The conversation continued a couple of years later, in the gardens of the American Academy of Rome, where I was a visiting scholar, and through multiple long email exchanges and voice messages that led to continuous realizations and propelled nomadic thoughts.

My first question for Danco was, "Who is Lost Soul, and what is her torment?" "Lost Soul is someone who doesn't want to, and doesn't know how to, function in social life. She doesn't know how to live; the only thing she can do is to raise doubts. A profound discontent and, at the same time, a vital tension put her in a condition of perennial yearning. A philosophical character, in this sense," she answered. "I wanted to represent an adult who maintains that penchant to question everything, as an adolescent would do, before being engulfed by the responsibilities of adult life."[11]

And, so she goes . . .

DRIFTING

A woman, Lost Soul, walks on a dirt road with the sea in the background. She keeps her eyes on the road; she seems anxious, frustrated. Now, she dangerously stands at a belvedere, on the edge of a ravine, outside the protective railing. Behind her, only partially visible, is the Roman Temple of Jupiter Auxur, while in front of her, at sea level, a myriad of homes and buildings interrupted by minuscule patches of green. The camera pans, leaving the woman at the edge of the shot and then off-screen, showing the sea and a promontory in the background. As the camera continues to pan in a descending movement, we can discern marinas, boats, and umbrellas on a beach. As will be reveled later in the film, Lost Soul/Danco is contemplating her hometown, the coastal town of Terracina, a Roman *colonia marittima* in southern Latium (fig. 5.1).

The landscape, like its observer, is informed by anguish, melancholy, and a sense of loss, but without drama. On the contrary, a derisive tone can be perceived in the woman's internal dialogue heard in voice-over: "Enough about these adolescent haunts, what are you doing here? Always going back, wasting time. I had such fun, I want to go on living like this. I can't manage to do anything. What should I do today? Look at yourself in the mirror; you're an adult. No one listens to you anymore. There are other expectations of you!"

While *N-Able* investigates the emotional struggle of being trapped in a state of transition from adolescence to adulthood, the film is not about immobility. Quite the opposite: the protagonist moves incessantly. Indeed, the expression *anima in pena*, often translatable as "lost (or perhaps, tormented) soul," is often used in Italian to refer to someone who is restless like a child.

Concerned with positionality, *N-Able* is a restless film with an erratic, multidirectional structure. The spatial and temporal trajectories of the film

Figure 5.1. Lost soul contemplates her hometown. Screen capture, *N-Able* (2014), directed by Eleonora Danco.

are confusing, building an indecipherable map from the unreliable quality of memory. The editing of the film, characterized by what Gilles Deleuze calls "incommensurable or irrational cuts" (a lack of logical connection between one shot and another), "shuns suture and works in a regime of radical disjunction."[12] The seeming incoherence accentuates the dreamlike atmospheres of the film and viewers' sense of displacement.

Psychogeography and its related idea of *dérive* (drifting), articulated below, seem appropriate critical tools for understanding mobility in Danco's film and the sort of "pedestrian speech acts" that the film conveys.[13] The merger of the terms *psychology* and *geography*, *psychogeography*, as Marilyn Coverley writes, comprises "a bewildering array of ideas [describing] everything from occult and urban walking to avant-garde experimentation and political radicalism." The idea, still popular among contemporary artists and writers, was launched by the French avant-garde Situationist International group founded by Marxist theorist and filmmaker Guy Debord in the mid-1950s, an epoch marked by artistic experimentation, mobility, technological advancement, and individualism, but also an era in which artists increasingly perceived and reacted against "the homogenizing effects of capitalist development."[14]

Psychogeography, according to Debord, is essentially an investigation of the emotional impact of the environment on human behavior. He acknowledges that such an approach is in line with the "materialist perspective of the conditioning of life and thought by objective nature." This is to say, from an ecocritical perspective developed decades after the publication of Debord's essays, psychogeography recognizes the entanglement of humans and the environment, their agencies and mutual influences. Thus, as defined by Debord, "psychogeography sets for itself the study of the precise laws and specific effects of the geographical environment, whether consciously organized or not, on the emotions and behavior of individuals."[15]

The concept of psychogeography was originally introduced by the poet Ivan Vladimirovitch Chtcheglov (alias Gilles Ivain) in *Formulaire pour un urbanisme nouveau* (*Formulary of a New Urbanism*) published in 1953. As an antidote to the banality of everyday life and alienation in modern cities, Chtcheglov envisions "a new urban environment in which architecture reflects an emotional engagement with its inhabitants."[16] In this formula Chtcheglov wishes for a "continuous *dérive*," or drifting, a concept that Debord will appropriate and elaborate on, first in *Introduction to a Critique of Urban Geography* (1955) and later in his *Theory of the Dérive* (1958).

The French term *dérive* (in Italian *deriva*) is a marine term that signifies deviation from a navigation route due to sea currents. A drifting boat, *alla deriva*, is transported by the currents and is in danger of sinking. The Italian expression *andare alla deriva* means not to resist and succumb to adversities. As intended by the Situationists, though, the term acquires positive, creative, and subversive connotations.

A dérive is an earthbound spatial practice that consists of walking through places to investigate how "different areas of the cities resonate with particular moods and ambiences."[17] Dérives, Debord continues, "involve playful-constructive behavior and awareness of psychogeographical effects and are thus quite different from classic notions of journey and stroll. In a dérive, one or more persons during a certain period drop their relations, their work and leisure activities, and all their other usual motives for movement and action, and let themselves be drawn by the attractions of the terrain and the encounters they find there."[18] Ultimately, the Situationists intended the dérive as a tool for a replanning of the city and a political program to eliminate the separation between art and life.

N-Able's approach to space is strongly reminiscent of the Situationists' practice. The protagonist's dérives take multiple forms and settings in the film, both natural and urban. In line with Chtcheglov's meaning of the dérive, it conveys a degree of critique toward modern society in its demand for productivity and restrictions on individual freedoms and claims the right to inactivity, disorientation, and melancholia. In some cases, it entails solastalgia, to recall Glenn A. Albrecht's earth emotion: a particular emotional distress triggered by natural disasters but also "war, terrorism, land clearing, mining, rapid institutional change and the gentrification of old parts of the city."[19] Furthermore, in *N-Able*,

Figure 5.2. A *dérive* at the station. Screen capture, *N-Able* (2014), directed by Eleonora Danco.

the dérive is a very intimate affair, and it has to do with personal conflicts, in particular the maternal one, as I will discuss later in the chapter.

A first example of a static, solo dérive appears at the beginning of Lost Soul's journey, the arrival at the station. Removing the separation between private and public space, between the house and the street, a bed appears in the middle of a train platform, in what looks like a deserted small town. No train is visible on the horizon, nor does it seem likely that one will arrive. A woman in her pajamas, looking rather fraught, sits on this bed (fig. 5.2).

Recalling Derrida's question in dealing with the unidentifiable narrative object, what are we looking at? Where does this absurd and powerful image originate? Most importantly, where is this bed positioned in the world and in the text? *N-Able* emerges from the play *Nessuno ci guarda* (Nobody Is Looking), also by Danco (2000).[20] In the opening scene of the play, a woman is stuck in bed. She is not ill; she is paralyzed by her memories, and, as the play unfolds, she re-enacts them, traveling through time: "The bed and the pajama are scenic elements that serve to communicate the idea of someone who's getting ready to leave the house," commented Danco.[21] But in the film, the bed, which appears repeatedly, having been relocated from the stage to urban space, assumes other and more poignant significances. The abandoned station with its dead tracks signifies an impossible mobility and evokes melancholia and malaise.

A similar instance of a static dérive (fig. 5.3) happens in a piazza in front of a church (barely visible at the edge of the shot, almost off-screen) in Danco's hometown of Terracina. It is a claim for nonbelonging to the religious community (as in Rohrwacher's *Corpo Celeste*), the display of which in the public space is subversive.

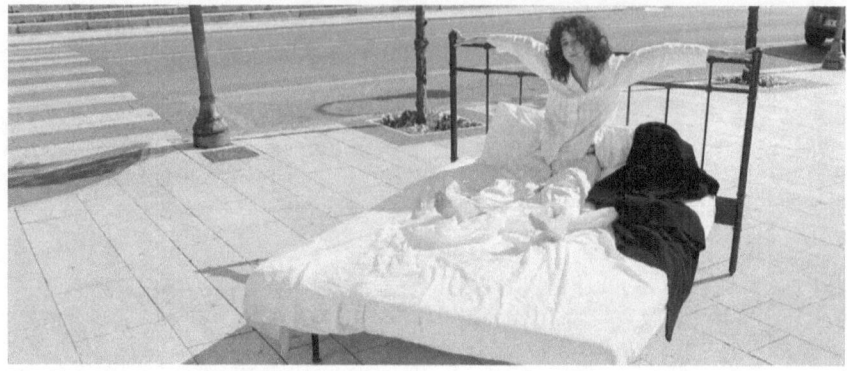

Figure 5.3. A religious *dérive*. Screen capture, *N-Able* (2014), directed by Eleonora Danco.

Deprived of sexual connotation, "the bed," Danco said, "is a form of rebellion, a refusal, a defense, as well as a form of resistance to reality."[22] Indeed, the woman in bed condenses the inability to function or to make choices while conforming to societal roles, including gender roles: "I'm anxious on Sundays. If you don't cook and set the table, you'd better kill yourself. If you don't stay home with your man you'll be alone forever!"—she hears from an inner critic.

To confirm that: here, even though her (female) character is in principle ungendered (the name, Anima in Pena, confirms that), Danco is articulating a discourse at the core of the feminist politics of space. Women's appropriation of public space is a form of resistance to the patriarchal control of that space, according to which women are confined to the domestic sphere. Lost Soul, as a childless adult woman who holds on to her adolescence, escapes every form of control.

As seen in chapter 4, "Coming of Age in the City," transitional or liminal spaces are occupied by individuals who lack a clear position in society and therefore wander in search of it. A similar marginal position is experienced by women directors in the world of film and media. Not coincidentally, the above-described dérive is also a performance of authorship.

The bed, placed in various settings, encapsulates the condition of liminality. While suggesting a sense of rest—that is, immobility—it is significant that the performances always happen in transitional spaces such as at a crossroad, on a pedestrian island, or on a station platform (fig. 5.2). Similarly, in other scenes—"intervals" in Lost Soul's peregrinations and search for truth(s)—the protagonist positions herself on thresholds and cliff edges.

In the body of films examined in *Wandering Women*, the process of becoming a woman aligns with that of becoming a director. As the opening image seen at the beginning of this chapter (and throughout the book) shows, the errant female protagonist replicates the gaze of the director. Positioning oneself in the landscape amounts to an authorial self-inscription, both in the world and in the cinematic text. Allison Butler, as mentioned in the introduction, observes that such self-reflexivity is recurrent in women directors, especially those who are at the early stages of their careers. "Performing as themselves and others, using their voices on the soundtrack and working with autobiographical content" are all ways of asserting authorship.[23] Danco, who performs the role of Lost Soul, who is also the director of a film about "an errant daughter who visits her father ten years after the death of her mother," is present in almost every shot either physically or in voice-over.[24] *N-Able* is, in Danco's words, "a performative film" insofar as it incorporates in the narrative the making of the film, the internal struggle of its director dealing with a merciless inner critic, and the efforts of guiding nonprofessional actors in the process of becoming actors or simply performing their own lives.[25] From the bed positioned in the city, she shifts in front of the camera from her role as actor to that of director, giving instructions to her crew members or asking a passerby carrying her groceries to appear in the film, even making sure (as a good production assistant would do) that she is willing to sign a release form, reminding us what an epic effort it takes to make a film, especially with very limited production means.

In *N-Able*, a film that "speaks from the articulated point of view of the filmmaker who readily acknowledges her subjective position," the assertion of female authorship becomes the raison d'être of the film itself.[26]

THE BEACH AND THE SILENT MOTHER

Further confirming Butler's insight regarding the autobiographical nature of women's films, *N-Able* deals explicitly with a major event in the director's own life: the loss of her mother. A marginal character in the film, Lost Soul's long-deceased mother appears in its margins, at its beginning and at its end, in a liminal place par excellence, the seashore, the limen between earth and water.

The seashore is ubiquitous in the cinema of the Italian peninsula. As Christian Uva shows in his recent book *Ultima spiaggia: Rive e derive del cinema italiano* (The Last Beach, Seashores and Drifts in Italian Cinema, 2021), countless films use the beach as a primary location or contain at least one or more significant marine scenes. "The beach," Uva writes, "is not just a physical and geographical territory, but an actual cultural *topos* in which the social and

Figure 5.4. Lost soul and her mother on the beach. Screen capture, *N-Able* (2014), directed by Eleonora Danco.

anthropological features and the identity of a population can be reflected in more or less evident forms."[27] Drawing from Mikhail Bakhtin, he observes that the beach has a carnival dimension: boundaries blur, hierarchies are disrupted, identities are negotiated or renegotiated, and bodies are displaced. The historical trajectory of his study demonstrates the ways connotations are attached to the beach as a site of change throughout different cinematic eras reflecting societal transformations.

In the late 1950s and mid-1960s, when an Italian beach movie genre developed, the beach was a space to showcase the euphoria of the economic miracle. The "scandalous" seminaked bodies of young people from various social classes "incarnate the idea of the rebirth of our country." As the euphoria of the brief boom progressively diminishes, the vital tension gives way to existential drifting, and the beach becomes the "theater of a series of anxious visions and distressing oneiric projections."[28]

In many of the films analyzed in *Wandering Women*, the sea and the seashore are often either intensely charged with symbolism or significantly kept off-screen. In Mangini and Barbanente's *Traveling with Cecilia*, set in a highly polluted Taranto, the sea is a conduit of toxicity that no longer provides sustenance for a community that once relied on fishing. In Rohrwacher's *Corpo Celeste*, the sea is imbued with spirituality. When the young protagonist reaches the beach after leaving the church, she perceives the sacredness of the earth. In *Lost Kisses* and *Domenica*, it is explicitly associated with femininity, imagined either as a monstrous or a benevolent mother. The sea is either erased within the bleak built-up environment or revealed in the ending as a hope for life-sustaining cities.

N-Able, with its erratic montages and surreal geographical discontinuities, frames and references the beach in various ways, having it fulfill a variety of diegetic functions. It is shown in connective mobile sequences as a narrow strip beyond rows of cars parked on the promenade, images that comment on limited access to nature in overconstructed seaside peripheries; it appears filled by crowds of young people, conveying a sense of joy and vitality, and melancholically deserted, it signals the end of the summer (i.e., the end of freedom and leisure). Along these lines, the beach is the setting for memory installations, dreamlike reenactments of childhood memories, or *dérive*, analogous to the anxious visions from the 1960s mentioned by Uva.

For Danco, though, the beach is perhaps above all a maternal landscape. Source of empowerment and disempowerment, or "the deepest mutuality and the most painful estrangement," as Adrienne Rich put it in her 1976 foundational text *Of Woman Born*, where she argues that the maternal figure is crucial to the process of "becoming women."[29] Hence, as mentioned in chapter 3, "Mothers and Daughters: Stories of Survival and Care," motherhood has been and continues to be a dominant theme in feminist scholarship and creative work by women. As Bernadette Luciano and Susanna Scarparo demonstrate in *Reframing Italy*, through the analysis of a cluster of contemporary Italian women's directed films on the subject, "the creation of a space in which to represent and create a different social subject and to address the spectator as female is tied to the search for the self, which in turn is linked to the search for the mother and the re-evaluation of the mother's perspective."[30]

In *N-Able*, though, the mother is an enigmatic and funereal figure, barely visible and audible, whereas it is the daughter's voice that is heard. An adult woman in her pajamas runs with open arms toward the water on a bright, deserted beach. At the edge of the shot appears an elderly woman, all bundled up in a black coat, hat, and gloves, turning her back to the camera and standing under an umbrella. She moves her arm up as if to say, "No! Come here!" Lost Soul's disembodied adult voice, says, "What time is it, Mom? How long until eleven? Let me swim. I've digested my meal, Mom. I won't die. Do I have to stay here with you, Mom? Here everything changes!" Kept from diving into the water, Lost Soul stands with arms crossed and head down in childlike frustration while her questions and entreaties remain unanswered.

The mother's silence, enhanced by hallucinatory electronic music by famed composer Marcus Aker, is highly meaningful considering that the perception of the maternal voice is a child's first auditory experience. As Kaja Silverman explores in her influential book *The Acoustic Mirror*, the maternal voice generates divergent fantasies that often manifest in classical narrative cinema. From different psychoanalytic perspectives and film theories, the sound of the maternal voice can be presented as an experience of pleasure or, at the opposite pole, an experience of distress. Psychoanalysts Guy Rosolato and Mary Ann Doane conceptualize this phenomenon in spatial terms as "a sonorous envelope" that immerses the infant in a "pleasurable milieu," surrounding and protecting it in a blissful union with the mother. Film theorist Michel Chion, as Silverman writes, "associates it with 'the terror of the umbilical night.'"[31] If, in Silverman's terms, the maternal voice can be "an emblem of impotence and entrapment," silencing the mother is, on behalf of the director, an assertion of agency that enables her to become a storyteller.[32]

Notably, in this dreamlike beginning, there are strong echoes of *8 ½* (1963), by Fellini, an auteur whom Danco worships and repeatedly pays homage to. As Uva reminds us, in *La Dolce Vita* (1960), like in *8 ½*, the beach is often the site of frightening fantasies. The latter is explicitly referenced in *N-Able*. In *8 ½*, the protagonist, tormented director Guido Anselmi, fraught by a creative crisis, dreams that he liberates himself from a traffic jam to fly over a windy beach. The asphyxiating city with endless lines of Fiats and the entrapment in the vehicle vividly expresses the protagonist's anxiety of being unable to finish his film and satisfy the demands of the production, whereas the sea, in a classic nature-culture dichotomy, functions, at least in the first part of the dream, as a metaphor for creative freedom. However, the liberating flight ends when a production person with a threatening laugh pulls him down with a rope tied to his foot, and he falls on the beach (fortunately, the protagonist wakes up before the crash!). Similarly, the mother in *N-Able*, who with her black coat, hat, and petite stature is strikingly reminiscent of Guido's mother, restricts the freedom of Lost Soul, who is also a tormented director. With this "reframing" of Fellini, Danco's memory installation functions as a fantasy of origin, the origin of the world created by the film.[33]

The deceased mother is a marginal yet present figure, like a ghost haunting the entire film, often evoked or addressed directly by Lost Soul while inhabiting the film's various locations. Unlike many women's films that place the maternal figure at the center of the narrative, in *N-Able*, a film about limits and borders, the mother/daughter relationship is not explored at length, but it is given primacy of place, in a sense, at the beginning and at the end of the film, enclosing (or containing) an unruly narrative.[34]

Such a framing strategy addresses a fundamental moment in the formation of female subjectivity and ties the loss of the mother to the daughter's artistic endeavor, which articulates "the daughter's desire for a brief reunion with her mother."[35] In other words, the act of filmmaking is part of the mourning process. It is the loss of the mother that initiates the errant daughter's journey.

PICKAXING

Proceeding "in a regime of radical [geographical] disjunction," to recall Deleuze's words, *N-Able* travels quickly and repeatedly from the seashore of southern Latium to the streets of Rome, where Lost Soul engages in more dérives that, as prescribed by Debord, "involve playful-[de]constructive behavior."[36] Wearing a white tunic that resembles the chiton (the garment both women and men wore in ancient Greece), Lost Soul wanders the Eternal City brandishing a pickax. Is she undoing the city? Arresting its changes? Recovering the past? Like a maddened *genius loci*, the protective spirit of a place, she intends to destroy what she considers to be ugly (and new), essentially "out of place" in Rome.[37]

This instance of dérive that might go well beyond the Situationists' original notion has a strong ecocritical dimension that echoes the concern of archaeologist, writer, and public intellectual Antonio Cederna, one of the fathers of the Italian environmentalist movement. In the same years in which the Situationists were active in Europe, at the dawn of the economic miracle, he published one of his most incendiary articles in the magazine *Il mondo*: "Il sacco di Roma" (The Sack of Rome). Establishing a continuity between the violent interventions on Rome's urban fabric from the fascist period to those of his times, he wrote, "The demolishing pickax furies in Rome, as in the good old days. Churches, convents, buildings, parks, houses, and streets are destroyed: it is like being back in the 30s, when the Capitolium was scraped and the Mausoleum of Augustus isolated. When the Renaissance district was disemboweled and the Borghi annihilated. Our local vandalism does not show tiredness."[38]

Cederna's indignation was shared by many intellectuals and writers, such as Elena Croce, Umberto Zanotti Bianco, Giorgio Bassani, and Desideria Pasolini dall'Onda, who in 1955, along with Cederna, founded Italia Nostra, the first Italian environmental organization. In contrast to current trends, this urban-focused organization was initially primarily concerned with the conservation of monuments and cultural heritage. "Vandalo è chi distrugge l'antico" (Whoever destroys antiquity is a vandal), wrote Cederna.[39]

Cederna's outrage is still pertinent. Not coincidentally, his major collection of essays, an exposé of Italian environmental malpractices during the postwar period, was republished in 2006 with the title *I vandali in casa: Cinquant'anni dopo* (The Vandals at Home: Fifty Years Later). His concern with conservation resonates in Danco's urban performances: "Living in the historical center of Rome I ride my *motorino* around, and I feel so much rage. I put that rage in my film," said Danco when I asked about her relationship with Rome and its environmental deterioration. Interestingly, Danco's dérives involve a pickax—per Cederna's observation—as a tool for digging and destruction.[40]

In line with Italia Nostra's initial focus on the preservation of monuments, Danco is preoccupied with ancient beauty and new ugliness.[41] This dichotomy is strongly reminiscent of the antimodernist discourse articulated in Pier Paolo Pasolini's documentary film *La forma della città* (The Shape of the City, 1974), in which he categorizes the new public housing buildings raised in the ancient city of Orte as "un'incrinatura, un turbamento della forma e dello stile" (a crack, a disturbance of form and style). Likewise, Italo Calvino, in his early environmentally conscious novella *La nuvola di smog* (*Smog*, 1958), proclaimed "una bellezza antica non può nulla contro una bruttezza nuova" (an ancient beauty can't do anything against a new ugliness).[42]

In *N-Able*'s tableaux shown in figure 5.5, the object of remonstration, being obscene, is left off-screen. This omission leaves the viewer who lacks knowledge of the geography of Rome wondering what these gestures of protest are about.

As we can observe in figure 5.5, the performer wants to tear down a travertine wall that "breaks the perspective," as Danco complained. Indeed, the wall tragically disrupts the view from the road of two landmarks of the Tiber: the seventeenth-century churches of San Girolamo and San Rocco, in the district of Campo Marzio. The wall, built in 2006, is part of an architectural structure characterized by glass, marble, and concrete, the Museum of the Ara Pacis Augustae, which, again, remains off-screen: "I shared my feelings about the museum of the Ara Pacis with an artist-friend, and he told me: 'don't show what's ugly; find a way to reverse it.' So, I showed up dressed like a statue and with a pickaxe and transformed that reality into something oneiric, absurd, and funny," said Danco.[43]

Among the few major works of contemporary architecture in Rome since the 1930s, the complex was designed by American architect Richard Meier to protect the sacrificial altar from 9 BCE that the Romans built to celebrate peace after military conquests. The remonstration encapsulates the feeling many Romans have had toward this aesthetically controversial work, which the notoriously belligerent art critic Vittorio Sgarbi described as "a highway rest stop (autogrill) or pizzeria, good for the outskirts of Las Vegas, but certainly not for the center of Rome."[44] It has been the object of vandalism, the wall sprayed with red pigment and decorated, so to speak, with a ceramic toilet underneath.

Figure 5.5. Tearing down walls. Screen capture, *N-Able* (2014), directed by Eleonora Danco.

Along the same lines, and in more sophisticated terms, the architecture critic Nicolai Ourossoff condemned it in a *New York Times* article as "absurdly overscale, [and] indifferent to the naked beauty of the dense and richly textured city around it."[45] Interestingly, in 2009, responding to the Copenhagen Climate Summit, the monument was used for a protest against climate change when a group of local environmental activists colored the water of its fountain green and affixed a banner on the side facing Via Tomacelli reading "Earth First! Act Now."[46] This monument is located along a bank of the Tiber River, near Piazza Augusto Imperatore, an area in Rome's historical center the protection of which has been the focus of urban planning debates and campaigns conducted by Italia Nostra to protect the *genius loci* of the place.

In *N-Able*, the tension between old and new, past and present, is acute. In a city like Rome, the past is magnificent, crumbling, and must be preserved, but it is also paralyzing and seems unable to allow anything new to serve Rome's contemporary needs, to emerge and function. This seems to be, at least in this film, an unresolvable and exhausting tension. Notably, many construction sites are shown and scrutinized by the errant character. As observed in chapter 2, devoted to Marina Spada's films, women's identities are aligned with cities'; therefore holes, barriers, and excavators are signifiers, for both characters and places, of crisis and potential transformations.[47]

An amusing and thought-provoking variant of this trope is offered by a dérive I called "A Nap at the Construction Site." As we can observe in figure 5.6, the dériveur/euse has put down the pickax and lies in a fetal position on the ground (in absence of the bed) accompanied by construction workers. Are they resting, playing dead, protesting passively, simply worn out? Why

Figure 5.6. A nap at a construction site. Screen capture, *N-Able* (2014), directed by Eleonora Danco.

there? What is this dérive about? If the bed, to recall Danco's words, "is a form of rebellion, a refusal, a defense, as well as a form of resistance to reality," and construction sites are signifiers for transformation and, depending on perspective, crisis, which are the dériveurs and the city experiencing? Which transformation might they be resisting? Once again, digging into the stories of the city unearths hidden meanings.

As the sign in Italian on the upper right side of the shot reads, "Lavori Linea C," this is a construction site for the third line of Rome's subway, which aims to connect the southeast periphery of the city with its northeast. Sardonically labeled "the metro of the mysteries," the project, inaugurated in 1990 and meant to be completed by the Jubilee of 2000, has endured countless interruptions.[48] Fortuitous discoveries of archaeological ruins hidden in Rome's millennial stratifications were brought to light while digging tunnels. For instance, in the area of San Giovanni shown in this shot, a massive Roman hydric basin along with agricultural tools from a first-century farm were uncovered.

Investigations on corruption and poor management of public funds contributed to inflated costs and the lengthened timetable for what represents "a vital project for Rome, a city with almost 3 million inhabitants and 2.5 million vehicles," and all the predictable ecological damage that result from that. Furthermore, as the subway is meant to connect the inhabitants of the city's "atomic peripheries" with the historical center, its incompleteness entails social exclusion and impeded mobility.[49]

This important, seemingly unattainable public project remains, at the time of this writing, only partially completed, exemplifying the city's struggle to preserve its memory and heritage while also securing its survival. In this light, Danco's dérive, which significantly involved a crew of construction workers, resists, as the rest of the film, univocal interpretation. It symbolizes a despair for an impossible timetable, or a necessary pause in time, but it also encapsulates people's frustration and exhaustion at the dysfunction of the city and its deterioration.

After taking a nap at the construction site, Lost Soul, brandishing her pickax, appears in Largo di Torre Argentina, home of the magnificent archaeological site that comprises four Roman temples (one of which is now a cat sanctuary) and site of the Teatro Argentina, a historical opera house and theater of Rome. There, Lost Soul wants to destroy a pedestrian island that has replaced the iconic cobblestones. By hammering the pavement, she reminds the most ecologically conscious viewers that, like many Italian cities, Rome has suffered, since the period of postwar reconstruction, from reckless overbuilding.[50] Between 2000 and 2007, in fact, Rome's real estate industry grew 80 percent in value. As urbanist Mose Ricci writes, "What damage to the urban environment and to the countryside landscape and to the image of Rome will the eighty-million square meters spread by the new master urban plan, or the seven million square meters built in 2007 and those previously built, do? This process of over-construction that is profoundly changing the image and the landscape of the Eternal City, while registered by statistics, is almost hidden by the media."[51]

By "not showing the ugly" directly, and "transforming that reality into something oneiric, absurd, funny," to use Danco's words again, *N-Able* avoids the tenor of the old-fashioned documentary film, a fact that the director seems eager to assert: "*N-Capace* is not a documentary film! It does not document anything!"[52] Here lies, in part, its originality and visual power. However, there is a cost to this "not showing" that must be noted. Namely, like Comencini's *The White Space*, the film ends up concealing the political resonance of its visual ecologies, especially to an international audience. In some ways, its playfulness can come off as an inside joke for those already attuned to the problems, or anyway to the domestic Italian audiences she addresses.

Another significant and rather cryptic dérive happens in the district of Testaccio, also known as Monte de Cocci, the mound of discharged amphorae used during the Roman Empire to store olive oil, today an archaeological site. In the background stands the iconic building of the ex-Mattatoio, the former slaughterhouse decommissioned in 1975. One of the suggestive exemplars of Rome's industrial archaeology, the space has hosted since the beginning of 2000 a branch of MACRO, the Museum of Contemporary Art, and the Faculty of Architecture of Roma Tre University.

Figure 5.7. Why did you remove the Testaccio Market? Screen capture, *N-Able* (2014), directed by Eleonora Danco.

The woman in the chiton with a pickax stares enraged at a marble-and-glass building (fig. 5.7), which is identified by a sign as the Hotel Re Testa, and shouts, "Why did you remove the Testaccio market? To make it horrible like this? I saw Mink DeVille with Guglielmina here in '94! You must eat, communicate, always be somewhere, loneliness is awful. Panino.com. Mamara nonstop beer and pizza. A shot, shottineria, damn it barbecue! A flask. Give it here. I was here first! I was here first!" Lost Soul screams, throwing herself on the floor (fig. 5.8), as if by touching it with her entire body she could appropriate the city: "I was here first!" (The humorous tone of the phrase as it is spoken is lost in translation: *ce stavo prima io!*)

What is this delirium about? The source of Lost Soul's rage is located off-screen, sixty-seven meters from the edges of the shot: the new market of Testaccio, a glass-roofed indoor market that, due to contemporary standards of food sanitation, replaced the former charming street market. This scene illustrates how memories are at play when individuals inhabit a place that they have previously experienced and that might have been later modified by urban design, affecting present perceptions, determining a certain aesthetic appreciation, and even provoking a sense of loss. As Monica Montserrat Degen and Gillian Rose put it in their study on walking and perceptual memories, "Buildings, streets and squares may be seen, heard and smelled through memories of what once was there but is no longer."[53] In short, new things, even if more efficient and hygienic, might be perceived as threatening to our own memories and bodies, wrapped in environments that can be nurturing or incapacitating.

Figure 5.8. I was here first! Screen capture, *N-Able* (2014), directed by Eleonora Danco.

But with an attentive listen to Lost Soul's ramblings, we understand that she is not nostalgically protesting change per se but asserting that urban design and certain alterations of the landscape are at one with the contemporary urge to sanitize emotions and conceal less pleasant emotions (inherent to human experience) behind a "shining" facade.

Danco's protests, however difficult to interpret, hint at the contradictions of Rome and Italy at large, "a country that seems to have forgotten its past urban excellence."[54] Her concern with beauty reminds us that Rome is both magnificent and degraded, buried by garbage, paralyzed by traffic, suffocated by air pollution, and its soil sealed by a never-ending flow of cement, resulting in poor urban quality of life. As defined by Pasolini in his heartrending 1957 "Pianto della scavatrice" (The Tears of the Excavator), Rome, my Rome, the city where I was born and educated, the city I have been and continue to be too distant from, is a "stupenda e misera città" (stupendous, miserable city).

A QUARRY

As *N-Able*'s nomadic narrative comes to an end and Lost Soul descends deeper into her memories, we leave, at least temporarily, the built-up environment. This shift from "the urban sphere to the geophysical," as media theorist Jussy Parikka argues, allows us "a more fundamental understanding of the modulation of the subject that is stretched between ecologies of capitalism and those of the earth."[55] This is an idea that reconfigures the sphere of film analysis and opens onto posthuman scenarios. While *N-Able* remains a deeply anthropocentric narrative, the captivating visual leitmotifs of the pickax, the recurrent gesture of digging, seemingly to peel off pavement from the streets or the topsoil off the surface of the earth, the symbolic attempt to destroy new construction, and the vertical trajectory of the film, all point toward a psycho-geology of the city.

In the powerful tableau shown in figure 5.9, Lost Soul stands on a boulder, against the backdrop of Mount Sant'Angelo, on top of which the Temple of Jupiter is erected, glimpsed in the opening aerial view I discussed at the beginning of this chapter. While her position on the edge reiterates the protagonist's liminality and search for a place, it is the corporeal blending with the matter of the mountain that seems more noteworthy.

The skeleton of the earth is laid bare, with exposed, thick strata of limestone from different eras on display, a legacy of the earth, ipso facto, constructing itself. Such framing, a quasi-autonomous landscape, to play with Martin Lefevre's definition, dwarfs human presence in the environment, reminding us of human-nonhuman shared vulnerabilities while enhancing the splendor of nature.[56]

To fully appreciate the lively beauty of this image, while interrogating the film's fascination with stones, a brief digression seems necessary. In *On Looking*, cognitive scientist Alexandra Horowitz takes twelve investigative walks in the city of New York, accompanied by experts in different subjects. As she demonstrates in her absorbing book, walkers' interests shape their field of vision, an idea that applies to any critical response to artistic expression, including film. In the amble described in the section of the book entitled "The Material of the Landscape," Horowitz walks with geologist Sydney Horenstein. Starting from the simple consideration that "[geology] is what is under us, but it is also what surrounds us," the author, as well as the reader, comes to understand where geology, the science that studies the physical structure of the earth, manifests in urban areas and how we can look at urban landscapes from a geological perspective. As Horowitz put it, "So-called man-made objects are just those that began as naturally occurring materials and are broken apart and recombined to form something customized to our purposes." This idea illuminates Lost Soul's last dérive and allows us to see a "less artificial" city.

In line with urban ecocriticism, which observes the ways the natureculture continuum manifests in the city, the emerging field of urban geology chooses the city, as opposed to the wilderness or a less built environment, as the geologist's field of research.[57] Indeed, even by looking at landscapes made of concrete, asphalt, and steel, we can reflect on the formation of rocks and sediments, about their geological cycles, and human and nonhuman temporalities.

Figure 5.9. A lime-scape. Screen capture, *N-Able* (2014), directed by Eleonora Danco.

As Horowitz explains, limestone is "a popular building material, is full of shells, remains, and other traces of ancient animals. In fact, it mostly *is* the fossils and fragments. Like schist, it formed in the Geologically-Long-Ago era, on the floor of the oceans.... The movement of ocean waters broke up the shells of the small invertebrate animals—snails, scallops, and other tiny organisms."[58] In this light, Lost Soul looks like a fossil, organic material that time could eventually morph into another stratum of the earth, perhaps to be uncovered epochs later as residue of previous life.[59]

While stones might be interpreted as symbols of resilience and strength, reflecting on the calcareous nature of the mountain featured in the film, we can read this landscape as a vulnerable, friable one.[60] The inherent vulnerability of the landscape is accentuated by the quarry that Lost Soul enters in the subsequent frame, toward the end of the film.

Reiterating the sense of vulnerability that the previous tableau conveyed (fig. 5.9), the protagonist appears tiny, in a vast empty space between some extracting machine, of which only the menacing shadow enters the scene, and the wall of the quarry (fig. 5.10). This enormous white chasm lies in proximity to the Natural Monument of Campo Soriano, a protected natural area of stunning beauty where karstic rocks take the shape of cathedrals.[61] My cine-geographical investigations led me to discover that in the same area lies a decommissioned quarry that, after decades of limestone extraction, was closed in the early 2000s without an adequate plan for environmental recovery. Subject to periodic episodes of cave-ins and landslides, and exposing the groundwater to contamination, it was turned into a dumpsite.

Figure 5.10. A lost soul in a quarry. Screen capture, *N-Able* (2014), directed by Eleonora Danco.

As Enrico Cesaretti demonstrates in *Elemental Narratives*, with his sophisticated analysis of "narratives of marble," this is a quite common story for quarries in Italy. "Quarries," he writes, referring to Apuan marble quarries, "have been contributing to the degradation of the local natural landscape, flora, and fauna (e.g., mountaintop removals, waste deposits, abandoned pits, and rivers and aquifers polluted by debris, fine marble dust, and hydrocarbons)" while also affecting the health and financial stability of local communities.[62] The quarry that Danco chooses as the site of Lost Soul's drifting is one of the 475 inactive quarries in the Latium region and one of 5,592 similar quarries in Italy.[63]

Quarries are representations of the Anthropocene par excellence. They are places where humans extract from the earth according to perceived need, sites where the earth has rendered previous life—the small invertebrate animals described by Horowitz—into limestone to be used for the renderings of human civilization. The quarry is a legacy of past life and an enabler of civilization, from ancient to contemporary. It is both earth laid bare as well as a scar upon its flesh. At the same time, the quarry is a tomb, both a vessel and container of what is no longer living, a memorial. And, in the process of extraction, there is an inevitable mourning for what, and whom, has been lost.

N-Able's tormented protagonist has lost her mother. Her corpse, although kept off-screen, symbolically lies in this quarry (fig. 5.10). While standing in the void, Lost Soul recalls the experience of seeing cadavers. As heard throughout the film, Danco mixes different tones and adds a playful note to a horrifying image. Absurdly, the memory of a dead man, a janitor from her school, whose face,

Figure 5.11. Permission to swim. Screen capture, *N-Able* (2014), directed by Eleonora Danco.

she thought, resembled a withered apple, overlaps with that of her mother: "This evening, Mom, my heart aches, because I want to feel your arm. . . . Your face was twisted, Mom. You had stockings without shoes. Flowers in hands across your stomach. Your mouth was open, and your nails were purple. They pushed me into the mortuary when the school janitor died. All allowed. I stopped eating apples because it seemed I was eating the janitor."

The jumble of confused thoughts and memories, spoken in such a suggestive setting, articulates the daughter's desire for "a brief reunion with the mother," permeated by ambivalent feelings. The scene, while inspiring compassion, leaves us with the vivid verbal image of a decomposing body.[64] The corpse, as Kristeva famously wrote, "seen without God and outside of science, is the utmost of abjection," a sense of repugnance involved in the process of differentiation from "the other."[65]

Abjection turns rapidly into moving tenderness when Lost Soul appears, via the umpteenth radical cut, walking (or sleepwalking) in her pajamas along a declining street of Rome, addressing her mother and sharing once again the emotional drifting that might come with grieving a loss: "What a confusion, Mom. What a confusion inside and outside of me that throws me from one place to another. But I have all these memories in my eyes that save my life. With all my tears, my most beautiful tears. You'll see, Mom. It'll be fine. Like always, right?"

Not entirely banned from the narrative, the mother, her back still to the camera but with arms open in a loving, enabling gesture, reappears on the beach and speaks the final words of the film: "Sono le undici, fatevi il bagno!" (It's eleven, go for a swim!).[66] She grants everyone permission to dive into the water. Moving from the quarry-tomb-vessel, to a quiet street, to an airy, deserted beach, we are left with a jumble of confused thoughts, memories, images, and a mix of ambivalent feelings: grief, disgust, longing, tenderness, and exhilarating anticipation, as Lost Soul runs toward the sea and remains suspended on the liminal space of the seashore, a moment before diving in, in a moment of *becoming*, or, in Danco's words, in a "condition of perennial yearning."[67]

NOTES

1. Di Giammarco, "Eleonora Danco, guardo al futuro con i vecchi film." Eleonora Danco speaks about writing during the shelter-in-place imposed due to the global COVID-19 pandemic.

2. Sainati, "Eleonora Danco, il suo è un teatro elettrico."

3. Eleonora Danco, interview by author, New York, June 10, 2015 (my translation).

4. Derrida, *H.C. for Life, That Is to Say*, 7.

5. In its memorandum on the New Italian Epic, the Italian collective Wu Ming uses the expression "unidentified narrative objects" to refer to experimental literary works produced in Italy after 2000 that crossed the porous border of fiction and nonfiction. See Willman, *Unidentified Narrative Objects and the New Italian Epic*, 21. Among the most popular Italian UNOs is Roberto Saviano's *Gomorrah* (2006).

6. Aprà, *Fuori norma*. Among the films I discuss in this book, Francesca Fini's *Ofelia non annega* (Ophelia Does Not Drown, 2016) might be also considered a UCO, an unidentifiable cinematic object. I dedicate to Fini's film a *fegatello*, in Italian film jargon a connecting scene or detail.

7. Papazian and Eades, *The Essay Film*, 6.

8. De Chirico's painting *Interno metafisico con biscotti* (Metaphysical Interior with Biscuits) provides inspiration for one of the transition shots (or acts of resistance) of the film, in which Lost Soul lies in a bathtub full of Gentilini biscuits, a traditional Italian brand of cookies.

9. "Psychogeographic Destination Kit," *Bureau of Unknown Destinations*, accessed September 10, 2020, http://unknowndestinations.org/files/destination _kit_1_0.pdf. This is an art project by Brooklyn-based artist Sal Randolph developed at the interdisciplinary gallery Proteus Gowanus in 2012.

10. Danco refers to her tableaux as "memory installations" in our interview. Eleonora Danco, interview by author, Zoom, September 6, 2021 (my translation).

11. Eleonora Danco, interview by author, New York, June 10, 2015 (my translation).
12. Deleuze, *Cinema 2*, 266.
13. De Certeau, *The Practice of Everyday Life*, 98.
14. Coverley, *Psychogeography*, 82.
15. Debord, "Introduction to a Critique of Urban Geography," 8.
16. Coverley, *Psychogeography*, 84.
17. Debord, "Theory of the Dérive," 62.
18. Debord, 62.
19. Albrecht, *Earth Emotions*, 39.
20. Danco's play *Nessuno ci guarda* is published in Danco, *Ero purissima*.
21. Eleonora Danco, interview by author, New York, June 10, 2015 (my translation).
22. Eleonora Danco, interview by author, Rome, June 20, 2018 (my translation).
23. Butler, *Women's Cinema*, 61.
24. As discussed in chapter 1, in *Traveling with Cecilia*, a participatory documentary film, directors Mangini and Barbanente are almost always in the scene as they conduct walking interviews. While many of the films I examine in these chapters have strong autobiographical components that became known to me only through interviewing the directors, *N-Able* is the only one that explicitly deals with the director's life.
25. Eleonora Danco, interview by author, Rome, June 20, 2018 (my translation).
26. Lebow, *The Cinema of Me*, 3.
27. Uva, *L'ultima spiaggia*, 13.
28. Uva, 73.
29. See Miller, *Subject to Change*.
30. Luciano and Scarparo, *Reframing Italy*, 66. One of the most compelling examples of this search for a female genealogy, as scholars such as Laura Mulvey and Emma Wilson also have explored, is Alina Marazzi's *Un'ora sola ti vorrei* (*For One More Hour with You*, 2002), a film often mentioned in relation to *N-Able*, which, incidentally, has the same producer, Angelo Barbagallo.
31. Silverman, *The Acoustic Mirror*, 72.
32. Silverman, 73.
33. Luciano and Scarparo conceive the act of reframing as a feminist reconfiguration. They argue that contemporary women directors in Italy "have reframed cinematic tradition by appropriating and rethinking ways of imagining Italy through realistic cinema and less conventional cinematic modes and by challenging traditional representations of women through female-centered narratives." Luciano and Scarparo, *Reframing Italy*, 9.

34. In *N-Able*, the quest for the mother is also pursued through the interviews of the father, the adolescents, and elderly people. Danco often asks her subjects, as part of their performances, to repeatedly call their mother. By doing so, she intimately connects with the interviewees and accesses their most fragile selves, the ones longing for their mother. This sense of vulnerability is enhanced by the fact that their call, like Lost Soul's, remains answered.

35. Luciano and Scarparo, *Reframing Italy*, 67.

36. Debord, "Theory of the Dérive," 62.

37. As Danco recounts in our conversation, her peculiar choice of costume was inspired by some comedies of Aristophanes she was reading during the development of the film.

For a definition of *genius loci*, see *A Dictionary of Architecture and Landscape Architecture*, 2nd ed., s.v. "genius loci": "Latin term meaning 'the genius of the place,' referring to the presiding deity or spirit. Every place has its own unique qualities, not only in terms of its physical makeup, but of how it is perceived, so it ought to be (but far too often is not) the responsibilities of the architect or landscape-designer to be sensitive to those unique qualities, to enhance them rather than to destroy them." Sebastiano Brandolini writes about contemporary architecture being considered "out of place" in Rome. *Roma: Nuova Architettura*, 19.

38. Cederna, *I vandali in casa*, 106. Cederna's book *Mussolini urbanista* features Mussolini brandishing a pickax.

39. Cederna, 45.

40. Eleonora Danco, interview by author, Rome, May 10, 2018 (my translation).

41. Calvino, *Difficult Loves*, 123.

42. Calvino, 123.

43. Eleonora Danco, interview by author, Rome, June 20, 2018 (my translation).

44. Strazulla, "War and Peace," 1.

45. Ourossoff, "An Oracle of Modernism in Ancient Rome."

46. Earth First! Italia (il blog 2007–2011): Blog di cultura ecologista, radicale e biocentrica. http://earthfirstitalia.blogspot.com/2009/12/earth-first-act-now.html.

47. The construction site as symbolic of societal transformation and potential crisis is central to Pasolini's poem "Il pianto della scavatrice" (The Tears of the Excavator), part of his 1957 renowned collection of poems *Le ceneri di Gramsci* (*The Ashes of Gramsci*), in which Pasolini meditated on the boundless growth of Rome's peripheries in the years of the economic miracle. For a detailed analysis of this poem, see Rhodes, "Pasolini, the Peripheral Sublime and Public Housing."

48. Nocera, *Metro C*, 29.

49. Nocera, 19.

50. In this scene, a streetcar billboard in the background shows the smiling face of Barbara D'Urso, a popular television host. While it is likely that the passage of the street might have been fortuitous, the protest against concrete, and potentially against the ruthless ongoing sprawling of the city, is linked to television culture, a link confirmed by Danco and Rohrwacher, as discussed in chapter 4.

51. Brandolini, *Roma: Nuova Architettura*, 12.

52. Several film critics speak of *N-Able* as a sort of remake of Pier Paolo Pasolini's documentary film 1963 *Comizi d'amore* (*Love Meetings*), an investigation Pasolini conducted during the period of Italy's economic miracle on people's ideas on sexuality, which revealed widespread misogyny and profound prejudices against homosexuality. Pasolini's influence on Danco's film is undeniable, principally through its exploration of youth living on Roman peripheries and its adoption of an antimodernist discourse, and that a substantial part of *N-Able* includes interviews exploring similar topics as *Love Meetings* (with both young and elderly people shockingly holding the same prejudices that Pasolini uncovered over fifty years ago). Nonetheless, Danco's film can by no means be classified as a documentary, even in the loose sense that the term *documentary film* has come to acquire in the last decade. Eleonora Danco, interview by author, Rome, May 10, 2018 (my translation).

53. Degen and Rose, "The Sensory Experiencing of Urban Design," 3282.

54. Gibelli, "Urban Crisis or Urban Decay?" 90.

55. Parikka, *A Geology of Media*, 61.

56. I discuss the definition of *autonomous landscape* in chapter 3. See Lefebvre, "Between Setting and Landscape in the Cinema," 19–59.

57. Nicholas Malone and Kathrin Ovenden provide the following definition of the neologism *natureculture*: "Natureculture is a synthesis of nature and culture that recognizes their inseparability in ecological relationships that are both biophysically and socially formed."

58. Horowitz, *On Looking*, 52. Along the same lines, Cesaretti speculates on marble's "dynamic sedimentation and metamorphoses." *Elemental Narratives*, 91.

59. Horowitz's explanation of the formation of limestone echoes Jeffrey Cohen's "Stories of Stone," in which, as summarized by Enrico Cesaretti, he "invites us to reconsider the supposed inertia and muteness of the stone." See also Bennett, *Vibrant Matter*.

60. I reflect on the vulnerability of Italian landscape in my article on Alice Rohrwacher's *Happy as Lazzaro*. See Di Bianco, "Ecocinema ars et praxis: *Lazzaro felice*," 11.

61. I am referring to a calcareous monolith called La cattedrale, also known as La rava di San Domenico, and other stunning karstic formations located in the

Park of Campo Soriano in Latium, featured in *N-Able* as a background of scenes involving the youth of Terracina.

62. Cesaretti, *Elemental Narratives*, 93.

63. "Legambiente, rapporto cave, 2014: una cava su sette è nel Lazio" (Legambiente, Quarry Report, 2014: One Quarry out of Seven Is in Latium. *Legambiente Lazio*, April 20, 2014, https://www.legambientelazio.it/legambiente-rapporto-cave-2014-una-cava-su-sette-e-nel-lazio/.

64. Luciano and Scarparo, *Reframing Italy*, 67.

65. In "Revisiting the Belly of Naples," O'Healy adopts Kristeva's concept of abjection in her analysis of Mario Martone's *L'amore molesto* (Troubling Love), adapted from Elena Ferrante's novel. The film, incidentally, opens with the image of a naked elderly woman floating in the sea. She is the protagonist's mother.

66. Lost Soul's mother, in her last words, uses the second-person plural, therefore addressing not only her daughter but also other imaginary children.

67. Eleonora Danco, interview by author, Rome, June 20, 2018 (my translation).

Fegatello: *In This World*

A ROCKY MOUNTAIN LANDSCAPE EMERGES from the mist rolling over it. A herd of sheep and goats grazes peacefully, seemingly oblivious, like rocks, to the changing conditions. The camera moves almost imperceptibly, framing in a long take a high-altitude pasture. Colors are changing, tenuous, shapes are blurred, animals into stones, grass against soil.

A nonhuman soundscape fills the frames: bells jingling, wind blowing, insects buzzing. A few inquisitive goats acknowledge, for a moment, the presence of the camera, then climb gracefully on rocks, the sound of their hooves clattering. As the fog thins, a human figure appears, walking slowly with a stick, followed by dogs panting: the shepherd. *She* looks around and, talking to herself, or to the camera intimately close to her, says, "I might still find it." The shepherd has lost a lamb. She sits on a rock and observes the surroundings. She recounts the harshness of the environment in which her flock grazes—hard grass brings on fever, feet become tender, and the animals lose their vigor. She nurses them with medicine, and they are restored to health.

This is the mesmerizing beginning of Anna Kauber's *In questo mondo* (In This World, 2018), a riveting and unselfconscious documentary film on the lives of women shepherds in Italy. With its slow and contemplative pace, it asks us to patiently observe and listen while preparing us for the wonders and beauty that a rural journey through Italy brings into view. Enclosing the narrative in a circular structure, the film also ends with this dreamlike scenario: a woman shepherd leading a flock.

A traditionally male job in a patriarchal rural world, pastoralism is embraced by the women portrayed in this film as a life of freedom and emancipation from the constraints of domestic and urban life, as well as symbiosis with nature and

Figure 5.12. Maria Pia, a shepherd. Photo by Anna Kauber. *In This World* (2018), directed by Anna Kauber. Director's personal archive.

nonhuman animals. "My home is everywhere I go, from here to Friuli!" says a cheerful young shepherd who plays the violin for her flock while practicing transhumance. And despite the physical challenges, the meager financial rewards, and the difficult social relationships that their nomadic lifestyle entails (not to mention the stench), many others—women of different ages, social backgrounds, and education—share the joy of taking care of the animals, the continuous movement, the freedom from domestic constraints.

Anna Kauber, who calls herself a director, a writer, and a *paesaggista* (a landscaper), vividly communicates that contentment throughout the film while accompanying the numerous protagonists in their daily lives, regulated by the animals' needs, often harsh natural environments, and the change of seasons. An unobtrusive, off-screen presence, she and her camera incessantly follow the wandering shepherds and their flocks through the high grasslands and the valleys, taking us out to pasture, letting us witness the milking, the birth of a lamb, and (alas) even the bloody slaughter of a sheep. Sometimes she pauses to observe nonhuman animals, who often powerfully return the gaze. Via the fine editing of Esmeralda Calabria, the choral tale takes us from region to region, through Italy's stunning landscapes and peculiar dialects.

In questo mondo is a beautiful example of what I call ecocinema *ars et praxis*, which places the relationships among humans, nonhumans, and the environment at the center of film narration. It shows a modus vivendi outside the logic of profit and consumption, and coherently with the world it presents, it employs an environmentally conscious filmmaking practice. Kauber, in fact, is a one-woman crew, who irrespective of the budget constraints of a self-production travels (with her yellow Panda car running on methane) and films at a slow pace, eager to contemplate, listen, and share.[1]

NOTE

1. A longer version of this piece, including an interview of Anna Kauber, was published on the website Gynocine, an online archive of interviews of women directors (https://www.gynocine.com/interview-kauber).

EPILOGUE

The Cities of Women

A HAZY CITYSCAPE FADES IN, framed by a large window. Crossing the screen is a woman who stands meditatively in front of the panorama, her back to the camera. She slowly exits the scene while the camera continues panning, following her gaze over the cityscape; another woman walks along a blustery dirt path, the sea in the background, her head down, her eyes on her road; a girl stands on the roof of an unfinished building gazing at a peripheral cityscape; her blurred silhouette on the left edge of the frame fades into rows of half-built *palazzi* (buildings). A barren, open space foregrounding two building blocks separated by a white-clouded blue sky appears abruptly; a girl, seen from the street, plays on a balcony. Another girl enters a culvert and walks slowly, precariously through the water. A man drags the body of a dead woman and dumps her on a pile of garbage under a freeway overpass. A musician plays the cello to a sparse audience that sits at a distance from one another on the steps of a white marble building, in cold light. A woman walks along a construction site. Another, framed in a crane shot, walks hastily through a deserted alley. Pedestrians pass, indifferent to the impressive marble sculpture of an erect middle finger in between two columns. The camera pans over a coastal town: marinas, boats, and umbrellas and a narrow strip of beach separates houses from the water. A girl walks down a street through a torrent of refuse scattered by the wind. A woman wearing a white tunic walks slowly, brandishing a pickax. She stops to pound the pavement. Meanwhile, the little girl who walks with trepidation through the water-filled tunnel has reached a trash-strewn beach. She stares at the sea, her back to the camera.

A few years ago, my friend, the artist Marinella Senatore, and I made a four-minute video entitled *Le città delle donne* (*The Cities of Women*), a montage of clips from all the films I had been examining while mapping women's cinema in Italy. Connecting steps and aligning gazes of women and girls, their trajectories and fields of view, we composed an on-foot, visual journey throughout a few Italian cities: Milan, Naples, Rome, Taranto, Catania, and Reggio Calabria. As I have always been fascinated by the meanings generated by the juxtaposition of images, I wanted to experiment using editing to develop writing.

My video research diary proved to be a useful tool to observe how the recurrent visual trope of the female city walker—the flaneuse, a woman who embarks on journeys throughout the city and scrutinizes its landscapes—constitutes a shared narrative strategy as well as a distinctive trait of the mise-en-scène. Indeed, in nearly all the films I screened, and as my description of the video let readers imagine, the camera would frequently follow the characters' walks along the streets in tracking shots. City views were shown through bird's-eye shots, presented as subjective camerawork, or through long takes that would frame, at the shot's edge, women pausing along the way to look at the landscape.

As I return to that video while writing this epilogue, I retrace the trajectories of *Wandering Women* from Marina Spada's view of Milan from the Torre Branca in *As the Shadow* to the Ionian Sea seen from Reggio Calabria's shore in Alice Rohrwacher's *Corpo Celeste*. I pause to commemorate the films left out from the final cut of the book, those discovered later and added in the unconventional form of the *fegatello*, and the unexpected discoveries I made while unearthing layers of meaning in women's nomadic narratives.

As the five chapters and the interludes that connect them discuss, women, as represented in these films, are often lonely and estranged from the world. They have suffered losses, they struggle to reconcile paid work and motherhood, or to embrace motherhood, but they also give voice to resilient communities, make gestures of hospitality, find the strength to fight abuses, learn to care, and spiritedly defend beauty; they take walks of mourning, they embark upon searches for lost friends and mothers (symbolic and real), they undertake marches of protest, and they take journeys of awakening and self-discovery to reengage with the world. They take life-restoring walks.

The Italian landscapes they behold from their peripheral positions are not the pleasing, harmonious views of the *Belpaese* but rather shifting, troubling landscapes of the Anthropocene, glimpses of "the loneliest and most disconsolate places."[1] The views from above that so often appear through these films show overwhelmingly built-up landscapes, streets strewn with garbage, or improbably sanitized, antiseptic streets. Piazzas that would normally appear teeming with people are empty, rather eerie. I repeatedly interrogated these voids, as the signifier of the absences of members of the community lost to pollution-induced illnesses or to the pandemic we—at the time of this writing—live in; the lack of nurturing mothers; individuals' (not only women's) isolation and invisibilities; uncertainties about the past and the future.

Green spaces are alarmingly absent in the cities represented in these films or reduced to a stretch of grass between the remains of a stone wall and the highway, an interstice on which a small flock of sheep might graze. But the sea, as a "silent epiphany," is often revealed at the end of the journey, bringing hope for cities built to sustain life.[2] As I have contended, we must see these landscapes to be aware of the progress of the Anthropocene and accept the invitation to reimagine those empty piazzas, streets, and alleys not merely as "pretrauma" scenarios or mournful landscapes but also as spaces of possibility, where communities might form and thrive.[3]

All the films analyzed in *Wandering Women*, with different degrees of ecological engagement, expose the entanglement of gender inequality, social injustice, alienation, violence, and the deterioration of the environment. Instances of an ecocinema, they cannot alone heal ecosystems, but they can, as Paula Willoquet Marcondi contends, lead to concrete changes in how individuals and societies live locally and globally.[4] Indeed, this is a minor cinematic production that, although deeply embedded in its national cinematic tradition, far transcends its national character in its treatment of women's conditions in contemporary society and for the ecological concerns it expresses. Thus, if released from invisibility, (women's) ecocinema can have a global impact. Films, as Sophie Mayer writes, "enter our imagination, our intimate and political fantasies, they shape our interactions, our conversations, possibly our revolutions.... They are the storks that deliver us, and we can be the storks that deliver them."[5]

Delivering to readers-viewers ecologically engaged films that "do justice to peripheral narratives" and are themselves peripheral films is one of the vital tasks of ecoscholars, a collective endeavor to which this book gives only a modest contribution.[6] As Italian cinema continues to address ecological crises and the body of documentaries about environmental justice, stories of urban resistance, and cohabitation, eco-melodramas, and eco-comedies grows, hopefully reaching broader audiences, our work continues.

This work does not only deal with the present. If ecocriticism creates the tools to broaden the view and shift perspectives, we can reread (and rewrite) film history from a nonanthropocentric perspective. We need to look back at the silent era, or even to film's origins. And if we continue to dig in the archive, we might retrieve forgotten, prophetic films that in their times, when the Anthropocene had not yet been named, conceived filmmaking as an earth-centered form of storytelling. This is a feminist project that embraces what Doreen Massey defines as "a gender-disturbing message: 'keep moving'!"[7] Thus, I cannot help but end this book with one more *fegatello*, the last nomadic narrative, at least for now.

FEGATELLO: HUMANITY
BY ELVIRA GIALLANELLA

In 2007, on the occasion of a conference on the role of women in silent cinema, the National Film Archive of Rome recovered a remarkable film made in 1919: *Umanità* (*Humanity*), written, directed, and produced by a woman named Elvira Giallanella.[8] Unlike her contemporary Elvira Notari, whose career as director of Neapolitan silent melodrama was long and productive (although neglected for decades), the even lesser-known Giallanella directed only one film, visionary, dystopian, incongruous, and splintered as it was. She intended it (as the opening credits define it) as a humorous, satirical, and educational film.

A boy named Tranquillino dreams. The world has been destroyed by the Great War; only he and his sister Sirenetta have survived. God entrusts Tranquillino (under the guidance of a hobgoblin) with the task of remaking the world. Overwhelmed and amused at the same time, Tranquillino, accompanied by Sirenetta, wanders through rubble, with its carcasses of airplanes, helmets, and soldiers' boots, when he hears that nonhuman animals are alive and gathering in assembly. They want to rebuild the world in their own way. He decides to attend their congress, where he hears the presiding lion make a radical statement:

> È naturale ch'io proclami il disarmo universale. Ma finché avevo l'unghie per graffiare ditemi: come lo potevo fare? Ognun di noi viva lontano, e così almen, sarà vegetariano. Chi poi ciò nonostante da molestia sia detto Uomo e più non bestia. (It is natural that it is I who proclaims universal disarmament. But as long as I had my claws to scratch, tell me: How could I do it? We should all live apart, and so at least we will be vegetarian. Nevertheless, whoever will continue harming others should be called Man, and no longer a beast.)

Offended, Tranquillino wages war against the animals. But persuaded by his sister Sirenetta to desist from his violent actions, he returns—trowel in hand—to his world-building task. Despite his good deeds and intentions, he ends up launching a torpedo into the sea and once more deliberately commits a vicious crime against animals. A dying turtle calls him both cruel and a fool. God (in the semblance of a white-haired old man), applying the so-called Dilbert

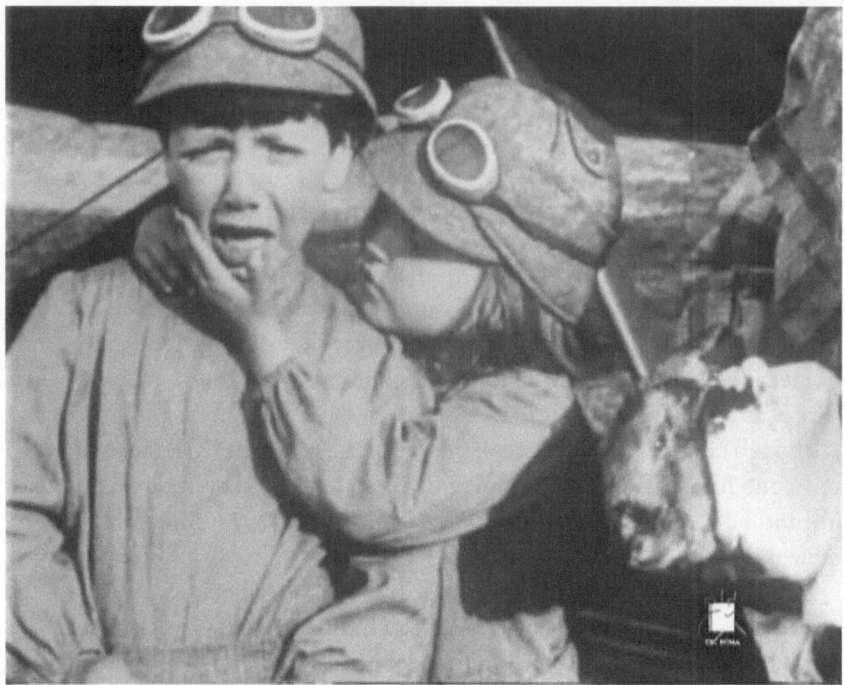

Figure E.1. Tranquillino, Sirenetta, and a nonhuman actor. Screen capture, *Humanity* (1919), directed by Elvira Giallanella.

principle of promoting someone so they can do less harm, takes him to Heaven. "[Tranquillino] si fece triste e non rifece il mondo" (Tranquillino became sad and did not rebuild the world), the caption says (fig. E.1).

Giallanella shifts from dream to reality and grafts documentary material to this fantasy, showing workers entering a factory, peasants harvesting wheat, and a shepherd grazing his flock. From Heaven, Tranquillino looks down at this peaceful world that (as suggested by the intertitle through hard work) will restore peace and prosperity. Though sister Sirenetta simply disappears from the scene, her pacifist impulse remains.

Humanity is a bizarre, visionary film and a remarkable cinematic effort for its time, shot *dal vero*, on the real ruins on the First World War, and in a zoo, engaging children and nonhuman actors. Most importantly, it might be one of the first examples—at least in the Italian context—of an ecofilm, imbued with Christian values, bearing witness to women's contributions to the pacifist movement that historically often intersected with environmentalism.

Even more original to our contemporary audience is the posthuman perspective that *Humanity* takes. Giallanella represents humankind as a destructive force, but she also envisions the possibility of a just world. In a radical decentering of man, nonhuman characters are given voice to deny human moral superiority and convey a pacifist message for a nonspeciesist world. Unwittingly or not, Giallanella's "humorous, satirical, and educational film" forges the path for the feminist ecocinema of today, one very much needed in the Anthropocene—a feminist ecocinema for all "earthothers," whose stories we "storks" continue to deliver.[9]

NOTES

1. Franco Arminio, "On Places and Looking: Italy's Silent Epiphanies," 110.
2. Arminio, 110.
3. See Ann E. Kaplan, *Climate Trauma*.
4. See Paula Willoquet-Maricondi, "Shifting Paradigms: From Environmentalist Films to Ecocinema," 45.
5. Sophie Mayer, *Political Animals*, 389.
6. Serenella Iovino, "Ecocriticism and a Non-Anthropocentric Humanism," 38.
7. Doreen Massey, *Space, Place, and Gender*, 11.
8. Micaela Veronesi, "Una donna vuol rifare il mondo. *Umanità* di Elvira Giallanella," 159–72.
9. I borrow the term *earthother* from leading feminist ecocritical thinker Greta Gaard. See Gaard, *Critical Ecofeminism*, xix. The image of the stork, as a metaphor for both stories that films tell and those who write about the films, comes from Sophie Mayer's *Political Animals*, referenced in this epilogue. Mayer, *Political Animals*, 389.

FILMOGRAPHY

Films are listed by their original title. I indicate in parentheses the English title in italics when a film was released with an English title, and in roman (that is, not italics) when it was not. When a film was released internationally with the original title, I only provide the original.

Accattone. 1961. Pier Paolo Pasolini. Italy.
All'armi siam fascisti (*To Arms! We Are Fascists*). 1962. Lino del Fra, Lino Miccichè, Cecilia Mangini. Italy.
Ambrogio. 1992. Wilma Labate. Italy.
Angelesse. 1991. Roberta Torre. Italy.
Arrivederci Saigon (Goodbye Saigon). 2018. Wilma Labate. Italy.
Bellissima. 1951. Luchino Visconti. Italy.
Biùtiful cauntri (Beautiful Country). 2007. Esmeralda Calabria and Andrea D'Ambrosio. Italy.
Brindisi '65. 1965. Cecilia Mangini. Italy.
Campania Infelix (Unhappy Campania). 2011. Ivana Corsale. USA, Italy.
Capriccio all'italiana (*Caprice Italian Style*). 1968. Mauro Bolognini, Mario Monicelli, Pier Paolo Pasolini, and Franco Rossi. Italy.
Carlo Giuliani, ragazzo (*Carlo Giuliani, Boy*). 2002. Francesca Comencini. Italy.
Checosamanca (What Is Missing). 2006. Chiara Bellosi, Marco Berrini, Enrico Cerasuolo, and Alice Rohrwacher. Italy.
Che cosa sono le nuvole? (*What Are the Clouds?*). 1968. Pier Paolo Pasolini. Italy.
Christine Cristina. 2009. Stefania Sandrelli. Italy.
Cléo de 5 à 7 (*Cléo from 5 to 7*). 1962. Agnes Varda. France.
Come l'ombra (As the Shadow). 2006. Marina Spada. Italy.
Comizi d'amore (*Love Meetings*). 1964. Pier Paolo Pasolini. Italy.

Corpo celeste. 2011. Alice Rohrwacher. Italy, Switzerland, France.
Documenti su Giuseppe Pinelli (Documents on Giuseppe Pinelli). 1970. Elio Petri and Nelo Risi. Italy.
Domenica. 2001. Wilma Labate. Italy.
Due scatole dimenticate (Two Forgotten Boxes). 2020. Cecilia Mangini and Paolo Pisanelli. Italy.
8 ½. 1963. Federico Fellini. Italy, France.
Essere donne (Being Women). 1965. Cecilia Mangini. Italy.
Firenze, il nostro domani (Florence Our Tomorrow). 2003. Francesca Comencini et al. Italy.
Forza cani (Come On, Dogs!). 2001. Marina Spada. Italy.
Gabriele Basilico. 2004. Marina Spada. Italy.
Gomorra (*Gomorrah*). 2008. Matteo Garrone. Italy.
Grazia Deledda, la rivoluzionaria (Grazia Deledda, the Revolutionary). 2021. Cecilia Mangini and Paolo Pisanelli. Italy.
I baci mai dati (Lost Kisses). 2010. Roberta Torre. Italy.
Ignoti alla città (Unknown in the City). 1958. Cecilia Mangini. Italy.
Il cielo in me: Vita irrimediabile di una poetessa (The Sky in Me: The Irreparable Life of a Poet). 2014. Sabrina Bonaiti and Marco Ongania. Italy.
Il deserto rosso (Red Desert). 1964. Michelangelo Antonioni. Italy, France.
Il grido (*The Outcry*). 1957. Michelangelo Antonioni. Italy, United States.
Il mio domani (*My Tomorrow*). 2011. Marina Spada. Italy.
Il tiburtino terzo (Tiburtino III). 2009. Roberta Torre. Italy.
In questo mondo (In this World). 2018. Anna Kauber. Italy.
Into Paradiso. 2010. Paola Randi. Italy.
In viaggio con Cecilia (My Travel with Cecilia). 2013. Mariangela Barbanente and Cecilia Mangini. Italy.
Io la conoscevo bene (*I Knew Her Well*). 1965. Antonio Pietrangeli. Italy, France, West Germany.
La bambina deve prendere aria (The Baby Needs Some Fresh Air). 2008. Barbara Rossi Prudente. Italy.
La briglia sul collo (The Bridle on the Neck). 1974. Cecilia Mangini. Italy.
La canta delle Marane (The Chant of Ditches). 1961. Cecilia Mangini. Italy.
La dolce vita. 1960. Federico Fellini. Italy, France.
Ladri di biciclette (Bicycle Thieves). 1948. Vittorio De Sica. Italy.
La gente resta (People Stay). 2015. Maria Tilli. Italy.
L'aggettivo donna (The Adjective Woman). 1971. Roni Daopuolo and Annabella Miscuglio. Italy.
La mia generazione (My Generation). 1996. Wilma Labate. Italy.
L'amore molesto (*Troubling Love*). 1995. Mario Martone. Italy.
La notte. 1961. Michelangelo Antonioni. Italy, France.

La notte quando è morto Pasolini (The Night Pasolini Was Murdered). 2009. Roberta Torre. Italy.
La pelle (*The Skin*). 1981. Liliana Cavani. Italy, France.
La terra trema. 1948. Luchino Visconti. Italy.
L'avventura. 1960. Michelangelo Antonioni. Italy, France.
Lazzaro felice (*Happy as Lazzaro*). 2018. Alice Rohrwacher. Italy, Switzerland, France, Germany.
L'eclisse. 1962. Michelangelo Antonioni. Italy, France.
Le meraviglie (*The Wonders*). 2014. Alice Rohrwacher. Italy, Switzerland, Germany.
Le notti di Cabiria (*Nights of Cabiria*). 1957. Federico Fellini. Italy, France.
Le parole di mio padre (The Words of My Father). 2001. Francesca Comencini. Italy, France.
Le ragazze di San Gregorio (The Girls of San Gregorio). 2009. Francesca Comencini. Italy.
Le sorelle Macaluso (The Macaluso Sisters). 2020. Emma Dante. Italy.
Lettere dalla Palestina (Letters from Palestine). 2003. Franco Angeli, Giuliana Berlinguer, Maurizio Carrassi, and Wilma Labate. Italy.
Le Vietnam sera libre (Vietnam Will Be Free). 2018. Cecilia Mangini and Paolo Pisanelli. Italy.
L'inverno (Winter). 2002. Nina Di Majo. Italy.
L'orchestra di Piazza Vittorio (The Orchestra of Piazza Vittorio). 2006. Agostino Ferrente. Italy.
Lo spazio bianco (*The White Space*). 2009. Francesca Comencini. Italy.
Mamma Roma. 1962. Pier Paolo Pasolini. Italy.
Mare nero (*The Dark Sea*). 2006. Roberta Torre. Italy, France.
Mi piace lavorare—Mobbing (I Like Working—Harassment). 2003. Francesca Comencini. Italy.
Mouchette. 1967. Robert Bresson. France.
My Marlboro City. 2010. Valentina Pedicini. Italy.
N-Capace (N-Able). 2014. Eleonora Danco. Italy.
Nina. 2012. Elisa Fuksas. Italy.
Non c'era nessuna signora a quel tavolo (There Wasn't a Lady at That Table). 2013. Davide Barletti and Lorenzo Conte. Italy.
Non perdono (I Do Not Forgive). 2016. Roberto Marsella and Grace Zanotto. Italy.
Ofelia non annega (Ophelia Does Not Drown). 2016. Francesca Fini. Italy.
Omelia Contadina (Funeral Homely). 2020. Alice Rohrwacher and JR. Italy.
Palermo bandita (Palermo Bandit). 1996. Roberta Torre. Italy.
Pasqualino settebelleze (*Seven Beauties*). 1975. Lina Wertmuller. Italy.
Per Sempre (Forever). 2005. Alina Marazzi. Italy, Switzerland.
Pianoforte. 1984. Francesca Comencini. Italy.
Poesia che mi guardi (Poetry You See Me). 2009. Marina Spada. Italy.

Qualcosa di noi (Something about Us). 2014. Wilma Labate. Italy.
Quando la notte (When the Night). 2011. Cristina Comencini. Italy.
Riccardo va all'inferno (Bloody Richard). 2017. Roberta Torre. Italy.
Roma città aperta (Rome, Open City). 1945. Roberto Rossellini. Italy.
Romanzo di una strage (Piazza Fontana: The Italian Conspiracy). 2012. Marco Tullio Giordana. Italy, France.
Roma ore 11 (Rome 11:00). 1952. Giuseppe De Santis. Italy.
Sátántangó. 1994. Béla Tarr. Hungary, Germany, Switzerland.
Shakespeare a Palermo (Shakespeare in Palermo). 1997. Francesca Comencini. Italy.
Signorina Effe (Miss F). 2007. Wilma Labate. Italy.
Stendalì, suonano ancora (Stendalì, Playing On). 1960. Cecilia Mangini. Italy.
Sud side stori (South Side Story). 2000. Roberta Torre. Italy.
Tano da morire (To Die for Tano). 1997. Roberta Torre. Italy.
Tommaso. 1965. Cecilia Mangini. Italy.
Tutto parla di te (All about You). 2012. Alina Marazzi. Italy, Switzerland, France.
Umanità (Humanity). 1919. Elvira Giallanella. Italy.
Un altro mondo è possibile (Another World Is Possible). 2001. Alfredo Angeli, Giorgio Arlorio, Mario Balsamo, and Wilma Labate. Italy.
Una montagna di balle (A Pile of Garbage). 2009. Nicola Angrisano. Italy.
Un complicato intrigo di donne, vicoli e delitti (Camorra: A Story of Streets, Women, and Crime). 1985. Lina Wërtmuller. Italy, Netherlands Antilles.
Un giorno speciale (A Special Day). 2012. Francesca Comencini. Italy.
Un'ora sola ti vorrei (For One More Hour with You). 2002. Alina Marazzi. Italy, Switzerland.
Uno virgola due (One Point Two). 2007. Silvia Ferreri. Italy.
Veleno (Poison). 2017. Diego Olivares. Italy.
Vesna va veloce (Vesna Goes Fast). 1996. Carlo Mazzacurati. Italy, France.
Vivre sa vie (My Life to Live). 1962. Jean-Luc Godard. France.

BIBLIOGRAPHY

Adorno, Theodor W. "The Essay as a Form." In *Notes to Literature,* edited by Rolf Tiedemann and translated by Shierry Weber Nicholsen, 13–23. New York: Columbia University Press, 1991.

Ahmed, Sara. "Happy Objects." In *The Affect Theory Reader,* edited by Melissa Gregg and Gregory J. Seigworth, 29–51. Durham: Duke University Press, 2010.

Alaimo, Stacy. "Insurgent Vulnerability and the Carbon Footprint of Gender." *Kvinder Køn & Forskning* 3, no. 3–4 (2009): 22–35. https://tidsskrift.dk/KKF/article/view/27969/24598.

Albrecht, Glenn A. *Earth Emotions: New Words for a New World.* Ithaca, NY: Cornell University Press, 2019.

Aleramo, Sibilla. *Una donna.* Milan: Feltrinelli, 2013.

Amelang, James S. "Mourning Becomes Eclectic: Ritual Lament and the Problem of Continuity." *Past & Present* 187, no. 1 (May 2005): 3–31. https://doi.org/10.1093/pastj/gti011.

Angelone, Anita. "Talking Trash: Documentaries and Italy's 'Garbage Emergency.'" *Studies in Documentary Film* 5, no. 2–3 (2011): 145–56.

Antonello, Pierpaolo. "The (Political) Forms of Technology: Antonioni, Olmi, De Seta, and Post–World War II Industrial Cinema." *The Italianist* 39, no. 2 (2019): 151–70.

Aprà, Adriano. *Fuori norma: La via sperimentale del cinema italiano.* Venice: Marsilio, 2013.

Arminio, Franco. "On Places and Looking: Italy's Silent Epiphanies." In *Italy and the Environmental Humanities: Landscapes, Natures, Ecologies,* edited by Serenella Iovino, Enrico Cesaretti, and Elena Past, 111–14. Charlottesville: University of Virginia Press, 2018.

Bakhtin, Michail. "Forms of Time and Chronotope in the Novel." In *The Dialogic Imagination: Four Essays*, edited by Michael Holquist and translated by Caryl Emerson and Michael Holquist 84–258. Austin: University of Texas Press, 1981.

Barthes, Roland. "The Death of the Author." In *Image, Music, Text*, edited and translated by Stephen Heath, 142–48. New York: Hill and Wang, 1977.

Baudelaire, Charles. *The Painter of Modern Life and Other Essays*. Translated by Jonathan Mayne. London: Phaidon, 1964.

Bauhardt, Christine, and Wendy Harcourt. "Introduction: Conversations on Care in Feminist Political Economy and Ecology." In *Feminist Political Ecology and the Economics of Care: In Search of Economic Alternatives*, 1–15. London: Routledge, 2019.

Bazin, André. *What Is Cinema?* Translated by Hugh Gray. Berkeley: University of California Press, 2005.

Benjamin, Walter. "Paris, the Capital of the Nineteenth Century." In *Selected Writings. Volume 3. 1935–1938*, edited by Howard Eiland and Michael W. Jennings, and translated by Edmund Jephcott, Howard Eiland, and Others. Cambridge, MA: Belknap Press, 2002.

Benjamin, Walter, and Asja Lacis. "Naples." In *Reflections: Essays, Aphorisms, Autobiographical Writings*, 163–76. Translated by Hannah Arendt. New York: Shocken, 1978.

Bennett, Jane. *Vibrant Matter: A Political Ecology of Things*. Durham, NC: Duke University Press, 2010.

Bernabò, Graziella. *Per troppa vita che ho nel sangue: Antonia Pozzi e la sua poesia*. Milan: Viennepierre, 2004.

Bertetto, Paolo. "Dall'ossessione alla rimozione: Figure del femminile negli autori degli anni Sessanta." In *Women in Italian Cinema: La donna nel cinema italiano*, edited by Caterina Tonia Riviello, 117–27. Rome: Edizioni Libreria Croce, 1999.

Bettinotti, Massimo, ed. *Kenzo Tange 1946–1996: Architettura e disegno urbano*. Rome: Electa, 1996.

Bevilacqua, Piero. "The Distinctive Character of Italian Environmental History." In *Nature and History in Modern Italy*, edited by Marco Armerio and Marcus Hall, 15–32. Athens: Ohio University Press, 2010.

Bowlby, Rachel. *Still Crazy after All These Years: Women, Writing, and Psychoanalysis*. London: Routledge, 1992.

Bowring, Jacky. *Melancholy and the Landscape: Locating Sadness, Memory and Reflection in the Landscape*. London: Routledge, 2017.

Braidotti, Rosi. "Afterword: The Proper Study of the Humanities Is No Longer 'Man.'" In *Italy and the Environmental Humanities: Landscapes, Natures, Ecologies*, edited by Serenella Iovino, Enrico Cesaretti, and Elena Past, 242–45. Charlottesville: University of Virginia Press, 2018.

———. *Nomadic Subjects: Embodiment and Sexual Difference in Contemporary Feminist Theory*. New York: Columbia University Press, 1994.

———. *The Posthuman*. Malden, MA: Polity Press, 2013.
Brandolini, Sebastiano. *Roma: Nuova Architettura*. Losanna, Italy: Skira editore, 2008.
Bruno, Giuliana. *Streetwalking on a Ruined Map: Cultural Theory and the City Films of Elvira Notari*. Princeton, NJ: Princeton University Press, 1993.
Bruno, Giuliana, and Maria Nadotti. *Off Screen: Women and Film in Italy*. New York: Routledge, 1988.
Buck-Morss, Susan. *The Dialectics of Seeing*. Cambridge, MA: MIT Press, 1989.
———. "The *Flâneur*, the Sandwichman and the Whore: The Politics of Loitering." *New German Critique* 39 (1986): 99–140.
Buffoni, Laura. *We want cinema: Sguardi di donne nel cinema italiano*. Venice: Marsilio, 2018.
Butler, Alison. *Women's Cinema: The Contested Screen*. New York: Wallflower, 2002.
Buzzati, Dino. *La famosa invasione degli orsi in Sicilia*. Florence: Giunti, 1966.
———. *Il segreto del bosco vecchio*. Milan: Mondadori, 2009.
Callahan, Vicki. *Reclaiming the Archive*. Detroit: Wayne State University, 2010.
Calvino, Italo. *Le città invisibili*. Turin, Italy: Einaudi, 1972.
———. *Difficult Loves; Smog; a Plunge into Real Estate*. Translated by William Weaver, D. S. Carne-Ross, and Ann Goldstein. London: Vintage Classics, 1999.
———. "La nuvola di smog." In *Romanzi e racconti*, edited by Claudio Milanini, 891–952. Milan: Mondadori, 1991.
Cardone, Lucia, Elena Marcheschi, and Giulia Simi, eds. "FAScinA 2020_Sperimentali: i contributi video," *Forum Annuale delle Studiose di Cinema e Audiovisivi*, accessed April 24, 2022, https://fascinaforum.org/fascina-2020-home/galleria-video-fascina-2020/.
Casson, Felice. *La fabbrica dei veleni*. Venice: La Toletta Edizioni, 2015.
Castelli, Valeria G. "The Filmmaker Is Present: Performance, Ethos, and Politics in *In viaggio con Cecilia* and *Io sto con la sposa*." *The Italianist* 38, no. 2 (2018): 235–57. https://doi.org/10.1080/02614340.2018.1477308.
Catalli, Claudia. "A Venezia Francesca Comencini: Ragazze non svendete la vostra bellezza." *Panorama*, September 7, 2012. http://cultura.panorama.it/cinema/.
Cavarero, Adriana. *Inclinations: Critique of Rectitude*. Stanford, CA: Stanford University Press, 2016.
Cederna, Antonio. *I vandali in casa*. Bari, Italy: Editori GFL Laterza, 1956.
———. *Mussolini Urbanista: Lo sventramento di Roma negli anni del consenso*. Venice: Corte del Fontego, 2006.
Cesaretti, Enrico. *Elemental Narratives: Reading Environmental Entanglements in Modern Italy*. University Park, PA: Penn State University Press, 2020.
Clarke, David. *The Cinematic City*. London: Routledge, 1997.
Conti, Francesca, and Giorgio Fonio. *I baci mai dati e altre storie: Il cinema irriverente di Roberta Torre*. Palermo, Italy: Edizioni di passaggio, 2011.
Conti, Laura. *Una lepre con la faccia di bambina*. Rome: Editori Riuniti, 1978.

Corona, Gabriella. *A Short Environmental History of Italy: Variety and Vulnerability.* Translated by Federico Poole. Cambridgeshire, UK: The White Horse Press, 2017.

Coverley, Merlin. *Psychogeography.* Harpenden, UK: Pocket Essentials, 2010.

Crainz, Guido. *Storia del miracolo italiano: Culture, identità, trasformazioni fra anni cinquanta e sessanta.* Rome: Donzelli editore, 2003.

Creed, Barbara. *The Monstrous-Feminine: Film, Feminism, Psychoanalysis.* London: Routledge, 1993.

Danco, Eleonora. *Ero purissima.* Rome: Minimum Fax, 2009.

Dassisti, Liliana, Angela Stufano, Piero Lovreglio, Luigi Vimercati, Pasquale Loconsole, and Ignazio Grattagliano. "Donne e uomini, autori e vittime di mobbing in Italia: Una revisione della letteratura." *La Medicina del Lavoro* 111, no. 6 (2020): 463–77.

D'Eaubonne, Françoise. *Le féminisme ou la mort.* Paris: Pierre Horay, 1974.

De Bonis, Maurizio G. "*Il mio domani*: Un film di Marina Spada." *CultFrame: Arti visive*, November 3, 2011. https://www.cultframe.com/2011/11/il-mio-domani-film-marina-spada/.

Debord, Guy. "Introduction to a Critique of Urban Geography." In *Situationist International Anthology*, edited and translated by Ken Knabb, 8–11. Berkeley, CA: Bureau of Public Secrets, 2006.

———. "Theory of the Dérive." In *Situationist International Anthology*, edited and translated by Ken Knabb, 62–66. Berkeley, CA: Bureau of Public Secrets, 2006.

De Certeau, Michel. *The Practice of Everyday Life.* Translated by Steven F. Rendall. Berkeley: University of California Press, 1984.

De Céspedes, Alba. *Dalla parte di lei.* Milan: Mondadori, 1949.

Degen, Monica Montserrat, and Gillian Rose. "The Sensory Experiencing of Urban Design: The Role of Walking and Perceptual Memory." *Urban Studies* 49, no. 15 (2012): 3271–87.

De Lauretis, Teresa. *Technologies of Gender.* Bloomington: Indiana University Press, 1987.

Deleuze, Gilles. *Cinema 2: The Time-Image.* Translated by Hugh Tomlinson and Robert Galeta. Minneapolis: University of Minnesota Press, 1989.

De Martino, Ernesto. *Morte e pianto rituale nel mondo antico: Dal lamento funebre antico al pianto di Maria.* Turin, Italy: Bollati Boringhieri, 2008.

———. *Sud e magia.* Milan: Feltrinelli, 2013.

De Pascalis, Ilaria. "La ricerca DEA-Donne e Audiovisivo: Il ruolo delle donne nell'industria dell'audiovisivo." In *We want cinema*, edited by Laura Buffoni, 259–66. Venice: Marsilio, 2018.

Derrida, Jacques. *H.C. for Life, That Is to Say.* Translated by Laurent Milesi and Stefan Herbrechter. Stanford, CA: Stanford University Press, 2006.

De Seta, Cesare. *Napoli*. Rome: Laterza, 1981.
Di Bianco, Laura. "Ecocinema *Ars et Praxis*: Alice Rohrwacher's *Lazzaro Felice*." *The Italianist* 40, no. 2 (2020): 151–64.
———. "La funzione salvifica dell'immigrato: *In to Paradiso* di Paolo Randi e *Mozzarella Stories* di Edoardo De Angelis." In *Italy A/R Migrazioni nel\del Cinema Italiano*, edited by Vito Zagarrio. Special issue, *Quaderni del CSCI: Rivista annual di cinema italiano* 8 (2012): 118–21.
———. "Interview with Alice Rohrwacher." In *Women Filmmakers and the Gendered Screen*, edited by Maristella Cantini, 247–52. New York: Palgrave Macmillan, 2013.
———. "Interview with Marina Spada." In *Women Filmmakers and the Gendered Screen*, edited by Maristella Cantini, 237–46. New York: Palgrave Macmillan, 2013.
———. "Women's Archiveology. Lost Mother, Found Footage." In *Radical Equalities and Global Feminist Filmmaking—An Anthology*, edited by Bernadette Wegenstein and Lauren Benjamin Mushro. Wilmington, DE: Vernon Press, 2022: 285–306.
Di Figlia, Luca. "Places in the Memory: Abandoned Villages in Italy." In *Proceedings of the Scholars Workshop on Architecture, Archeology, and Contemporary City Planning*, Florence, June 16–18, 2014, edited by Giorgio Verdiani and Per Cornell, 47–58.
Di Giammarco, Rodolfo. "Eleonora Danco, guardo al futuro con i vecchi film." *La Repubblica*, March 31, 2020.
"Dissenso Comune." *Il manifesto*, February 2, 2018. https://ilmanifesto.it/dissenso-comune/.
Doane, Mary Ann. "Woman's Stake: Filming the Female Body." *October* 17 (1981): 23–36.
D'Souza, Aruna, and Tom McDonogh, eds. *The Invisible Flâneuse? Gender, Public Space, and Visual Culture in Nineteenth-Century Paris*. Manchester, UK: Manchester University Press, 2006.
Faleschini Lerner, Giovanna. "Cybermoms and Postfeminism in Italian Web Series." *gender/sexuality/italy* 5 (2018): 142–59.
Faleschini Lerner, Giovanna, and Maria Elena D'Amelio. Introduction to *Italian Motherhood on Screen*, edited by Giovanna Faleschini Lerner and Maria Elena D'Amelio, 1–20. Cham, Switzerland: Palgrave Macmillan, 2015.
Ferrante, Elena. *La figlia oscura*. Rome: Edizioni e/o, 2015.
———. *L'amore molesto*. Rome: Edizioni e/o, 2015.
Ferrari, Ivano. *Slaughterhouse* (Macello). Translated by Matteo Gilebbi. Mineola, NY: Legas, 2019.
Fiore, Teresa. *Pre-Occupied Spaces: Remapping Italy's Transnational Migrations and Colonial Legacies*. New York: Fordham University Press, 2017.

Fiorini, Lorena, et al. "Land Take and Landscape Loss: Effect of Uncontrolled Urbanization in Southern Italy." *Journal of Urban Management* 8, no. 1 (April 2019): 42–56.

Foot, John. *Milan since the Miracle: City, Culture and Identity*. Oxford: Berg, 2001.

Forgacs, David. "Antonioni: Space, Place, Sexuality." In *Spaces in European Cinema*, edited by Myrto Konstantakaros, 101–11. Exeter, UK: Intellect, 2000.

Foucault, Michel. "Of Other Spaces." Translated by Jay Miskowiec. *Diacritics* 16, no. 1 (1986): 22–27.

Friedberg, Anne. *Window Shopping: Cinema and the Postmodern*. Berkeley: University of California Press, 1994.

Gaard, Greta. *Critical Ecofeminism*. London: Lexington Books, 2017.

Gaard, Greta, Simon C. Estok, and Serpil Oppermann, eds. *International Perspectives in Feminist Ecocriticism: Making a Difference*. London: Routledge, 2013.

Galetto, Manuela, Chiara Lasala, Sveva Magaraggia, Chiara Martuccie, Elisabetta Onori, and Charlotte Ross. "Feminist Activism and Practice: Asserting Autonomy and Resisting Precarity." In *Resisting the Tide: Cultures of Opposition under Berlusconi (2001–06)*, edited by Daniele Albertazzi, Clodagh Brook, Charlotte Ross, and Nina Rothenberg, 190–203. New York: Continuum, 2009.

Gandhy, Matthew. "The Cinematic Void: Desert Iconographies in Michelangelo Antonioni's *Zabriskie Point*." In *Landscape and Film*, edited by Martin Lefebvre, 315–32. New York: Routledge, 2006.

Garlaschelli, Barbara, and Valentina Pedicini. *Nostalgie urbane*. Florence, Italy: Editpress, 2021.

Gaybor, Jacqueline. "Menstrual Politics in Argentina and Diverse Assemblages of Care." In *Feminist Political Ecology and the Economics of Care: In Search of Economic Alternatives*, edited by Christine Bauhardt and Wendy Harcourt, 230–46. London: Routledge, 2019.

Gianicolo, Emilio Antonio Luca. "Acute Effects of Urban and Industrial Pollution in a Government-Designated 'Environmental Risk Area': The Case of Brindisi, Italy." *International Journal of Environmental Health Research* 23, no. 5 (2013): 446–60.

Gibelli, Maria Cristina. "Urban Crisis or Urban Decay? Italian Cities Facing the Effects of a Long Wave towards Privatization of Urban Policies and Planning." In *City of Crisis: The Multiple Contestation of Southern European Cities*, edited by Frank Eckardt and Javier Ruiz Sánchez, 89–108. Bielefeld, Germany: Transcript, 2015.

Gilebbi, Matteo. "Becoming Human in the Slaughterhouse." In *Slaughterhouse (Macello)*, by Ivano Ferrari, translated by Matteo Gilebbi. Mineola, New York: Legas, 2019.

———. "Witnessing the Slaughter: Human and Nonhuman Animals in Ivano Ferrari's Poetry." In *Italy and the Environmental Humanities: Landscapes,*

Natures, Ecologies, edited by Serenella Iovino, Enrico Casetti, and Elena Past, 47–56. Charlottesville: University of Virginia Press, 2018.

Gilloch, Graeme. *Myth and Metropolis: Walter Benjamin and the City*. Cambridge: Polity Press, 1996.

Glynn, Ruth. "Engendering Occupation: The Body as a War Zone in Liliana Cavani's *La pelle*." *Romance Notes* 55, no. 3 (2015): 345–55.

Grusin, Richard. *Anthropocene Feminism*. Minneapolis: University of Minnesota Press, 2017.

Harcourt, Wendy, and Christine Bauhardt. "Introduction: Conversations on Care in Political Feminist Economy and Ecology." In *Feminist Political Ecology and the Economics of Care: In Search of Economic Alternatives*, edited by Christine Bauhardt and Wendy Harcourt, 1–15. London: Routledge, 2019.

Harrison, Robert Pogue. *Gardens: An Essay on the Human Condition*. Chicago: University of Chicago Press, 2008.

Helbert, Maryse. "Australian Women in Mining: Still a Harsh Reality." In *Feminist Ecologies: Changing Environments in the Anthropocene*, edited by Lara Stevens, Peta Tai, and Denise Varney, 231–46. Cham, Switzerland: Palgrave Macmillan, 2018.

Heyer-Cáput, Margherita. *Grazia Deledda's Dance of Modernity*. Toronto: Toronto University Press, 2008.

Hipkins, Danielle. "'Whore-ocracy': Show Girls, the Beauty Trade-Off, and Mainstream Oppositional Discourse in Contemporary Italy." *Italian Studies* 66, no. 3 (2011): 413–30.

———. "Who Wants to Be a TV Showgirl? Auditions, Talent and Taste in Contemporary Popular Italian Cinema." *The Italianist* 32, no. 2 (2012): 154–90.

———. "Why Italian Film Studies Needs a Second Take on Gender." *Italian Studies* 63, no. 2 (Autumn 2008): 213–34.

Horowitz, Alexandra. *On Looking: A Walker's Guide to the Art of Observation*. New York: Scribner, 2013.

Horowitz, Jason. "In Italy, #MeToo Is More Like 'Meh.'" *New York Times*, December 16, 2017. https://www.nytimes.com/2017/12/16/world/europe/italy-sexual-harassment.html.

Iovino, Serenella. "Ecocriticism and a Non-Anthropocentric Humanism: Reflections on Local Natures and Global Responsibilities." In *Local Natures, Global Responsibilities: Ecocritical Perspectives on the New English Literatures*, edited by Laurenz Volkmann, Nancy Grimm, Ines Detmers, and Katrin Thomson, 29–54. Amsterdam: Rodopi, 2010.

———. "Naples 2008, or, the Waste Land: Trash, Citizenship, and an Ethic of Narration." *Neohelicon* 36, no. 2 (2009): 335–46.

———. "Restoring the Imagination of Place: Narrative Reinhabitation and the Po Valley." In *The Bio-Regional Imagination: Literature, Ecology, and Place*, edited by

Tom Lynch, Cheryll Glotfelty, and Karla Armbruster, 110–17. Athens: University of Georgia Press, 2012.

———. "Toxic Epiphanies: Dioxin, Power, and Gendered Bodies in Laura Conti's Narratives on Seveso." In *International Perspectives in Feminist Ecocriticism*, edited by Greta Gaard, Simon C. Estok, and Serpil Oppermann, 37–54. London: Routledge, 2013.

Johnston, Claire. "Women's Cinema as Counter-cinema." In *Notes on Women's Cinema*, edited by Claire Johnston, 24–31. London: Society for Education in Film and Television, 1973.

Kaplan, E. Ann. "The Case of the Missing Mother: Maternal Issues in Vidor's *Stella Dallas*." In *Feminism and Film*, edited by E. Ann Kaplan, 466–78. New York: Oxford University Press, 2000.

———. *Climate Trauma: Foreseeing the Future in Dystopian Film and Fiction*. New Brunswick, NJ: Rutgers University Press, 2016.

———. "Traumatic Dystopian Futurist Scenarios: Documentary Film, Gender, and Witnessing in Jennifer Baichwal's *Manufactured Landscapes*." In *Contemporary Women's Cinema, Global Scenarios and Transnational Contexts*, edited by Veronica Pravadelli, 15–28. Milan: Mimesis International, 2017.

Karagoz, Claudia. "Motherhood Revisited in Francesca Comencini's *Lo spazio bianco*." In *Italian Women Filmmakers and the Gendered Screen*, edited by Maristella Cantini, 103–19. New York: Palgrave Macmillan, 2013.

Kristeva, Julia. *Powers of Horror: An Essay on Abjection*. Translated by Leon S. Roudiez. New York: Columbia University Press, 1982.

Lakhous, Amara. *Scontro di civiltà per un ascensore a piazza Vittorio*. Rome: Edizioni e/o, 2011.

Lebow, Alisa, ed. *The Cinema of Me: The Self and Subjectivity in First Person Documentary*. London: Wallflower Press, 2009.

Lefebvre, Martin. "Between Setting and Landscape in the Cinema." In *Landscape and Film*, edited by Martin Lefebvre, 19–60. New York: Routledge, 2006.

Lewis, Charlton T., and Charles Short. *A Latin Dictionary*. Oxford: Clarendon Press, 1879.

Longo, Abele. "Palermo in the Films of Ciprì and Maresco." In *Italian Cityscapes: Culture and Urban Change in Contemporary Italy*, edited by Robert Lumley and John Foot, 187–95. Exeter: University of Exeter Press, 2004.

Lucamente, Stefania. "A Quiet Revolution: Illness as Resilience in Grazia Deledda's *La chiesa della solitudine*." *Modern Language Review* 115, no. 1 (2020): 83–106.

Luciano, Bernadette, and Susanna Scarparo. "Gendering Mobility and Migration in Contemporary Italian Cinema." *The Italianist* 30, no. 2 (2010): 165–82.

———. "Maternal Ambivalence in Contemporary Italian Cinema." In *Italian Motherhood on Screen*, edited by Giovanna Faleschini Lerner and Maria Elena D'Amelio, 45–70. Cham, Switzerland: Palgrave Macmillan, 2017.

———. *Reframing Italy: New Trends in Italian Women's Filmmaking*. West Lafayette, IN: Purdue University Press, 2013.

Lukács, György. "On the Nature and Form of the Essay." In *Soul and Form*, edited by John T. Sanders and Katie Terezakis, and translated by Anna Bostock, 1–19. London: Merlin Press, 1974.

MacDonald, Scott. "The Ecocinema Experience." In *Ecocinema Theory and Practice*, edited by Stephen Rust, Salma Monani, and Sean Cubitt, 17–42. New York: Routledge, 2013.

———. "Toward an Eco-Cinema," *ISLE: Interdisciplinary Studies in Literature and Environment* 11, no. 2 (2004): 107–32.

Malaparte, Curzio. *La pelle*. Milan: Adelphi, 2010.

Malone, Nicholas, and Katrin Ovenden. "Natureculture." In *The International Encyclopedia of Primatology*, edited by Agustin Fuentes. Hoboken: John Wiley & Sons, 2017. https://doi.org/10.1002/9781119179313.wbprim0135.

Marcomin, Franca, and Laura Cima, eds. *L'ecofemminismo in Italia: Le radici di una rivoluzione necessaria*. Padua: Il Poligrafo, 2017.

Marcus, Millicent. "Postmodern Pastiche, the *Sceneggiata*, and the View of the Mafia from Below in Roberta Torre's *To Die for Tano*." In *After Fellini: National Cinema in the Postmodern Age*, 234–49. Baltimore: Johns Hopkins University Press, 2002.

———. "Unnatural Child Birth: Naples, the Neo-Natal Intensive Care Unit, and the Blank Space of Possibility in Francesca Comencini's *Lo spazio bianco*." In *Italian Motherhood on Screen*, edited by Giovanna Faleschini Lerner and Maria Elena D'Amelio, 195–210. Cham, Switzerland: Palgrave Macmillan, 2017.

Marini-Maio, Nicoletta. "The Children Are Still Watching Us: The 'Visual-Psyco-Mimesis' of *Il cielo cade* and *Certi bambini*." In *Coming of Age on Film: Stories of Transformation in World Cinema*, edited by Anne Hardcastle, Roberta Morosini, and Kendall Tarte, 40–55. Newcastle, UK: Cambridge Scholars, 2009.

Marlow-Mann, Alex. *The New Neapolitan Cinema*. Edinburgh: Edinburgh University Press, 2011.

Massey, Doreen. *Space, Place, and Gender*. Minneapolis: University of Minnesota Press, 1994.

Mayers, Sophie. *Political Animals: The New Feminist Cinema*. London: I. B. Tauris, 2016.

Miller, Nancy K. *Subject to Change: Reading Feminist Writing*. New York: Columbia University Press, 1990.

Missero, Dalila. "Cecilia Mangini: A Counterhegemonic Experience of Cinema." *Feminist Media Histories* 2, no. 3 (2016): 54–72.

Modini, Laura. Perché desidero che tutte/i vedano il film *Come l'ombra* di Marina Spada." https://www.libreriadelledonne.it/_oldsite/news/articoli/contrib201206.htm.

Momigliano, Anna. "'The Ferrante Effect': In Italy Women Writers Are Ascendant." *New York Times*, December 9, 2019. https://www.nytimes.com/2019/12/09/books/elena-ferrante-italy-women-writers.html.

Mortimer-Sandilands, Catriona. "Eco/feminism on the Edge: A Commentary." *International Feminist Journal of Politics* 10, no. 3 (2008): 305–13.

———. "An Ecofeminist Perspective in the Urban Environment." In *The Nature of Cities: Ecocriticism and Urban Environment*, edited by Michael Bennett and David W. Teague, 191–209. Tucson: University of Arizona Press, 1999.

Mulvey, Laura. *Afterimages: On Cinema, Women and Changing Times*. London: Reaktion Books, 2019.

———. *Visual and Other Pleasures*. Bloomington: Indiana University Press, 1989.

———. "Visual Pleasure and Narrative Cinema." *Screen* 16, no. 3 (1975): 6–18.

Nixon, Rob. *Slow Violence and the Environmentalism of the Poor*. Cambridge, MA: Harvard University Press, 2011.

Nocera, Enrico. *Metro C: Roma, capitale degli sprechi*. Rome: Round Robin Editrice, 2015.

O'Healy, Áine. "Anthropological Anxieties: Roberta Torre's Critique of Mafia Violence." In *Visions of Struggle in Women's Filmmaking in the Mediterranean*, edited by Flavia Laviosa and Laura Mulvey, 83–101. New York: Palgrave Macmillan, 2010.

———. "Are the Children Watching Us? The Roman Films of Francesca Archibugi." *Annali D'Italianistica* 17 (1999): 121–36.

———. "Border Traffic: Reimagining the Voyage to Italy." In *Transnational Feminism in Film and Media*, edited by Katarzyna Marciniak and Anikó Irme, 37–52. New York: Palgrave Macmillan, 2007.

———. "Revisiting the Belly of Naples: The Body and the City in the Films of Mario Martone." *Screen* 40, no. 3 (1999): 239–56.

Oppermann, Serpil. "A Posthumanist Direction in Ecocritical Trajectory." In *International Perspectives in Feminist Ecocriticism: Making a Difference*, edited by Greta Gaard, Simon C. Estok, and Serpil Oppermann, 19–55. London: Routledge, 2013.

Ortese, Anna Maria. *Corpo celeste*. Milan: Adelphi, 1997.

Ourossoff, Nicolai. "An Oracle of Modernism in Ancient Rome." *New York Times*, September 25, 2006. https://www.nytimes.com/2006/09/25/arts/design/an-oracle-of-modernism-in-ancient-rome.html.

Pandian, Anand. "Landscapes of Expression: Affective Encounters in South Indian Cinema." *Cinema Journal* 51, no. 1 (2011): 50–74.

Papazian, Elizabeth, and Caroline Eades. *The Essay Film: Dialogue, Politics, Utopia*. New York: Wallflower Press, 2016.

Parikka, Jussi. *A Geology of Media*. Minneapolis: University of Minnesota Press, 2015.

Pasolini, Pier Paolo. *Le ceneri di Gramsci*. Milan: Garzanti, 1957.
Past, Elena. "Documenting Ecomafia." In *Italian Political Cinema: Public Cinema, Public Life, Imaginary, and Identity in Contemporary Film*, edited by Giancarlo Lombardi and Christian Uva, 82–91. Bern, Switzerland: Peter Lang, 2016.
———. *Italian Ecocinema Beyond the Human*. Bloomington: Indiana University Press, 2019.
Piccino, Cristina. "Marta ragazzina arrabbiata in cerca d'indipendenza." *Il Manifesto*, May 18, 2011.
Pitt, Roger, and Danielle E. Hipkins. *New Visions of the Child in Italian Cinema*. Oxford: Peter Lang, 2014.
Povoledo, Elisabetta. "A Legendary Documentary Maker Closes 'an Open Wound.'" *New York Times*, January 24, 2020. https://www.nytimes.com/2020/01/24/world/europe/cecilia-mangini.html?searchResultPosition=1.
Pozzi, Antonia. *L'età delle parole è finita: Lettere 1923–1938*. Edited by Alessandra Cenni and Onorina Dino. Milan: Archinto, 2002.
Pravadelli, Veronica, ed. *Contemporary Women's Cinema, Global Scenarios and Transnational Contexts*. Milan: Mimesis International, 2017.
Ranieri, Daniele. *Il lavoro molesto: Il mobbing; Cos'è e come prevenirlo*. Rome: Ediesse, 2003.
Rascaroli, Laura. *How the Essay Film Thinks*. New York: Oxford University Press, 2017.
Recalcati, Massimo. *Le mani della madre: Desiderio, fantasmi, ed eredità del materno*. Milan: Feltrinelli, 2015.
Rhodes, John David. "Pasolini, the Peripheral Sublime and Public Housing." In *Stupendous Miserable City: Pasolini's Rome*, 75–109. Minneapolis: University of Minnesota Press, 2007.
Riva, Gigi. "La puglia dei veleni." *L'Espresso*, March 30, 2007.
Rose, Deborah Bird. "Val Plumwood's Philosophical Animism: Attentive Interactions in the Sentient World." *Environmental Humanities* 3, no. 1 (2013): 93–109.
Rose, Gillian. *Feminism and Geography: The Limits of Geographical Knowledge*. Minneapolis: Minnesota Press, 1993.
Sainati, Augusto. "Eleonora Danco, il suo è un teatro elettrico." *Il Fatto Quotidiano*, December 9, 2018.
Sala, Roberto. "Moratti boccia la Comencini." *La Repubblica.it*, October 22, 2006. http://ricerca.repubblica.it/repubblica/archivio.
Salleh, Ariel. "Deeper than Deep Ecology: The Eco-Feminist Connection." *Environmental Ethics* 6, no. 4 (1984): 339–45.
Schirinzi, Tatiana. *Il Petrolchimico a Brindisi (1969–1972)*. Bologna: La Scribacchina, 2013.
Sciamanneo, Giancluca. *Con ostinata passione: Il cinema documentario di Cecilia Mangini*. Bari, Italy: Edizioni dal Sud, 2011.

Scott, A. O. "Happy as Lazzaro Review: This Modern Fairy Tale Is an Instant Classic." Review of *Happy as Lazzaro*, by Alice Rohrwacher. *New York Times*, November 29, 2018. https://www.nytimes.com/2018/11/29/movies/happy-as-lazzaro-review.html?searchResultPosition=1.

Seger, Monica. *Landscape in Between: Environmental Change in Modern Italian Literature and Film.* Toronto: University of Toronto Press, 2015.

———. "Narrating Dioxin: Laura Conti's *A Hare with the Face of a Child*." *ISLE: Interdisciplinary Studies in Literature and Environment* 24, no. 1 (2017): 47–65.

———. "Thinking through Taranto: Toxic Embodiment, Eco-catastrophe and the Power of Narrative." In *Italy and the Environmental Humanities: Landscapes, Natures, Ecologies*, edited by Serenella Iovino, Enrico Cesaretti, and Elena Past, 184–93. Charlottesville: University of Virginia Press, 2018.

———. *Toxic Matters: Narrating Dioxin in Contemporary Italy.* Charlottesville: University of Virginia Press, 2022.

Silverman, Kaja. *The Acoustic Mirror: The Female Voice in Psychoanalysis and Cinema.* Bloomington: Indiana University Press, 1988.

———. *The Subject of Semiotics.* New York: Oxford University Press, 1983.

Siviero, Giulia. "È vero che in Italia il #MeToo non c'è mai stato?" *Internazionale*, May 10, 2021. https://www.internazionale.it/opinione/giulia-siviero/2021/05/10/metoo-italia.

Solnit, Rebecca, and Joshua Jelly-Schapiro. "City of Women: The Power of Names." In *Nonstop Metropolis: A New York City Atlas*, 85–90. Berkeley: University of California Press, 2016.

Stam, Robert. "Palimpsestic Aesthetics: A Meditation on Hybridity and Garbage." In *Performing Hybridity*, edited by May Joseph and Jennifer Fink, 59–78. Minneapolis: University of Minnesota Press, 1999.

Stendhal. *Rome, Naples, and Florence.* Translated by Richard N. Cole. London: John Calder, 1959.

Strazulla, Maria José. "War and Peace: Housing the Ara Pacis in the Eternal City." *American Journal of Archeology Online Museum Review* 113, no. 2 (April 2009): 1–10.

Svevo, Italo. *La coscienza di Zeno.* Milan: Feltrinelli, 2014.

Tabanelli, Roberta. *I "pori" di Napoli: Il cinema di Mario Martone, Antonio Capuano e Pappi Corsicato.* Ravenna, Italy: Angelo Longo Editore, 2011.

Tester, Keith. *The Flâneur.* New York: Routledge, 1994.

Torre, Roberta. "Intervista per Antonio Vitti." http://www.robertatorre.com/about/Preview/about.html.

Tronto, Joan C. *Moral Boundaries: A Political Argument for an Ethic of Care.* New York: Routledge, 1993.

Ulfsdotter, Boel, and Anna Backman Rogers. *Female Authorship and Documentary Image: Theory, Practice and Aesthetics*. Edinburgh: Edinburgh University Press, 2018.

Uva, Christian. *L'ultima spiaggia: Rive e derive del cinema italiano*. Venice: Marsilio Edizioni, 2021.

Vasquez, Daniele. *Manuale di psicogeografia*. Cuneo, Italy: Nerosubianco, 2010.

Verdicchio, Pasquale. "This Nostrum that Is Neither Sea nor Remedy: Mediterranean Revisions." In *Italy and the Environmental Humanities: Landscapes, Natures, Ecologies*, edited by Serenella Iovino, Enrico Cesaretti, and Elena Past, 203–14. Charlottesville: University of Virginia Press, 2018.

Veronesi, Michela. "Una donna vuol rifare il mondo. *Umanità* di Elvira Giallanella." In *Non solo dive pioniere del cinema italiano*, edited by Monica Dell'Asta, 159–72. Bologna, Italy: Cineteca di Bologna, 2008.

Vitale, Antonella. "The Body of Law. Redefining Rape in Italy." In *Rape Cultures and Survivors: International Perspectives*, edited by Tuba Inal and Merril D. Smith, 253–64. Santa Barbara, CA: Praeger, 2018.

White, Patricia. *Women's Cinema, World Cinema: Projecting Contemporary Feminisms*. Durham, NC: Duke University Press, 2015.

Wichterich, Christa. "Transnational Reconfigurations of Re/production and the Female Body: Bioeconomics, Motherhoods and the Case of Surrogacy in India." In *Feminist Political Ecology and the Economies of Care: In Search of Economic Alternatives*, edited by Christine Bauhardt and Wendy Harcourt, 211–29. London: Routledge, 2019.

Williams, Linda. "When the Woman Looks." In *The Dread of Difference: Gender and the Horror Film*, edited by Barry Keith Grant, 17–36. Austin: University of Texas Press, 2015.

Williams, Raymond. *The Country and the City*. New York: Oxford University Press, 1973.

Willman, Kate Elizabeth. *Unidentified Narrative Objects and the New Italian Epic*. Cambridge: Legenda, 2019.

Willoquet-Maricondi, Paula. "Shifting Paradigms: From Environmentalist Films to Ecocinema," in *Framing the World: Explorations in Ecocriticism and Film*, edited by Paula Willoquet-Maricondi, 43–61. Charlottesville: University of Virginia Press, 2010.

Wilson, Elizabeth. "The Invisible *Flâneur*." *New Left Review* 191, no. 1 (January 1, 1992): 90–110.

———. *The Sphinx in the City: Urban Life, the Control of Disorder, and Women*. Berkeley: University of California Press, 1991.

Wilson, Sheena, Adam Carlson, and Imre Szeman. "Introduction: On Petrocultures: Or, Why We Need to Understand Oil to Understand Everything

Else." In *Petrocultures: Oil, Politics, Culture*, edited by Sheena Wilson, Adam Carlson, and Imre Szeman, 3–20. Montreal: McGill-Queen's University Press, 2017.

Wolff, Janet. "The Invisible *Flâneuse*. Women and the Literature of Modernity." *Theory, Culture and Society* 2, no. 3 (November 1985): 37–46.

Zagarrio, Vito. *Gli Invisibili: Esordi italiani del nuovo millennio*. Turin: Kaplan, 2009.

Zavattini, Cesare. "Some Ideas on the Cinema." Translated by Pier Luigi Lanza. *Sight and Sound* 23, no. 2 (1953): 64–69.

Zylinska, Joanna. *The End of Man: A Feminist Counterapocalypse*. Minneapolis: University of Minnesota Press, 2018.

INDEX

Page numbers in italics refer to figures

AAMOD. *See* Fondazione Archivio Audiovisivo del movimento operaio e democratico
abortion, 24, 41n36
Abruzzo earthquake, 86
Accattone (Pasolini), 129
Aker, Marcus, 161
All About You (Marazzi), 12, 96, 111–12
All'armi siam fascisti (Mangini), 17
Ambrogio (Labate), 125
Angela (Torre), 135
Anthropocene, 6–7, 10, 143, 172, 187; landscapes of, 48, 116–17, 183–84
anthropocentrism, 24
antimodernism, 164, 177n52
Antonia (Filomarino), 82n31
Antonioni, Michelangelo, 1, 39n3, 40n20, 48–49, 53, 60
Apulia, 18–19, 21, 23, 26, 28, 30
Arcades Project, The (Benjamin), 3
architecture, 52–53, 156, 163–65
Arendt, Hannah, 95
Argento, Asia, x
Arrivederci Saigon (Labate), 126
Ashes of Gramsci, The (Pasolini), 176n47
As the Shadow (Spada), 10, 27, 45–49, 52, 53, 56–57; film diary of, *50–51, 54–55*; and Milan, 62

authorship, 2, 9, 13, 41n31; performance of, 20, 22, 46, 115, 142–43, 153, 158; self-inscription of, 5, 10, 48, 60, 134, 159. *See also* autobiography; Spada, Marina
autobiography, 5, 59, 66, 85, 114; and authorship, 159, 175n24. *See also N-Able* (Danco); *Pianoforte* (Comencini, F.); *Poetry You See Me* (Spada)

Barbanente, Mariangela, 2, 5, 17, 19, 21; interview with, 40n21. *See also Traveling with Cecilia* (Barbanente and Mangini)
Basilico, Gabriele, 53, 80n1
Baudelaire, Charles, 2, 49
Being Women (Mangini), 17, 20, 23, 24, 35, 41n31
Benjamin, Walter, 3, 49, 124
Berlusconi, Silvio, x, 99
Bicycle Thieves (De Sica), 105, 142
bird's-eye view. *See* view from above
Biùtiful cauntri (Calabria, D'Ambrosio, and Pepe), 109n24
Blaché, Alice Guy, 4
Bloody Richard (Torre), 135
Bresson, Robert, 124, 129, 145n28
Brindisi, 9, 20–21, 32–36, 41n30
Brindisi 65 (Mangini), 20, 32, 36
Buñuel, Luis, 152

207

208 INDEX

Calabria, Esmeralda, 109n24, 145n22, 180
Calvino, Italo, 25, 164
Camorra, 87
Campania, 92
Campania infelix (Corsale), 109n24, 145n22
Campion, Jane, ix
Campo Soriano, 177n61
capitalism, 98, 102, 104, 155, 169. See also neoliberalism
Caprice Italian Style (Bolognini), 145n29
Cardone, Lucia, xiv
care. See practice of care
Carlo Giuliani, ragazzo (Comencini), 86
Catania, 115–16, 134, 136, 183. See also Librino
Catholic Church, 60, 124; collapse of, 11, 115–17; critique of, 120, 122–23, 144n18; rejection of, 157, 158; as shelter, 129, 140–41
Cavani, Liliana, ix, xiii, xvn11, 39n3, 146n43
Cavarero, Adriana, 94–95, 97
Cederna, Antonio, 163
cementification: and industry, 24; of the landscape, 6, 48, 116, 118, 137, 170; protest against, 177n50; and urban building, 47, 58, 75, 88, 164, 169
censorship, xiii, 36, 67, 81n29
Centro Sperimentale di Cinematografia, 16, 39n3
Checosamanca (Rohrwacher), 114
Che cosa sono le nuvole? (Pasolini), 124, 145n29
Chtcheglov, Vladimirovitch, 156
cinema, xi, xiii, 8; ecological footprint of, 13; and environmentalism, 44; and flânerie, 4; and gender, 16; as mapping, 47; margins of, 143, 184; maternal voice in, 161; narrative, 5, 142, 161; postmodern, 135; as voyeurism, 142. See also ecocinema; feminist cinema; film industry; Global Women's Cinema; Italian neorealist cinema; women's cinema; world cinema
cinema d'impegno, 86
Cinema e Donne di Firenze, xii
cinema studies, xiv. See also feminist film studies; film criticism and theory
Cineteca di Bologna, 36, 39n6, 41n38
cities: as characters, 114; deserted, 27–28, 32, 40n20, 49, 52, 56, 92; ecological destruction of, 11, 18, 20, 115, 120; emotional geography of, 86; and the flaneur, 3–4, 96; landscapes of, 3, 6; mourning of, 35; psychogeography of, 12, 153; sustainability of, 58; transformation of, 62, 165; walking in, 2, 143. See also Brindisi; cementification; Milan; Naples; Reggio Calabria; Rome; Taranto; urban space
Cities of Women, The (Di Bianco and Senatore), 182
Cixous, Hélène, 152
Clash of Civilizations Over an Elevator in Piazza Vittorio (Lakhous), 110n48
class, xiii, 10, 33, 130, 134, 160. See also gentrification; labor; space
Cléo de 5 à 7 (Varda), 4
climate change, 53, 165
Come l'ombra. See *As the Shadow* (Spada)
Comencini, Cristina, 96
Comencini, Francesca, 2, 10–11, 85–87, 99–100, 106, 108n17. See also *I Like to Work—Harassment* (Comencini, F.); *White Space, The* (Comencini, F.)
Comencini, Luigi, 85
coming of age story, 11, 115, 122, 126
Comizi d'amore (Pasolini), 177n52
Communist Party, 17
concrete. See cementification
Confederazione Generale Italiana del Lavoro (CGIL), 99
Consiglio Nazionale di Ricerca, xii
consumerism, 33, 56, 80n3, 121
Corpo Celeste (Ortese), 145n30
Corpo Celeste (Rohrwacher), 11, 87, 114–24, 125, 140–41, 143; critical reception of, 144n5, 144n18; the sea in, 160; and waste, 145n22
countercinema, xiii, 8
Cousins, Marc, xiii, 114
COVID-19, 53, 151, 184
Cresto-Dina, Carlo, 114
Cristo si è fermato a Eboli (Levi), 30
crowdfunding, 80n1

Danco, Eleonora, 2, 5, 11–12, 59, 151–54; authorship of, 159, 175n24; interview with, 174n10, 176n37, 177n50; in Rome, 164; and the sea, 162. See also *N-Able* (Danco)

Dante, Emma, 12, 149
Daopuolo, Roni, xi
Dark Sea (Torre), 135
da Vinci, Leonardo, 95
DEA (Donne e audiovisivo), xii
Debord, Guy, 155–56, 163
De Chirico, Giorgio, 152
Deledda, Grazia, 38. See also *Grazia Deledda, la rivoluzionaria* (Mangini and Pisanelli)
Del Fra, Lino, 17, 36, 38
De Martino, Ernesto, 30
dérive, 12, 153, 155–58, 163–66, 170. See also *N-Able* (Danco)
De Santis, Giuseppe, 84n2
De Sica, Vittorio, 105, 142
d'Eubonne, Françoise, 23, 39n12
dEVERSIVO (Danco), 153
directors. *See* filmmakers
documentary films, xi, 83, 167; committed, 86; environmental, 38n1; of Mangini, 16–20; participatory, 22, 35, 175n24; strategies of, 29, 33, 41n31; and visibility, 75. See also *Being Women* (Mangini); *In questo mondo* (Kauber); *Traveling with Cecilia* (Barbanente and Mangini)
Documenti su Giuseppe Pinelli (Petri), 145n34
Domenica (Labate), 11, 28, 115–16, 126–33, 143, 145n28, 146n43; and Naples, 146n36; the sea in, 160
Dora Film, xiii
Due scatole dimenticate. See *Two Forgotten Boxes* (Mangini and Pisanelli)

earthquakes, 108n14. *See also* Abruzzo earthquake
ecocinema, 8, 20, 106, 116, 136, 153; *ars et praxis* of, 180; contribution of, 184; women's, 143, 187. *See also* ecofilm
ecocriticism, 2, 87, 136, 163, 170, 184. *See also* feminist ecocriticism
ecofeminism, 7–8, 23–24, 91, 133, 184
ecofilm, 20, 186. *See also* ecocinema
ecology, 5–6, 8, 184; and care, 89; crisis of, 87, 94, 120, 143; feminist, 46, 106; and gender, 104; urban, 12, 153, 166. *See also* Anthropocene; nonhuman world
ecomafia, 109n23

ecomedia, xv
ecopoetry, 147n59
8 1/2 (Fellini), 162
ENI, 26
Enichem, 34
environment, 6–7; activism for, 24, 36, 163; and capitalism, 104; crimes against, 29, 87; destruction of, 9, 31–33, 120, 127, 184; and filmmaking, 181; human relationships to, 34, 48, 155–56, 170; and race, 122; urban, 58, 93; women and, 21, 35, 133. *See also* cementification; landscape; pollution; psychogeography; waste
environmental humanities, xiv, 6
environmental justice, 9, 20, 36, 87, 184
Essere donne (Mangini). See *Being Women* (Mangini)
ethnicity, 89, 100–101, 110n48, 130. *See also* race
European Social Forum (Florence), 86
European Women's Audiovisual Network, xii

Faces, Places (Varda, JR), 144n3
FAScinA, xiv
fascism, xiii, 39n3, 67, 131, 147n48
fegatello, 12, 15n37
Fellini, Federico, 1, 138, 141, 152, 162
feminism, ix–x, xiii–xiv, 184; in film, 4, 7, 128; Italian, 4, 57, 111; and space, 158. *See also* feminist cinema; feminist ecocriticism; practice of care
feminist cinema, 8, 29, 87, 112, 132, 175n33
feminist ecocriticism, xiv, 2, 5, 7, 11, 13, 20; and care, 89, 91, 106–7; and dialogue, 153; and ecofeminism, 24; and urban ecologies, 87, 136, 155, 163. *See also* ecology; landscape; psychogeography; urban ecocriticism
feminist film collective of Rome, 132
feminist film studies, 1, 38n1, 87, 112, 139
feminist political ecology, 98
Ferrante, Elena, xi, 178n65
Ferreri, Silvia, 99
film criticism and theory, 8, 13, 16, 184. *See also* cinema studies; ecocinema; feminist ecocriticism

film industry, x, xii–xiii, 1–2; Italian, 85, 113; margins of, 114; women in, 20, 38, 158. *See also* cinema; filmmakers; women's cinema
filmmakers, xi, 4–5, 6–7, 9, 16, 159
Fini, Francesca, 12, 83–84, 174n6
Firenze, il nostro domani (Comencini, F.), 86
Fiumicino, 13, 133
flânerie, 2–4, 49, 96, 137
flaneur, 2–3, 124
flaneuse, 4–5, 14n16, 49, 100, 104, 183
Fondazione Archivio Audiovisivo del movimento operaio e democratico (AAMOD), 39n6, 41n38
Forever (Marazzi), 112n1
Formulaire pour un urbanisme nouveau (Chtcheglov), 156
For One More Hour With You (Marazzi), 112n1, 175n30
Forum annuale delle studiose di cinema e audiovisivi, xiv
Forza cani (Spada), 80n1
found footage, xi, 17, 75, 111
framing, 7–8, 22, 87; angles, 69; of the city, 88, 91, 93; of landscape, 170, 179; strategies of, 47, 49, 59, 65, 101, 123. *See also* perspective; reframing; street view; view from above
Franceschini law, xii
Fuksas, Elisa, 40n20
Fukushima, 43

Gabriele Basilico (Spada), 80n1
garbage. *See* waste
Garrone, Matteo, 92
gaze, 2–5; active, 49; of the director, 159; female, 9, 24, 113–14, 142, 183; feminist, 56; gendered, 39n9, 43–44; male, 116, 128, 131; of nonhuman animals, 180; patriarchal, 10, 47
G8 Summit (Genoa), 86, 126
gender, x, xii, xiv, 2, 185; and the environment, 7, 22, 104; and filmmaking, 9, 113, 184; and harassment, 89, 99–101, 103; and identity, 140; roles, 158; and space, 5, 59, 146n42
"Gennariello films," 129
gentrification, 80n10, 156

Giallanella, Elvira, 185. *See also Umanità* (Giallanella)
Giordana, Marco Tullio, 145n34
Girl Has Flown, The (Labatte), 126
globalization, 87, 126. *See also* capitalism; neoliberalism
Global Women's Cinema, xiv
Godard, Jean-Luc, 49
Gomorra (film, Garrone), 92
Gomorrah (book, Saviano), 174n5
Gomorrah (TV series), 86, 93
Grazia Deledda, la rivoluzionaria (Mangini and Pisanelli), 21
Gynocine Project, The, xiv

Happy as Lazzaro (Rohrwacher), xvn11, 114, 122, 144n5
Hare with the Face of a Child, A (Conti), 41n36
heterotopia, 137
Hiroshima Mon Amour (Resnais), 43
Horowitz, Alexandra, 1, 5, 170–71

I baci mai dati. See Lost Kisses (Torre)
Ignoti alla città (Mangini), 16
I Knew Her Well (Pietrangeli), 1
Il cielo in me: Vita irrimediabile di una poetessa (Bonaiti and Ongania), 82n31
Il deserto rosso, 1
Il grido (Antonioni), 81n20
I Like to Work—Harassment (Comencini, F.), 10–11, 87–89, 98–106. *See also* mobbing
Il mare non bagna Napoli (Ortese), 133
Il mio domani. See My Tomorrow (Spada)
"Il Petrolchimico," 32–34, 36
"Il pianto della scavatrice" (Pasolini), 169, 176n47
Ilva steel plant, 25–27, 29, 40n15
Immaginaria International Film Festival of Lesbian and Rebellious Women, xii
immigrants, 105, 146n45. *See also* migrants
individualism, 155
industrialization, 2–3, 6, 8–9, 18, 26, 39n4, 49
In questo mondo (Kauber), 12, 179–81
Into Paradiso (Randi), 146n45
In viaggio con Cecilia. See Traveling with Cecilia (Barbanente and Mangini)

INDEX　211

Io la conoscevo bene (Pietrangeli), 1
Italian (language), 3, 147n59
Italian neorealist cinema, xiii, 11, 105, 114, 142–43
Italia Nostra, 163–65
Italian Studies, xv
Italy, x–xii, 1; cities of, 169; ecological crises of, 18, 20, 121, 124, 163; economic crisis of, 87, 144n18; economic miracle of, 6, 9, *18*, 23–24, 26, 48, 160, 176n47; fascist, xiii, 67, 131, 147n48; film funding in, 80n1; motherhood in, 87; pandemic in, 53; and race, 105; women in, 8, 133
Ivain, Gilles. *See* Chtcheglov, Vladimirovitch

JR, 144n3

Kauber, Anna, 12–13, 179–81. *See* also *In questo mondo* (Kauber)
Koudelka, Joseph, 81n22

La Bambina deve prendere aria (Prudente), 109n24, 145n22
Labate, Wilma, 2, 11, 125–27, 133, 140; interview with, 145n32, 146n36. *See* also *Domenica* (Labate)
labor, 24, 29; of care, 88, 98; crisis of, 87; exploitation of, 33, 64; liberalization of, 99
La briglia sul collo (Mangini), 21
La canta delle marane (Mangini), 16
La città senza notte. *See Nightless City, The* (Pescetta)
La Dolce Vita (Fellini), 141, 162
Ladri di biciclette (De Sica), 105
La fabbrica dei veleni (Casson), 41n33
La forma della città (Pasolini), 164
La gente resta (Tilli), 40n17
L'aggettivo donna (Miscuglio and Daopuolo), xi
La mia generazione (Labate), 125
L'amore molesto (Martone), 178n65
landscape, 1, 3, 5–6, 8; affective, 12, 153; Anthropogenic, 116–17, 119–20; in ecocinema, 20, 136; industrial, 25–26, 53; instability of, 108n14; and loss, 53; material of, 170–71; nonhuman,

58–59; observers of, 21–22, 24, 34, 56, 114, 183; postindustrial, 10, 137; the sea, 160–62; transformation of, 143, 167, 169; women in, 46, 48, 133, 159, 184. *See* also Anthropocene; cementification; cities; environment
La Notte (Antonioni), 1, 48
La notte quando morì Pasolini (Torre), 147n57
La nuvola di smog (Calvino), 25–26, 164
La pelle. *See Skin, The* (Cavani)
La ragazza ha volato (Labate), 126
La terra trema (Visconti), 142
Latium, 132, 154, 163, 172, 177n61
L'avventura (Antonioni), 49
Lazzaro felice. *See Happy as Lazzaro* (Rohrwacher)
Le ceneri di Gramsci (Pasolini), 176n47
Le città delle donne (Di Bianco and Senatore), 182
L'eclisse (Antonioni), 40n20, 53
Legambiente, 109n23
"Legge Biagi," 99
Le meraviglie (Rohrwacher). *See Wonders, The* (Rohrwacher)
Le notti di Cabiria (Fellini), 1
Le prenóm de Dieu (Cixous), 152
Le ragazze di San Gregorio (Comencini, F.), 86
Le sorelle Macaluso. *See Macaluso Sisters, The* (Dante)
Lettere dalla Palestina (Angeli, Berlinguer, Carrassi, Labate), 126
Levi, Carlo, 30
Le Vietnam sera libre (Mangini), 36
Libreria delle donne di Milano, 57
Librino, 11, 115, 134–37, 140, 147n59, 147n61
liminality, 2, 11, 143, 150, 152, 158, 174
L'orchestra di Piazza Vittorio (Ferrante), 110n48
Lo spazio bianco. *See White Space, The* (Comencini, F.)
Lost Kisses (Torre), 11, 115–16, 134–43, 160
Love Meetings (Pasolini), 177n52

Macaluso Sisters, The (Dante), 12, 149–50
Macchi, Egisto, 27
Mafia, 135, 146n42. *See* also ecomafia
Mamma Roma (Pasolini), 1, 81n14, 129

Mangini, Cecilia, 2, 5, 9, *17–19*, 20–21; career of, 38, 40n21, 41n31; censoring of, 36; environmental activism of, 39n4; interview with, 16, 36–37. See also *Being Women* (Mangini); *Brindisi 65* (Mangini); *Tommaso* (Mangini); *Traveling with Cecilia* (Barbanente and Mangini)
Marazzi, Alina, xi, 12, 96, 112, 112n1, 175n30. See also *All About You* (Marazzi)
Mare nero (Torre), 135
Marghera Petrochemical, 32, 34, 41n33
Marsé, Juan, 129
Marsella, Roberto, 35
Martano, *30*, 31
Martone, Mario, 178n65
Mattarella, Sergio, x
media industry, x, 138, 141, 144n20, 158, 177n50
Mediterranean Sea, 26, 40, 121. See also *N-Able* (Danco)
Meier, Richard, 164
#MeToo movement, x, xi
migrants, 87, 121–22
Milan, 10, *19*, 27; Cathedral Square of, 65–66; deserted, 52–53; redevelopment of, 62, 75, 80n10, 147n61; remapping of, 68–69; views of, *46, 47–49*, 183. See also *As the Shadow* (Spada); *My Tomorrow* (Spada)
Milano, ritratti di fabbriche (Basilico), 53
Milan's Women Book Store, 57
"minor cinema," 2, 14n3
Mi piace lavorare—Mobbing. See *I Like to Work—Harassment* (Comencini, F.)
Miscuglio, Anna Bella, xi
misogyny, 132, 177n52
mobbing, 99–100, 102–3, 110n43. See also gender; *I Like to Work—Harassment* (Comencini, F.); sexual harassment
mobility, 1, 3–4, 13, 57, 154–55; restriction of, 101, 129, 157, 166; social, 33, 60. See also *dérive*; flânerie; *N-Able* (Danco); nomadism; psychogeography; walking
modernity, 1–2, 4–5
Montedison, 34
Morante, Else, 86
motherhood, 3, 85, 87–89, 106, 108n15, 183; and capitalism, 102; demonization of,

59; inclination toward, 94–97, 109n33; in popular culture, 140; and the public sphere, 91; of the sea, 161–62. See also *White Space, The* (Comencini, F.)
Mouchette (Bresson), 124, 129, 145n28
Mount Vesuvius, 91, 93, *94*, 108n14
Museum of the Ara Pacis Augustae, 164
My Marlboro City (Valentina), 40n30
My Tomorrow (Spada), 10, 27, 46, 57–60, 65; film diary of, *61, 63*, 81n22; and Milan, *62, 64*

N-Able (Danco), 11–12, 151–53, 174n8, 175n30, 177n52, 177n61; as autobiographical, 22, 59, 159, 175n24, 176n34; geology of, 170–72; movement in, 154–58; in Rome, 163–65, 167–69; the sea in, *160*, 161–62, 173
Naples, 4, 10–11, 27–28, 87–89, 108n12, 115; belonging to, 129–30, 146n45; cityscape of, 91, 126–27; deserted, 97–98; geography of, 130–31; image of, 92–93, 108n17, 146n36; street children in, 128–29; and women, 146n42, 183. See also *Domenica* (Labate); *White Space, The* (Comencini, F.)
National Film Archive (Rome), xi, 185
National Research Council. See Consiglio Nazionale di Ricerca
nature. See nonhuman world
natureculture, 170, 177n57
N-Capace. See *N-Able* (Danco)
Neapolitan Quartet (Ferrante), xi
neoliberalism, 10, 60, 64, 104; violence of, 88–89, 101, 106. See also capitalism
Nessuno ci guarda (Danco), 157
New Italian Epic, 174n5
Nightless City, The (Pescetta), 12, 43, 44
Nights of Cabiria, The, 1
Nina (Fuksas), 40n20
Nobody Is Looking (Danco), 157
nomadism, 2, 6–7, 62, 124, 126, 185. See also flânerie; streetwalking; walking
nonhuman animals, xv, 11–12, 114, 185–87; care for, 106, 180; crisis of, 87; in ecocinema, 20, 150; as waste, 122. See also speciesism
nonhuman world, 6, 48, 59, 65, 87–88, 179; human domination of, 91; human sharing of, 97, 147n59, 170

Non perdono (Zanotto and Marsella), 35
Non una di meno, x
Nostalgie urbane (Garlaschelli and Pedicini), 41n30
Notari, Elvira, xiii, xviii4, 129, 185

Ofelia non annega. See *Ophelia Does Not Drown* (Fini)
Omelia Contadina (Rohrwacher, JR), 144n3
Ongania, Marco, 82n31
Open Roads: New Italian Cinema festival, 151
Ophelia Does Not Drown (Fini), 12, 83, 84, 174n6
Ortese, Anna Maria, 145n30
Outcry, The (Antonioni), 81n20

Palermo, 134, 137, 149–50
Palermo Bandita (Torre), 147n57
Paris, 2, 14n16
Pasolini, Pier Paolo, 1–2, 16–17, 31, 38, 152; films of, 81n14, 124, 145n29, 164, 177n52; novels of, 129; poetry of, 169, 176n47
Pasqualino settebellezze (Wertmuller), ix
Past, Elena, xiv–xv, 6, 8, 92–93
patriarchy, ix, 5, 11, 28, 60, 98; and space, 158; violence of, 115, 132; and women's bodies, 122
peace movement, 24
Pedicini, Valentina, 41n30
performance art, 83, 152
Per sempre (Marazzi), 112n1
perspective, 6–7, 47–48, 95, 137, 161. *See also* framing; street view; view from above
Pescetta, Alessandra, 12, 43, 44
Petri, Elio, 145n34
petrochemical industry, 32, 34, 36, 41n33, 104. *See also* Brindisi; "Il Petrolchimico"
Pianoforte (Comencini, F.), 85–86
"Pianto della scavatrice" (Pasolini), 169, 176n47
Piazza Fontana: The Italian Conspiracy (Giordana), 145n34
Pietrangeli, Antonio, 1
Pisanelli, Paolo, 21, 36–38, 39n6, 41n31
Poe, Edgar Allan, 2
Poesia che mi guardi. See *Poetry You See Me* (Spada)

Poetry You See Me (Spada), 10, 27, 46, 65–66, 68, 69; as compilation film, 75, 80; film diary of, 70–74, 76–79
polis, 91, 108n13, 152. *See also* public space
pollution, 6, 9; of agricultural, 144n3; and capitalism, 104; of cities, 18, 25–28, 34, 56, 64, 169; and illness, 87, 184; of quarries, 172. *See also* waste
Ponti, Gio, 48
posthumanism, 12, 97, 150, 169, 187
postindustrialism, 6, 10, 32–34, 41n37, 49, 62
postmodernity, 5, 49, 135, 137
poverty, 18, 20, 87, 133; and industrialization, 24, 32; and women, 35
Pozzi, Antonia, 10, 46, 65–69, 75, 80; films about, 82n31; writing of, 81n28, 81n29. *See also Poetry You See Me* (Spada)
practice of care, 10, 22, 87–89, 91, 106, 183; choice of, 95–96, 109n33; and time, 103–4; value of, 98. *See also* motherhood; *White Space, The* (Comencini, F.)
Prague, 81n22
"pretrauma," 53, 184
private sphere, 2, 4, 49, 59, 153
prostitution, 3, 49. *See also* streetwalking
psychogeography, 11–12, 153, 155–56. *See also N-Able* (Danco)
psychogeology, 153, 170
public space, 4, 12, 35, 91–92, 153, 157–58. *See also polis*; urban space
public sphere, 2–4, 7, 49, 75

Qualcosa di noi (Labate), 126
Quando la notte (Comencini, C.), 96
#quellavoltache, x

race, 7, 21, 35
racism, 105, 120, 122
Ragazzi di Vita (Pasolini), 129
rape, 126–28, 131–32, 147n48
Red Desert, 1
reframing, 161–62, 175n33
refugees, 122
Reggio Calabria, 11, 115, 118–19, 183
Riccardo va all'inferno (Torre), 135
Riva, Emilio, 29, 40n21

Roghudi, 122–23, 145n24
Rohrwacher, Alice, xiii, xvn11, 2, 11, 114–15, 144n3; interview with, 113, 119–20, 123, 177n50. See also *Corpo Celeste* (Rohrwacher); *Happy as Lazzaro* (Rohrwacher); *Wonders, The* (Rohrwacher)
Romanzo di una strage (Giordana), 145n34
Roma ore 11 (Santis), 84n2
Rome, 10–12, 53, 81n14, 87, 89, 183; architecture of, 110n46; development of, 176n47, 177n50; multiethnicity of, 100–101, 105, 110n48; vandalization of, 163–68. See also *I Like to Work—Harassment* (Comencini, F.); *N-Able* (Danco)
Ronda del Guinardò (Marsé), 129

Sant'Anna, la Madonna e il bambino con l'agnello (da Vinci), 95
Sátántangó (Tarr), 121
Saviano, Roberto, 174n5
Scontro di civiltà per un ascensore a Piazza Vittorio (Lakhous), 110n48
secularization, 87
Senatore, Marinella, 182
Seven Beauties (Wertmuller), ix
Seveso, 35
sexism, x, 89
sexual harassment, x. See also mobbing
Sguardi Altrove (Milan), xii
Shakespeare a Palermo (Comencini, F.), 86
Shape of the City, The (Pasolini), 164
Sherman, Cindy, 81n22
Sicily, 134–35. See also Palermo
Signorina Effe (Labate), 126
silent film, xiii, xvn2, 129, 185
Sironi, Mario, 53
Situationists, 12, 153, 155–56, 163
Skin, The (Cavani), xvn11, 146n42, 146n43
Smog (Calvino), 25–26, 164
social justice, 9, 20, 184
solastalgia (Albrecht), 123, 127, 133, 156
space, 3, 6, 48–49, 137; and class, 96, 130, 161; confined, 101; empty, 52, 60, 108n15, 110n37; as a film character, 114; movement through, 153, 156–58. See also cities; landscape; liminality; private sphere; psychogeography; public space; public sphere; urban space
Spada, Marina, 2, 10, 27, 46, 80n1; authorship of, 48, 53, 59, 62; diaries of, 47, 60, 65–66, 68, 70–74, 76–79; interview with, 45, 49, 52. See also *As the Shadow* (Spada); *My Tomorrow* (Spada); *Poetry You See Me* (Spada)
speciesism, 7. See also nonhuman animals
Stendalì, Playing On (Mangini), 17, 20, 30, 31
Storaro, Vittorio, 39n3
Street in Palermo, A (Dante), 149
Street Kids, The (Pasolini), 129
street view, 7, 22, 27, 46
streetwalking, 1, 3–4, 49, 146n43. See also mobility; nomadism; walking
Sud side stori (Torre), 135

Tange, Kenzo, 136, 147n63
Tano da morire (Torre), 135, 140
Taranto, 9, 20–21, 24–27, 32, 40n17, 160; toxicity of, 35–36; views of, 183; walking in, 29–31
"Tears of the Excavator, The" (Pasolini), 169, 176n47
technology, 83, 104, 108n12, 108n15, 155; digital, x, xvn2
Terracina, 11, 154
Tommaso (Mangini), 20, 32–33
Torre, Roberta, 2, 11, 134–36. See also *Lost Kisses* (Torre)
trash. See waste
Traveling with Cecilia (Barbanente and Mangini), 9–10, 17, 19–24, 39n6, 41n31; availability of, 41n38; and the industrial city, 25–26, 27–28, 32; politics of, 35–36, 87; the sea in, 160; and walking, 29, 31, 34, 175n24. See also Brindisi; Taranto
Troubling Love (Martone), 178n65
Turin, 111, 126
Tutto parla di te. See *All About You* (Marazzi)
Two Forgotten Boxes (Mangini and Pisanelli), 21, 36–37, 39n6, 41n31

Umanità (Giallanella), 185–87
Una lepre can la faccia di bambina (Conti), 41n36

Un altro mondo è possibile (Labate), 125
Una montagna di balle (Angrisano), 109n24
Una vita violenta (Pasolini), 129
Un complicato intrigo di donne, vicoli e delitti (Wertmuller), 146n42
Une Dame vraiement bien (Blaché), 4
Un giorno speciale (Comencini, F.), 86
Unidentified Cinematic Object, 152, 174n6
Unidentified Narrative Object, 152, 174n5
United States, x, 36, 38
Un'ora sola ti vorrei (Marazzi), 112n1, 175n30
Uno virgola due (Ferreri), 99
urban ecocriticism, 170. *See also* feminist ecocriticism
urban geology, 170
urban space, 2–5, 14n16, 49, 130, 146n45, 157; dangers of, 104; as generative, 93, 184; reconfiguration of, 41n38, 48, 65, 96, 150. *See also* cities; ecology; landscape; psychogeography; public space

Varda, Agnès, 4, 144n3, 152
Veleno (Olivares), 109n24
Venice, 32
Venice Film Festival, 57, 81n27
Very Fine Lady, A (Blaché), 4
Via castellana bandiera (Dante), 149
video art, 43, 83
view from above, 6–7, 20, 22, 46, 117–18, 183; of Naples, 88, 92, 97–98, 126–27; of Taranto, 24–25; trope of, 47, 153
violence, x, 10–11, 184; of capitalism, 101, 106; of cities, 115; of industrialization, 24; in Italy, 120; psychological, 99; sexual, 131–32, 147n48; "slow," 32; against women, 88, 116. *See also* mobbing; neoliberalism; rape; sexual harassment
Violent Life (Pasolini), 129

Virgin and Child with St. Anne, The (da Vinci), 95
Visconti, Luchino, 142
Vivre sa vie (Godard), 49
Vogliamo anche le rose (Marazzi). *See We Want Roses Too* (Marazzi)
voice-over, 23, 31, 33, 36, 41n31
volcanos, 108n14. *See also* Mount Vesuvius

walking, 1–3, 5, 12; in the city, 115–16, *121*, 129–30, 155–56, 170; in documentaries, 29, 175n24; and memory, 168; perspective of, 97; and time, 64; women and, 49, 183. *See also* cities; flânerie; mobility; nomadism; psychogeography; streetwalking
waste, 26, 33–34, 43–44, 92–94, 119–22, 169; disposal of, 88, 102, 109n23; in film, 145n22; re-use of, 124. *See also* pollution
Wertmuller, Lina, ix, xiii, 146n42
We Want Roses Too (Marazzi), xi, 112n1
White Space, The (Comencini, F.), 10, 27, 87–89, *90–97*, 106, 167; setting of, 108n12. *See also* Naples
Women in Audiovisual Industry. *See* DEA (Donne e audiovisivo)
Women Make Film: A New Road Movie (Cousins), xiii, 114
women's cinema, ix, xi, xiv, xvn2, 1–2; environmental practices in, 7; in Italy, 175n33. *See also* Global Women's Cinema
women's liberation movement, xi, xiv, 112n1, 131
Wonders, The (Rohrwacher), 114, 144n5, 144n20
workplace harassment. *See* mobbing
world cinema, 4, 38

Zanotto, Grace, 35

LAURA DI BIANCO is Assistant Professor of Italian Studies and is affiliated with the Center of Advanced Media Studies, the Program for the Study of Women, Gender, and Sexuality, and Environmental Science and Studies at Johns Hopkins University. She is the coeditor of the academic journal *MLN* (*Modern Language Notes*), Italian edition.

www.ingramcontent.com/pod-product-compliance
Lightning Source LLC
Chambersburg PA
CBHW030106170426
43198CB00009B/512